Vital Signs

Nature, Culture, Psychoanalysis

D1706888

Charles Shepherdson

ROUTLEDGE

New York and London

Permissions to reprint

Chapter one was published as "Biology and History: Some Psychoanalytic Aspects of the Writing of Luce Irigaray," *Textual Practice* 6 (Spring 1992): 47–86. Permission from Routledge to reprint is gratefully acknowledged.

Chapter three was published as "The Role of Gender and the Imperative of Sex," in *Supposing the Subject*, ed. Joan Copjec (London: Verso, 1994), pp. 158–84. Permission from Verso to reprint is gratefully acknowledged.

A longer version of chapter five was published in *Postmodern Culture*, an electronic journal published by Johns Hopkins University Press, and was reprinted in a shortened form by Yale University Press. The references are "History and the Real: Foucault with Lacan," *Postmodern Culture* 5 (January 1995); "History and the Real: Foucault with Lacan," in *Rhetoric in an Anti-Foundational World: Language, Culture, and Pedagogy*, ed. M. Bernard-Donals and R. Glejzer (New Haven, CT: Yale University Press, 1997), 496–544. I thank Johns Hopkins University Press and Yale University Press for permission to reprint.

Published in 2000 by
Routledge
29 West 35th Street
New York, New York 10001

Published in Great Britain by
Routledge
11 New Fetter Lane
London EC4P 4EE

Library of Congress Cataloging-in-Publication Data
Shepherdson, Charles.
    Vital signs: nature, culture, psychoanalysis / Charles Shepherdson.
        p.   cm.
    Includes bibliographical references and index.
    ISBN 0-415-90879-5 (hardcover). — ISBN 0-415-90880-9 (pbk.)
    1. Psychoanalysis—France. I. Title.
BF173.S4975   1999
150.19'5—dc21   99-29671
                                                                    CIP

For Paul Mann, who knows better.

Contents

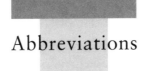

Abbreviations

Lacan

E   Jacques Lacan, *Écrits* (Paris: Seuil, 1966). A portion of this volume has appeared in English as *Écrits: A Selection,* trans. Alan Sheridan (New York: Norton, 1977). References will be given to both volumes whenever possible, French pagination first, English second. Translations are occasionally modified.

FS   *Feminine Sexuality: Jacques Lacan and the école freudienne,* ed. Juliet Mitchell and Jacqueline Rose, trans. Jacqueline Rose (New York: Norton, 1985).

SII   *The Seminar of Jacques Lacan, Book II: The Ego in Freud's Theory and in the Technique of Psychoanalysis, 1954–55,* ed. Jacques-Alain Miller, trans. Sylvana Tomaselli, with notes by John Forrester (New York: Norton, 1988).

SVII   *Le Séminaire, livre VII: L'ethique de la psychanalyse, 1959–60,* ed. Jacques-Alain Miller (Paris: Seuil, 1986). *Seminar VII: The Ethics of Psychoanalysis 1959–60,* ed. Jacques-Alain Miller, trans. Dennis Porter (New York: Norton, 1992). References will be given to both volumes, French pagination first, English second; translations are occasionally modified.

SXI   *Le Séminaire, livre XI: Les quatres concepts fondamentaux de la psychanalyse,* ed. Jacques-Alain Miller (Paris: Seuil, 1973). *The Four Fundamental Concepts of Psychoanalysis,* trans. Alan Sheridan (New York: Norton, 1978). References will be given to both volumes, French pagination first, English second; translations are occasionally modified.

T   "Television," trans. Denis Hollier, Rosalind Krauss, and Annette

Michelson, *Television: A Challenge to the Psychoanalytic Establishment,* ed. Joan Copjec (New York: Norton, 1990).

Foucault

BC   *The Birth of the Clinic: An Archaeology of Medical Perception,* trans. A. M. Sheridan Smith (New York: Vintage, 1975).

DP   *Discipline and Punish: The Birth of the Prison,* trans. Alan Sheridan (New York: Vintage, 1977).

LCMP   *Language, Counter-Memory, Practice: Selected Essays and Interviews,* ed. Donald F. Bouchard (Ithaca: Cornell University Press, 1977).

MC   *Madness and Civilization: A History of Insanity in the Age of Reason,* trans. Richard Howard (New York: Vintage, 1965).

OT   *The Order of Things: An Archaeology of the Human Sciences,* trans. Alan Sheridan (New York: Random House, 1970).

HS   *The History of Sexuality: An Introduction,* trans. Robert Hurley (New York: Vintage, 1990).

Freud

SE   *The Standard Edition of the Complete Psychological Works of Sigmund Freud,* trans. James Strachey, ed. James Strachey et al. (London: The Hogarth Press, 1953). 24 vols. Works will be cited by volume and page number.

Acknowledgments
Go little book

In the years since I wrote these papers—among them my earliest attempts to come to terms with the notoriously obscure work of Jacques Lacan—I have managed to stumble my way toward something like a thesis that might explain why they should be grouped together. The introduction that books require (if they are ever to find their place within the genre, and thereby take leave of their authors) provides me with the chance or obligation to formulate that argument more clearly, though it is perhaps worth noting that the essays themselves—despite my having tacked on a paragraph here and there—do not always have this larger horizon clearly in mind.

For the most part, in fact, they are concerned with relatively local details: a case study by an author who is not well known; a single article that is discussed only briefly; a rather narrow clinical topic, presented in a more or less "underground" book that is not widely available. "I seriously advise you not to join my audience a second time," Freud writes in 1915. And if, he continues, "there should actually turn out to be one of you who did not feel satisfied by a fleeting acquaintance with psychoanalysis but was inclined to enter into a permanent relationship with it, I should not merely dissuade him from doing so, but actively warn him against it" (*SE*, 15:15–6). *Caveat lector.*

That these fragments are grouped together at all is due in part to Maureen MacGrogan, formerly of Routledge, who—at a time when I was only beginning to write about these things—generously asked me whether I had a manuscript in progress, and, upon hearing that I did not (and moreover did not expect to: "I only write articles," I told her), cunningly planted the idea in my mind that the things I had already done might make up a volume in themselves. In principle, then, the book could well have been finished the very moment she suggested it, as though sneaking up on me from behind, imposing its poor existence on its author before I had any intention of producing it. It turned out, moreover, that she was right, and that much of the work had in fact been completed (in a partial and somewhat haphazard way); but I was unwilling to admit it, and steadfastly refused to imagine that the tentative efforts I had made to understand this strange material—which might make it possible to think of writing a book one day—could in themselves already pretend to comprise one. I therefore tried to ignore her suggestion, but it was too late, the words had already been planted; and since that time, many other forces have likewise conspired to thwart me, foiling my best efforts at reticence and circumspection. I am happy now to admit defeat, and to express my gratitude to a range of valiant conquerors.

Interested and often highly motivated students have repeatedly compelled me to elaborate arguments that I might otherwise have neglected, demanding by the sheer pressure of their energy and attention a more developed exposition, tolerating my relentless preoccupation with textual details, stubbornly returning week after week despite my efforts to exhaust them, and patiently enduring classes that often ran (it seems brutal in recollection) some two hours overtime. I am grateful for their stamina and intellectual vitality. In a climate of public opinion where research and teaching are often said to be in conflict, I have experienced again and again the strongest refutation of this dogma: I could not have read this material as carefully without the obligation to explain it with the clarity and detail that my students demanded, nor would my teaching have generated such interest as it did, had I not been permitted to pursue material that I myself was eager to explore and understand. Thanks to Maureen, then, for her subterfuge and cunning, and to my students, especially Ben Pryor and Laurie Glover; Annie Pulis, David Beran, Tim Spence, and Mehdi Semati; Rob Hughes and Jennifer Shaw.

I thank the Henry and Clare Boothe Luce Foundation for its generous support during a two-year period in which I first began to work on this material, which amounted to a significant departure from my doctoral work. I thank the Pew Charitable Trust for sponsoring a faculty seminar on "Law and Transgression" at Pomona College that led me to develop some of the details in chapter five. I thank Arden Reed and Paul Mann for including me in their discussions and their lives, for repeatedly rescuing me from the dangers of southern California, and for much more in the way of conversation and friendship over the years. I owe them both a lot.

The Commonwealth Center for Literary and Cultural Change at the University of Virginia provided money and time to write when I first began to publish in this area, and hosted a semester-long seminar on "Cultural Evolution" that exposed me to a number of arguments concerning contemporary evolutionary theory. These are arguments that my own theoretical work has led me to resist, but they are far more subtle and interesting than their opponents often suppose. I am grateful to Ralph Cohen and Dell Hymes for organizing this interdisciplinary seminar, and for pitching the material at a serious level. The support of the center allowed me to complete the first stages of this project, and encouraged me to think through in more detail the difference between psychoanalysis and biological knowledge, particularly with respect to the way in which historical time is conceived.

When four of the chapters were complete, the National Endowment for the Humanities sponsored a summer institute titled "Embodiment: The Intersection of Nature and Culture," which brought together scholars from a variety of fields to address the question of embodiment, which has been central to the development of a number of disciplines in recent years. I am grateful to David Hoy and Hubert Dreyfus for organizing this interdisciplinary project, which helped me to situate my arguments in a broader intellectual context. The seminar had a substantial impact on my conception of this project as a whole, and has affected my introductory remarks.

I especially want to acknowledge an extremely useful and productive year of support from the Pembroke Center for Teaching and Research on Women at Brown University, where I was the Artemis and Martha Joukowsky Fellow in 1996–97. This was a particularly important period in my development: it not only allowed me to write the final chapter (given here as chapter four), and to pull these separate pieces together with some attention to their frame, but also gave me time to complete a number of related essays, and to begin two other projects. The work of the Pembroke Center also considerably broadened my exposure to a range of scholarly literature in contemporary feminist theory, by sustaining a yearlong seminar on "The Limits of Gender." Here again, I was pushed to set the particular details of my work within a wider intellectual context, and to elaborate my claims in a way that is, I hope, both more responsible and more ambitious.

I would particularly like to thank Elizabeth Weed for her generous encouragement and support, for her friendship and fine intellectual companionship, and for insisting that I learn to consider my contribution not simply as having an exegetical function, but—*mirabile dictu*—as making an argument in its own right. Under her admirable direction, the Pembroke Center not only gave me the courage to imagine that my own work might actually be of some interest, in addition to the work I was trying to address, but also put me in excellent and lively company. Jean Walton, Mary Caputo, and Lynne Joyrich were each an amazing source of life: their intelligence and creativity, their seriousness of purpose, and their relentless and sparkling humor kept me on earth in more ways than one, and helped me to see the future. I am truly grateful for their company and friendship. I thank Nancy Armstrong for finding time under pressure, for her interest in my work, for the example of her indefatigable wit, and for doing major surgery on a minor piece of narrative.

I have been fortunate not only in these many sources of support, but also in the fact that these different institutional contexts have encouraged me to confront the complex relations between the sometimes quite baroque details that occupied me in these pieces, and the much larger and more schematic questions that these interdisciplinary institutions have done so much to cultivate. The theoretical transformations that have marked so many academic fields in recent decades are difficult to engage in a way that is intellectually serious. The institutional support that sustains these transformations is crucial to the responsible development of intellectual life, particularly at a time of such rapid disciplinary upheaval. Money and time are thus only part of what I owe to these generous institutions.

Many other friends and colleagues have contributed in important ways to this work at various stages. I am especially grateful to Charles Scott for introducing me to Continental philosophy (especially Heidegger and Foucault), as well as for his friendship over many years, for sharing his life, and for many profitable summers of work at the *Collegium Phaenomenologicum* in Perugia, Italy. He also tolerated an especially protracted and labyrinthine contribution to *Research in Phenomenology,* which would have made a less permissive editor wince (if not recoil). Bill Richardson has represented for me an exemplary mix of persistent and skeptical engagement with Lacan, and I appreciate the interest he has shown in my work. Catherine Belsey kindly invited me to lecture to her seminar at the Folger Institute, and was the first person to publish my work in psychoanalysis (there is always someone to blame). She sustained me at a number of crucial moments with her enthusiasm, her irreverence, and her professional support, as well as by sharing her work and taking an interest in mine. I am grateful for her friendship and wry humor. Tina Chanter did her best to encourage me to finish this project some time ago, and I am grateful for her efforts and support, and for many conversations.

I would also like to thank Joan Copjec, who has been especially generous in support of my work since we attended a symposium on Lacan with members of the École Freudienne, at the Centre for Psychoanalytic Research in Australia. In addition to her unwavering endorsement of my work in the face of political difficulties, she has invited me to contribute to a number of publications, and to speak on several occasions at the Center for the Study of Psychoanalysis and Culture at the University of Buffalo. I appreciate her encouragement and steadfast support in the heat of various controversies.

A number of people read and commented on portions of the manuscript: Catherine Belsey, Rob Hughes, Ewa Ziarek, Tim Dean, and Frances Restuccia all gave me useful feedback, though much of the original damage will still be visible. Judith Feher Gurewich kindly invited me to speak to her seminar on Lacan at the Center for Literary and Cultural Studies at Harvard on several occasions, and I am grateful for her interest and enthusiastic support. She has maintained a genuine and respectful debate between the clinical and academic communities, and has generously opened her home to numerous informal seminars, where I have spent many fruitful and productive hours. Her own contributions have helped me to keep an eye on the clinical dimension of Lacan's work, and her intellectual independence has been an important example to me of the constant discovery that becomes possible with a refusal of academic pieties. I appreciate her friendship and her energy. The group that formed in conjunction with that seminar, including especially Francis Restuccia and Kalpana Seshadri-Crooks, broke a long-standing conviction of mine by providing my first experience of a successful reading group. To Kalpana I am grateful not only for this, but for her friendship and honesty, for the seriousness of her intellectual engagement, for a home away from home, and for the ferocity of her judgment, which helped to put me at ease.

Ana Rueda and Kim Schäfermeyer dragged me in out of the rain on more than one occasion, and I cherish their friendship and their solid affection. Sherod Santos and Lynne McMahon did much to keep me intellectually alive and connected to another language, and I am most gladly indebted to them both.

Finally, I want to thank Joan Scott and Judith Butler, who turned out to be something like the bookends of this project. Judith Butler generously helped to get the project off the ground at a time when I scarcely knew her, and did not even realize I was receiving her support; and since then, her encouragement has helped to keep me from abandoning the project at several crucial moments. It is truly remarkable and impressive that someone under such heavy professional demands, with commitments to so many colleagues and students, should have found the time and energy—much less the generosity of spirit—to attend to a project by someone whom she had not the slightest obligation to support or even to read. In the current climate of academia, her example is exceptional and genuinely heartening. And as for Joan Scott, she simply expected the book to appear, and that was enough, though I gladly confess that her support, and my time at the Institute for Advanced Study, allowed me to finish another manuscript, and thereby to distance myself sufficiently from this one that I might let it go. So I thank her for that as well, and for much more.

To all of them I say, as Catullus to his patron Cornelius:

> *quare habe tibi quidquid hoc libelli*
> *qualecumque . . .*

> [So then, take this little book for yourself,
> such as it is . . .]

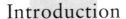

Introduction

*Factus sum mihi terra difficultatis
et sudoris nimii.*
　　　St. Augustine, *Confessions*

[I have become to myself
a land of trouble and infinite sweating.]

I.

In recent years, psychoanalytic theory has witnessed an extraordinary revival as a means of interdisciplinary research in gender and social theory. Many accounts of literature and culture have turned to psychoanalysis as a way of breaking the impasse between general, socio-historical modes of analysis, and approaches that seek to specify subjectivity more precisely. In addition, psychoanalysis highlights questions of embodiment and sexual difference that have often been neglected by other theoretical approaches. Psychoanalytic theory has also come to play an increasingly pivotal role in the debates between the French and Anglo-American philosophical traditions, with particular impact on the social sciences that have been affected by these debates.

Despite this renewal of interest, however, the basic theoretical orientation of contemporary French psychoanalysis still remains obscure. The most important work is extremely abstract and technical, while more popular accounts have often consisted of concrete applications that combine various methods, thereby blurring the psychoanalytic conception of the subject, or interpreting it through the vocabulary

1

and the disciplinary lens of philosophy, or film theory, or cultural studies. Moreover, literary and cultural uses of psychoanalysis have largely neglected its clinical dimension, a fact that has led to considerable distortion in the American reception of a number of important figures in contemporary European thought.

To take only one of the most obvious examples, we might note that the technical vocabulary of French psychoanalysis—in which the term "sexual difference" plays an important part—has been received in the Anglo-American community by reference to the distinction between "sex" and "gender," a distinction that allows psychoanalysis to coincide with a more familiar paradigm (the debate between nature and nurture), but at the cost of displacing its basic terminology. This is one reason why French feminists have had such a difficult reception in the United States, where psychoanalysis is either celebrated for demonstrating that sexual difference is a "symbolic" phenomenon (a "contingent historical formation"), or else denounced as a form of "biological essentialism," a return to anatomical difference that is ultimately ahistorical, despite its notorious emphasis on language. In fact, however, neither of these assessments does justice to the phenomenon that psychoanalysis is intended to address: psychoanalysis does not advocate a "biological" account of sexual difference, or even a version of "psychic essentialism" (grounded in a fixed ideal of "masculinity" and "femininity"), but neither does it amount to a form of historicism, focused on the symbolic construction of "gender." This is the great enigma, but also the theoretical importance, of contemporary French psychoanalysis: sexual difference is neither "sex" nor "gender."[1]

This difficulty is not limited to the problem of sexual difference, but extends through the entire conceptual apparatus of French psychoanalytic theory.[2] At the broadest theoretical level, then, my principal claim is that the contemporary French revision of Freud has been interpreted through an inappropriate paradigm, which has not only obscured the theoretical specificity of psychoanalysis, but has also distorted the reception of a number of influential European writers who are grounded in this emerging tradition. We are now familiar with debates between those who seek to demonstrate the biological foundations of consciousness and sexuality, and those who argue for the cultural construction of subjectivity, insisting that human life has no automatically natural form, but is always decisively shaped by contingent historical conditions. No theoretical alternative is more widely publicized than this, or more heavily invested today. And yet, this very debate, in which "nature" and "culture" are opposed to one another, amounts to a distortion of psychoanalysis, an interpretive framework that not only obscures its basic concepts, but erodes the very field of psychoanalysis as a theoretically distinct formation.

This distortion affects the technical vocabulary of psychoanalysis at every level, and is particularly important for the problem of embodiment. The body in psychoanalysis is not a natural fact, governed by biological laws. At the same time, however, the body is not simply a product of representation, a contingent historical formation capable of being analyzed with the same techniques that a historian or social scientist might use to account for the rise of democracy, or the formation of the nation-state. From the standpoint of psychoanalysis, the body is not a natural phenomenon, but this does not mean it can be regarded as the invention of a particular culture, or the product of a specific historical moment—something that was invented *in historical time,* and that might be treated in the same way that we treat other historical phenomena, such as agricultural practices, or the invention of money, or the rise of genetic engineering. (Time is, in fact, one of the pressing but insufficiently developed issues in this book, an issue that both biological and sociohistorical modes of analysis take far too easily for granted: for what really is the time of the body, if—as psychoanalysis suggests—it cannot be immediately inscribed in the developmental or evolutionary time of biological nature, or in the chronological time of public and social history?)[3] This is not to say that biological accounts of health and disease, or historical accounts of "the Renaissance experience of madness," or "homosexuality in ancient Greece," are inappropriate or incorrect, but only that the theoretical specificity of psychoanalysis cannot be adequately grasped on the basis of these models. As a result, when readers seek to determine once and for all whether psychoanalysis is a theory of the "symbolic order," aimed at demonstrating the "social construction of gender," or whether it amounts to a return to "biological difference" that is based on a natural anatomy, the entire theoretical orientation of psychoanalysis has already been lost, displaced by a more familiar paradigm.

This argument not only addresses the *theoretical* specificity of psychoanalysis in relation to biological and sociohistorical models, but also seeks to clarify the unique *historical* position of psychoanalysis, the peculiar challenge it represents in relation to the inherited configuration of our knowledge. From this genealogical perspective, current debates between nature and nurture are strictly anachronistic, grounded in a conceptual framework that was formed in the nineteenth century, when the disciplines of biology and history as we know them today were first organized as academic fields.[4] The great debate between *Naturwissenschaften* and *Geisteswissenschaften* still governs the reception of psychoanalysis today, but it was made possible through an organization of knowledge that had already begun to erode at the time when Freud was writing. The contemporary French engagement with Freud thus represents an attempt to break (once again) with that inherited framework, and thereby to bring into view the most far-reaching philosophical consequences of Freud's work. And yet when terms such as "the symbolic order," or "sexual difference," or the "body," or the "drive" are understood in terms of the alternative between biological essentialism and historical construction, the basic vocabulary of psychoanalysis has already been abandoned— drawn back into the very framework it was intended to contest. In this respect, I follow Foucault's archaeological account of psychoanalysis, which suggests a radical disjunction between psychoanalysis and the "human sciences" on precisely this point.[5]

II.

The title of the book is explicitly intended to mark this basic theoretical and historical difficulty. And in fact, the title underwent a transformation that turned on precisely these issues. For I had initially called the book *Vital Signs,* intending to stress the peculiar conjunction between language and the body that I had seen in Freud's earliest work, where he spoke of the formation of hysterical symptoms, which he was forced to regard not as having a natural cause, but rather as being due in some way to "representation." In "A Comparative Study of Organic and Hysterical Motor Paralyses," for example, he explicitly spoke of hysterical paralysis as "representation paralysis," and noted with some surprise (in keeping with his neurological training) that unlike organic paralysis, in which a physical cause—and indeed a material "lesion"—can always be found, in hysterical paralysis by contrast one finds a concrete, bodily disturbance in which the organism itself remains undamaged. "I will try to show," Freud writes, "that there can be a functional alteration without a concomitant organic lesion" (*SE*, 1:170). This is what led to Freud's famous remark that "hysterics suffer mainly from reminiscences" (*SE*, 2:7), in which it seemed perfectly clear that—far from suggesting the hysteric is "only imagining things," or that it is "all in her head"—Freud was trying to understand the mechanisms by which representations could give rise to bodily effects (the "reminiscence" being a somatic symptom rather than merely a "psychological" memory). It was precisely this notion of "representation paralysis" that initially led me to expect that I might approach the entire domain of psychoanalysis, and clarify its conceptual specificity, by focusing on this question concerning the effect of representation on the material dimension of the body. Following Freud's famous remark, I thus expected that psychoanalysis as a whole would be a theory of the peculiar intersection between the organism and language—the vital domain and the signifier. Far from being a "psychological" theory, or a theory of representation, the discipline of psychoanalysis would be defined as an account of the processes by which, as Freud said, "the material conditions" of the body "are profoundly altered" (*SE*, 1:170). Not only the conceptual specificity of psychoanalysis, but also its unique historical position, would be more clearly defined in this manner. Even if psychoanalysis wished at all cost (perhaps for the sake of its prestige) to maintain the traditional medical language of "lesions," so admirably discussed by Foucault in *The Birth of the Clinic*, it would still have to follow Freud: "The lesion in hysterical paralysis," he writes, is not a simple organic alteration, as in the case of a medical disease, but is rather "an alteration of the *conception, the idea*, of the arm, for instance" (*SE*, 1:170).[6] Some material part of the body is inaccessible, or paralyzed, or loses its function, Freud says, but "without its material substratum . . . being damaged." "The lesion," he concludes, "must therefore be *the abolition of the associative accessibility of the conception of the arm*. The arm behaves as though it did not exist for the play of associations" (170). It is this peculiar conjunction of representation and the organic domain that led

Freud to the notorious statement: "Hysteria behaves as though anatomy did not exist" (1:169).

Eventually, however, I came to the conclusion that this account was not really adequate. In keeping with the general argument of the book, I was forced to conclude that the very framework I had adopted in initially posing the problem was itself undergoing a certain transformation as Freudian theory developed, and that the vocabulary with which I had begun remained attached to the very conceptual apparatus that psychoanalysis should have led me to rethink. For in fact, as Monique David-Ménard has shown in her admirable book *Hysteria from Freud to Lacan*, it was not a question of an "organic" or "biological" domain being somehow subjected to the force of representation—as if "nature" and "culture" somehow collided or overlapped in the phenomenon of human embodiment.[7] This was indeed the case for the early account of symptom formation, as explained by the "conversion theory" of hysteria, in which a certain "idea" or "image" (an unconscious "thought" or "memory") somehow came to be somatized, lodged in the organic world—as though the divine abstraction of the signifier were suddenly "converted" into the material and fleshly form of the body, itself understood as a natural substratum that occasionally falls prey to the work of representation (or more precisely to its occasional malfunction). This was, to be sure, an early hypothesis, but as David-Ménard argues, such an account actually conceals the very concept of the erotogenic body, by maintaining a pre-Freudian framework in which the biological organism is subject to peculiar symbolic or imaginary effects (under conditions that are strictly aberrant and unusual—a symptomatic exception that should quickly be corrected and overcome).[8] It was not long, moreover, before Freud himself abandoned this early account in favor of a more precise description (in his *Three Essays on the Theory of Sexuality* and elsewhere), in which the body itself was to be understood in terms of a process of libidinal organization that necessarily cut against the grain of nature—not in the exceptional or merely pathological case, but as such, and in its very constitution. This libidinal organization of the body (which Lacan would later develop through the "imaginary," "symbolic," and "real") explains why "sexuality" in the Freudian sense is a uniquely human problem. It also explains why there can be such a thing as a "history of sexuality," for it suggests that human existence is not so decisively bound to the mechanisms of instinct, the force of evolution, and the singular telos of reproduction. And yet, this very capacity to have a history, and this peculiar, constitutive, and even "formative" relation to the domain of representation, so insistently emphasized by Lacan, should not lead us to conclude that "sexuality," or indeed the phenomenon of embodiment, is simply a "discursive product," the contingent construction of a particular culture or a given historical moment. On the contrary, Freudian theory confronts us with an emerging theoretical formation in which the very alternative, and even the occasional conjunction, between biology and language, was no longer adequate.

This transformation in my understanding is silently marked in the subtitle of the book. For its original form, *Nature and Culture in Psychoanalysis*, eventually had to be replaced by a more disjunctive formulation: *Nature, Culture, Psychoanalysis*. Whereas the first version indicated my belief that psychoanalytic theory might be explored as a kind of intersection between biology and the symbolic domain, the later version was more hesitant, as if to say "nature," "culture," and then ". . . psychoanalysis?" It was thus no longer a question of regarding psychoanalysis as an arena in which nature and culture would overlap, but rather of considering psychoanalysis as a theoretical development in which these other two domains, as they are commonly understood, no longer function as the absolute points of reference. And here again, I would like to stress (precisely by this disjunctive use of the terms) that it is not a question of simply dismissing arguments that are devoted to demonstrating the "historical construction of subjectivity," or indeed accounts of disease and health that remain wedded to the biomedical model. Knowledge, it seems to me, is simply far too diverse and too lacking in theoretical unity for such absolute claims to be made. It is therefore not a matter of banishing other perspectives or exposing their glaring stupidity to the lacerating gaze of a triumphant Lacanian theory, but simply a question of doing justice to the theoretical specificity of psychoanalysis, which has been almost entirely absorbed in disputes between the other two domains, which even today remain more familiar to us. One might well wonder, in fact, if the loud and tendentious arguments between biology and social construction, displayed not only in the academy but also in the popular press (where they struggle to explain almost everything today—from alcoholism and depression to intelligence, homosexuality, and career choice), are not the angry voices of a knowledge suddenly made aware that it no longer has the ultimate word.

III.

These remarks should be enough to indicate some of the concerns that occupy me in what follows: the place of psychoanalysis in relation to other forms of knowledge; the historical challenge that psychoanalytic theory presents to inherited modes of explanation; the peculiar way in which the theoretical specificity of Lacanian theory is constantly eroded in the very course of its reception; and the impact that the Lacanian reading of Freud should have on our understanding of a series of basic problems, above all the question of sexual difference, and the problem of human embodiment. But there are perhaps two other things that are worth mentioning in an introductory way.

For I may as well confess that this book did not originally aim at such grand and comprehensive claims, but began as a rather limited effort to explore some relatively narrow aspects of contemporary French psychoanalysis—to sort out a few of its local details, which (particularly in the case of Jacques Lacan) are notoriously difficult and obscure. For the most part, its internal affairs are governed by nothing more than this exegetical interest: I simply wanted to understand what was happening in this enigmatic but remarkably vital domain of contemporary continental thought.

I was therefore not especially concerned with producing an argument or generating a thesis—or indeed with entering into the grand and often volatile debates that have characterized so many discussions of French psychoanalysis, whether they seek to denounce it as a purely charismatic, mystical, or hyperrational dogma, or to celebrate it as the ultimate truth of subjectivity, and indeed as the final standard by which every other discourse can finally be measured. One is all too familiar with such gestures today (profoundly anti-intellectual, in my view), which litter both the high discourse of the academy and the domain of the popular press, explaining to us in somber or apocalyptic tones (but with a wide range of conclusions) that psychoanalysis, whether of the tortured French variety or its classical Freudian counterpart, is a fascinating but ultimately corrupt and outmoded enterprise, a pseudo-scientific discourse that must finally be dismissed (a view that is commonly and often hysterically expressed in the *New York Times*), or a crucial and subversive theoretical endeavor that nevertheless remains crippled by its attachment to a number of conservative, metaphysical, or normalizing notions (a canonical judgment in some areas of cultural studies), or indeed—to take a more enthusiastic tone—the most exemplary new conceptual development, in which sexuality is for once accorded its rightful place, while at the same time the contingent, discursive formation of subjectivity is at last conclusively demonstrated, allowing us finally to purge psychoanalysis of the last vestiges of Freud's biological vocabulary (a view that is widely held among some proponents of psychoanalysis).

Having just begun to read this strange material, I was not prepared to defend or refute such positions, despite the fact that successful and even somewhat formulaic genres have now developed in all these modes. From my tentative and still exploratory perspective, the Lacanian elaboration of Freudian theory had far too many aspects and seemed far too diverse—too intimately linked with other theoretical domains, and still too poorly understood—for such summarizing judgments to be useful (much less true). And apart from the enormous complexity of its internal machinery, its relationship to other forms of knowledge—particularly biomedical knowledge on the one hand, and sociohistorical knowledge on the other—was still far too undeveloped for such conclusions to be meaningful. In addition, my academic training (grounded in close and often exacting encounters with lyric poetry and philosophy) had taught me to be far more hesitant and circumspect in the face of a theoretical formation that was at once so conceptually intricate (like philosophy) and so verbally nuanced, so subtly bound up (like poetry) with the mysteries of subjectivity.

Thus it happened that in the midst of a remarkably fertile and especially strident period in the history of psychoanalysis—a moment of crisis and rebirth, full of moral fervor, utopian passion, and scientific righteousness—I sought to pose, mainly for myself and my students, some very local and elementary questions. I did so not with the aim of producing a grand conclusion, but simply with the desire to grasp somewhat more clearly the basic architecture of Lacan's work, and in the hope of gaining some sense of how this discourse—so massively dependent on other disciplines, and so open to being influenced, and even conceptually altered, by developments in other fields—might nevertheless lay claim to its own conceptual integrity, distinct from its disciplinary neighbors even as it drew on their resources, and cast its light upon them in return.

I therefore sought simply to explore a few elements of French psychoanalysis, in a rather limited way, without aiming at a broader account, and to do so, moreover, by focusing on at least a few texts by authors other than Lacan himself. This choice was guided partly by my interest in considering some clinical material (which was more readily available in other writers, and which has been sorely neglected in the American reception of Lacanian theory), and partly by the fact that, after several years of reading Lacan, I wanted to gauge just how far his thinking might extend into the work of other figures in the French analytic tradition, and whether their writing, cast in a different style and sometimes a different vocabulary, might shed light on Lacan's own work, and clarify it further. In addition, I wanted to address the work of women writers, in order to understand more clearly what Lacanian theory might contribute to the contemporary effort to rethink the question of sexual difference.

The chapters in this book are thus defined by relatively local questions, posed in a more or less exploratory way. My general aim was thus (1) to clarify the distinctive theoretical position of psychoanalysis in relation to biomedical and sociohistorical models, and (2) to suggest how this argument might affect the reception of several major figures in contemporary French thought (above all Kristeva, Irigaray, and Foucault). My initial and more immediate aim, however, was (3) to introduce some clinical material into the American discussion of Lacan, and (4) to elaborate in a very localized way the relation between Lacan's work and several important women writers in contemporary French thought. To this last point may be added a wish to expand the canon of received authors to some extent, by speaking not only of Kristeva and Irigaray, but also of figures who are less well-known in the United States—in particular Eugénie Lemoine-Luccioni and Catherine Millot. Since Lacan's reception in America has been so thoroughly intertwined with feminist theory, these relations seemed worthy of attention.

IV.

This brings me to the chapters themselves. If one aim of the book is broadly theoretical and historical, another is to contribute to the American reception of French feminist theory. By clarifying the manner in which "sexual difference" functions, and by initiating a discussion of the "body" that does not remain determined by the opposition between biological law and historical construction, it becomes possible to elucidate the work of several influential French feminist thinkers who have often been misinterpreted, due to a lack of clarity about the psychoanalytic terminology that orients their work. The chapters that follow also seek to fulfill the third aim of the book, by introducing a number of clinical issues: anorexia (in chapter one, on Lemoine-Luccioni), the distinction between "maternity" and "femininity" (in chapter two, on Kristeva), transexuality (in chapter three, on Millot), and the incest taboo (in chapter four, on Freud and Lacan).

The first chapter deals with the recently translated work of Eugénie Lemoine-Luccioni, whose book *The Dividing of Women* addresses the mother-daughter relation from a Lacanian perspective, focusing in particular on the question of *inheritance*. The theoretical stakes of the entire project are evident here. On the one hand, the *Diagnostic and Statistical Manual of Mental Disorders* (DSM) notes that anorexia "cannot be accounted for by a known *physical disorder*." From the standpoint of organic medicine, no biological cause is recognized for anorexia. The "body" in anorexia therefore cannot be adequately grasped by the techniques of biomedical knowledge. On the other hand, arguments about the "social construction of femininity," though commonly used in cultural theory—for example, to account for the "invention of hysteria" in the Victorian period—are not sufficient to explain why one subject rather than another becomes anorexic. As the *DSM-IV* also notes, anorexia is far more common among those whose sisters or mothers have been anorexic than it is in the general population. The medical community has used this statistic to suggest that a genetic factor is behind anorexia, but Lemoine-Luccioni's work allows us to argue (she herself does not make this claim) that anorexia can be understood in terms of the *mother-daughter relation*: it is thus a *symbolic inheritance*, a particular relation to the "symbolic order," that is transmitted from one generation to another—a "historical" inheritance that cannot be understood biologically, but that also cannot be grasped by the familiar techniques of sociohistorical knowledge. Since anorexia is almost exclusively found in women (though not entirely: because some men are anorexic, it is not *genetically* specific to women), we may add that this relation to the "symbolic order" is bound up with the symbolization of sexual difference. One begins to see from this that the term "sexual difference" is not used biologically, but also that it does not refer to general social representations of "gender," since it concerns a more particular formation of the "subject." The first chapter thus introduces an important thinker in contemporary feminist theory whose work has not been widely discussed, while also contributing (I hope) to the general theoretical project of the book.

If the first chapter deals with the "relation to the mother" and "maternity" (Lemoine-Luccioni's book discusses women who become pregnant during the course of their analyses), the second chapter moves on to the distinction between the "mother" and the "woman." In a reading of Kristeva's essays "Stabat Mater" and "Freud and Love," I argue for a fairly substantial revision of the canonical reception of her work, based on a more precise understanding of its psychoanalytic framework.

Recent accounts of psychoanalysis often argue that the mother belongs to the "imaginary" domain, a dual relation of intersubjectivity that must be abandoned when the child passes into the "symbolic order" of language, where the dual relation of the imaginary is superseded by a triangular structure, mediated by the paternal function. This account is said to parallel Freud's analysis of the "pre-Oedipal" and "Oedipal" stages. One of the difficulties American feminists have had with psychoanalysis is that the mother appears—on this account—to have no place in the "symbolic order" and to be confined to the "imaginary." Similar objections have been made in relation to Freud, who is said to consider the maternal as a "pre-Oedipal" figure who must be abandoned if the child is to develop. As a result of this "abjection" of the maternal, it follows that the place of women in the symbolic order is not adequately established. Psychoanalytic theory appears not only to describe this difficulty, but also to perpetuate it.

This popular account of the "imaginary" and "symbolic," however, is inaccurate in two important ways. First, it tends to identify the "imaginary" with the "maternal" and "feminine," while identifying the "symbolic" with the "paternal" and "masculine." In fact, however, it is insufficient to say that the mother is confined to the imaginary: "Stabat Mater" shows that the position of the "mother" emerges only *in the symbolic order*. The same point is made in Lacan's essay on psychosis, and I show (in an account of "schema R") that contrary to popular belief, the mother *does not appear in the imaginary*. Thus, when we speak of the "imaginary," we cannot rightly say that we are speaking of "mothers" or "women." As Kristeva argues in "Stabat Mater," it would be more precise to say that the image is a *concealment* of maternity, what Freud called an "archaic image" in which maternity remains veiled. In different language, one could say that sexual difference emerges only in the symbolic order, and that Kristeva is therefore seeking to distinguish the "imaginary mother" (who is not sexually marked) from the "symbolic mother." Once this distinction is made, however, it remains necessary to distinguish in turn between "maternity" and "femininity." This leads to the second point: the "mother" and the "woman" should not be so quickly identified with one another, as happens when they are regarded as "confined to the imaginary." Kristeva's work has often been taken as an effort to recover a lost or abjected "maternity," an "imaginary" (or "semiotic") domain that is lost when the symbolic order is established; but her work should be read in almost the opposite way—as an attempt to insist upon the mother in her symbolic function, but also as an attempt to show how the question of "femininity" remains beyond the maternal image, which seeks to "contain" the woman.

This is precisely the issue that Freud's late work addressed, when he spoke (in notoriously problematic language) of the way in which woman remains "resistant" to castration. Lacan's late seminar on "feminine sexuality" returns to these issues in Freud's late work, and the entire discourse of "feminine *jouissance*" can be read as an attempt to show why the "question of woman" cannot be resolved—as Freud was often tempted to think—by appeal to "maternity" (to "accept castration" by taking the child as a substitute, and so on). Thus, even for women who in fact become mothers, the question of "sexual difference" cannot be resolved by appeal to the distinction between "men" and "mothers." And the effort to *reduce* the feminine to the maternal has clinical consequences (and theological underpinnings) that Kristeva explores. I read her texts in conjunction with Lacan's "sexuation graph" from *Encore,* and with "schema R" (from the psychosis essay) to elaborate the problem of "sexual difference," and to suggest its bearing on Freud's late work.

The third chapter is focused on Catherine Millot's book *Horsexe,* which deals with some clinical issues in the treatment of transsexuals. Here, too, the basic thesis of the book is addressed: in current cultural theory, the transsexual is often celebrated as the most radical instance of the "construction of gender." According to Millot, however, more specific clinical information suggests that the transsexual should not be unequivocally celebrated, or construed as a liberatory figure, since the case histories often show evidence of abuse, of speech disorders, and of a suffering that is not recognized by those who (from too far away) take the figure of the transsexual to be heroic or defiant or liberatory. This chapter also discusses the relation of "sexual difference" to historical developments in medical technology.

The fourth chapter deals with the relation between Freud's *Totem and Taboo* and his discussion of the Oedipal myth. Having explored to some extent the relation between the "imaginary" and the "maternal," and then the relation between the "maternal" and the "feminine," I wanted to understand more clearly the position of the "father," so apparently univocal, authoritative, and unproblematic in Lacan—to judge from his reception. Here again, the expectation I had been given on the basis of secondary reading did not prepare me for what I found. As I read Lacan's own account of the position of the father, it seemed to me that whereas his early work indeed appeared to place the father in the position of a "third term," mediating between the child and the mother, it was in fact necessary to distinguish between the "imaginary father" and the "symbolic father," and that these two versions of the father were often confused with one another. What interested me more, however, was that even the more "correct" reading, in which the symbolic father could be regarded, roughly, as a liquidation of the imaginary father, was itself eventually complicated and even overturned by Lacan. For around 1960, at the time he wrote *The Ethics of Psychoanalysis*, Lacan began to speak of a deficiency in the law, a certain dimension of incompleteness in the symbolic order, which corresponded to the increasing attention he gave to terms such as *jouissance* and the "object a." And this development in Lacan's account of the paternal function, I thought, corresponded quite precisely to the development of Freud's own work, and the movement of thought that had led him to turn from Oedipus to *Totem and Taboo*.

The final chapter turns to Foucault, whose "historical" analyses are often thought to conflict with a purportedly "ahistorical" psychoanalysis. I suggest that, although he certainly remained wary of psychoanalysis, Foucault saw clearly that it represented a radical break with nineteenth-century thought, and particularly with the debate between *Naturwissenschaften* and *Geisteswissenschaften*. In *Madness and Civilization*, *The Order of Things*, and even in his late work, Foucault argued that the philosophical challenge of psychoanalysis lay in its break with the opposition between "nature" and "history." If he turned, in his late work—as do many theorists today—to questions of the "body," it was precisely because the body was the clearest point at which this inherited debate proves inadequate: like "sexual difference," the body can be adequately grasped neither as a natural fact nor simply as a "product" of history. Such is the challenge of psychoanalytic theory, which will only be read when this paradigm has come into question.

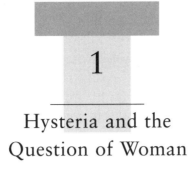

Hysteria and the Question of Woman

DEVENIR-FEMME

In *Partage des Femmes*, Eugénie Lemoine-Luccioni tells of a client, Anne-Marie, who becomes pregnant after she has been in analysis for some time.[1] It is a biologically normal pregnancy, but this does not altogether deprive it of *significance*. It would be a mistake, therefore, to pretend that the question of sexuality can come to a close at this point. This will not keep Anne-Marie from taking refuge from the question by appealing to her supposed proof—as though woman and mother were one and the same. When the pregnancy is confirmed, Anne-Marie goes not to her husband but directly to her analyst and declares that her analysis can come to an end: she now has nothing more to say.

Five years earlier, when she was eighteen, Anne-Marie began to suffer from anorexia and amenorrhea, and for two years, her periods stopped altogether—*exactly as her mother's had when she was the same age* (61–62). Her analyst, Lemoine-Luccioni, is reminded of another client whom she calls Blanche, a young woman who was also anorexic and amenorrheic, just as her mother had been at the same age. There is a history here that does not belong to the order of genetics.

Biology *and* History

We must be attentive to this history, and the theoretical difficulty it presents. On the one hand, we have a bodily symptom, but it does not reduce to the order of biology. The *Diagnostic and Statistical Manual of Mental Disorders* sagely observes, without further comment, that "the disturbance [anorexia, which is usually accompanied by amenor-rhea] cannot be accounted for by a known *physical* disorder."[2] On the other hand, in addition to this bodily but not simply physiological symptom, we have a history of some kind, linking mother and daughter, but this history does not reduce to the order of cultural determination, as though it were a matter of what is so quickly called "the social construction of femininity." For as Lemoine-Luccioni suggests, what is at stake is the handing down of a phenomenon from generation to generation, something, in other words, that happens not at the general level of culture, but rather in a more specific relation between mother and daughter.[3] Again, as the *Diagnostic and Statistical Manual* observes, without troubling itself further, this disturbance "is more common among sisters and mothers of individuals with the disorder than in the general population." This remark might suggest to the medical community that the cause will one day prove to be genetic. One hears this sort of hope expressed today about alcoholism as well, by a community of research that does not take the history that confronts us here as seriously as it might. What binds the generations here is not in fact a genetic endowment, nor a matter of what we call the "social construction of the subject," but a more intimate transmission of the signifier, inherited at the level of the flesh. It is therefore a question of the *relation between* the symbol and the organism—a question that has led psychoanalytic feminism to rethink the categories of biology and history.

We are dealing, in short, with what one might call a transmission of the question of sexual difference, and the peculiar historicality of this question: the question *repeats*, and the subject is produced as a particular answer to this question—an answer that, being always more or less inadequate, is frequently also a symptom. Such a history is still virtually unthinkable for us, but it gives us a central and neglected trajectory of Irigaray's work. An inheritance between generations of women, which functions at the level of the body, without answering to physiology; a history, then, which at the same time is not susceptible to the usual, broad cultural analysis—such phenomena lead Irigaray to question the accepted tools of biological and cultural analysis. This is precisely the theoretical contribution of psychoanalysis: when it is a question of sexuality, feminism cannot have recourse to the usual arguments about cultural and political determination, any more than it can rely on biology.[4]

It is ironic that both of these arguments have been attributed to Irigaray—the one, which pretends she is celebrating female anatomy and is therefore ahistorical, insufficiently political, and guilty of biological essentialism; and the other, which imagines that she reduces everything to language, as if the question of sexual difference were a matter of nothing more than discourse and representation, nothing more, in short, than what is hastily called the symbolic order.[5] For Irigaray, neither of these positions even begins to encounter the question of sexuality; to read her in terms of these two options is therefore to close out the very basis of her writing.

We know that Irigaray has written on the mother-daughter relation.[6] But she has not done so in order to celebrate a community of women, as has sometimes been said.[7] She is not as optimistic here as one might wish.[8] Perhaps what is handed down in this relation is precisely the question of sexual difference—"Am I a man or a woman?"

"The Fable of the Blood"

Anne-Marie explains to her analyst that sometime after the beginning of her symptoms, her father died of a cerebral hemorrhage (her mother's father had died in a similar way); at the time of his death, her physician gave her advice, evidently hoping that she would be able to resume her life. "'One year after my father's death,' Anne-Marie explains, 'I put on lipstick, as a physician had advised, and my periods came back'" (62). What is this relation between the symbol and the organism?[9] Shortly after this moment, which we might all too quickly call her "return to womanhood," she was engaged to be married, and now, carrying the news of her pregnancy, Anne-Marie will declare to her analyst that she has nothing more to say: she has a job (she is a psychologist and she takes care of children), and now that she is pregnant she *does not wish for her analysis to continue*.

Her analyst refuses to comply with this demand. She notices that her client's discourse has suddenly changed. Instead of being a pleasure, the prospect of analysis now brings with it a high degree of anxiety: "I am not even analyzable," Anne-Marie says. Besides, "I have stopped dreaming. . . . And what am I doing here anyway: I'm pregnant" (63). Faced with a client who stops eating, who stops bleeding, who stops dreaming, and who brings her pregnancy forward in order to stop analysis in this particular way, Lemoine-Luccioni can only regard these details as a chain, a symptomatic repetition. The pregnancy, she believes, is being used as a resistance. "Conceiving the child" is intended *to put a stop to the question* that has governed the entire analysis, namely: "If I do not have periods" (65), if I do not eat, *if I do not become a mother, am I nevertheless a woman?*

Let me pause for a moment at this question to cite the interview with Irigaray titled "Questions":

> It is the first question, and all the others lead right back to it.
> It is this one: "Are you a woman?"
> A typical question.
> A man's question? I don't think that a woman—unless she has been assimilated to masculine, and more specifically phallic, models—would ask me that question. . . . In other words, in response to the person who asked the question, I can only refer it back to him and say: "It's your question." . . .
>
> If I had answered: "My dear sir, how can you have such suspicions? It is perfectly clear that I am a woman," I should have fallen back into the discourse of a certain "truth" and its power. And if I were claiming that what I am trying to articulate, in speech or writing, starts from the *certainty* that I am a woman, then I should be caught up once again within "phallocratic" discourse. I might well attempt to overturn it, but I should remain included within it. (120–21/120–22)

Desire

I cannot take time to follow this case presentation in the detail it deserves; let me simply mention a few points. The first concerns the register of Anne-Marie's desire. Although she claims to have stopped dreaming, this is not the truth; as the analysis continues, it turns out that she "has a clearly homosexual dream." Anne-Marie says she is astonished at this dream, she does not understand it, and she has never had the slightest idea of being a lesbian (63–67). This is the first detail, then: her pregnancy appears to be offered as proof that she is not a lesbian. This is why Anne-Marie wishes to claim this pregnancy as the last word, the end of analysis. Such is the register of her desire, which will not be spoken.[10]

"Mother" and *"The* Woman"

The second point concerns a series of remarks Anne-Marie makes about her mother, and the meaning of the term "woman"—a term, according to Lemoine-Luccioni, around which all her client's symptoms have been constructed. Despite her recent marriage, the pregnancy makes Anne-Marie no longer a wife, the partner, in other words, of her new husband. "The pregnancy makes her a kind of universal woman, a woman for everyone"(64).[11] Her analyst recalls another client who says, "I do not want to get married just to get married. I want to be a married mother for my mother" (67). In addition, Anne-Marie says there is something criminal about woman: "Woman is guilty."[12] "Anne-Marie," her analyst says, "is balanced between not being a woman and dying in blood because woman is guilty of theft and murder." Her mother, whose husband was a widower when she met him, figures strongly at this point. According to Anne-Marie, her mother "stole her father from a dead woman" (64). Anne-Marie, of course, is herself the product of this theft. A final detail:

> A little before Anne-Marie's pregnancy, her mother brought her "a child": in a delusional episode, this mother believed herself to be pregnant. . . . Anne-Marie was very shaken by this event. . . . "It is I who am pregnant, not my mother," she says. (65)

The Body, The Signifier, Totality

We can elaborate here the meaning of *La femme*. In conceiving of the body as a relationship between the signifier and the flesh, psychoanalysis points out that the organization of the body—which is not given at birth but which has rather to be constructed—is accomplished by virtue of a certain relation to language. We cannot enter here into the important difference between the signifier and the image, but we can note that if the image plays a part in the construction of the body—and certainly it has a decisive role in anorexia—it is another thing to speak of the signifier, which, insofar as it gives rise to the constitution of objects, will play an organizing role in giving *limits* to the body, in allowing the subject to distinguish, in other words, between what is inside and what is outside. This is what gives the concept of erotogenic zones—those orifices by means of which the body establishes its exchange with exteriority—their decisive relation, not simply to the image, but to language.

It will be evident, I think, that in distinguishing between the signifier and the image I am suggesting the necessity of drawing a sharp line where there is normally some confusion. We hear people speak of "imagining" a possible femininity, and "symbolizing" femininity, as though these were roughly the same; we hear the concept of "the symbolic" used as though it were something one could also do, in the sense that one is said to "symbolize" things, or to "symbolize" women in a fashion that will give a place to more than the mother, as Whitford suggests Irigaray wishes to do. This usual meaning of the word is not inappropriate, but it must be remembered that, within the psychoanalytic field, the symbol is distinct from the image, a point Freud broached with his discussion of "word-presentations" and "thing-presentations." Freud's distinction concerns different modes of "presentation" (visual and verbal), different modes of "re-presentation" (memory), and a difference in register between a hypothetical level of "perception" and the order of "consciousness" as it is linguistically organized. Hence one cannot say that the generation of "images" of women would automatically be a means of adding to and altering the "symbolic" (an argument that also misconstrues the symbolic as a rough equivalent for "the sociohistorical context"). As Irigaray herself says, the most positive and apparently affirmative images of woman one can find "are capable of nurturing repeatedly and at length all the masquerades of femininity that are expected of her" (26/27). This is precisely why Irigaray finds it necessary to be unusually wary of the strategy of simply offering "positive images," a wariness that separates her work from that of some other feminists.[13] It also suggests that her conception of what it would take to "change history" must be complicated accordingly. And clearly this conception will be shaped in part by the psychoanalytic understanding of how the subject's relation to the past is altered in such a way that the future may be something other than a repetition of that past.

I cannot pursue this problem of the symbol and the image within the scope of this argument, and the importance of this distinction for the concept of history, but I can suggest two things. First, Lemoine-Luccioni is being careful with this distinction when, in effect, she refuses the image in favor of *speech*: thus, even if the structure of this speech is a *question* (man or woman?) difficult to bear, and not simply an affirmation (which one finds in some nonpsychoanalytic forms of therapy), and even if this question is quite literally a grammatical structure that does not *solidify*—in the way the image sought by Anne-Marie offers solidity and takes the form of a totality—such a question is nevertheless to be preferred, Lemoine-Luccioni suggests, to the "quick fix" that Anne-Marie has attempted. Second, Irigaray frequently says—we have seen it in the quotation cited already—that her project is not to *represent* "woman," but to "*articulate*, in speech or in writing," something that starts precisely from her *not beginning with the certainty* that she is a woman.[14] For the moment, let us only note this role of the symbol in the constitution of the body's organization, that sense of its own limits that is necessary for what one might call the body's containment within its skin.

If this *limitation* of the body, through the mediation of the symbol, is not achieved in some manner, one can say that the "body," strictly speaking, is not present for the living being.[15] Let me cite Monique David-Ménard:

> The paradoxical relation between the hysteric and her body has become clearer: in a sense, the hysteric lacks a body. . . . [F]or a hysteric (male or female), certain zones of the erotogenic body—*those whose symbolization refers to the first constitution of an object-relation* [emphasis mine]—are in fact condemned to nonexistence. But another aspect of the paradox comes to light here: if the hysteric lacks a body, it is because he or she passionately rejects the lack.[16]

We see here not only the figure of *La femme*, the idea of a totality which in fact does not exist ("woman," as Lacan puts it, is "*pas toute*"; or, in another formulation, "*La femme n'existe pas*"; or, in yet another, this sex is "not *one*"); we also see the relation between *La femme* and the figure of the mother.[17] David-Ménard continues: one sees here not only the failure of symbolization that makes the relation to the object, and hence the limitation of the body itself, unstable, but also

> a desperate declaration that there is nothing but body and that whatever lacks body must be disallowed. There is *obliteration of the subject* [emphasis mine] by a body that could be figured as a whole and adored as Dora adores the Madonna or Frau K. . . . The hysteric suffers in that she considers the body the only reality, she is unable to know the order of language. When the resources of the symbolic order take into account the void that inhabits a body, they do not suppress it; *they give it limits.* (see note 23)

In this way, Dora comes to be dominated by the question "What is Woman?"—a question that seems to her to have only one overwhelming and one might as well say ontotheological answer, in the Madonna. In short, because she was unable to symbolize the "void that inhabits the body," David-Ménard suggests, "Dora becomes passionate about the form of an adorable body, and her own body has no configuration, no limit."

"Man or Woman?"

Fourth point. Let us pause for a moment with this question, "Man or woman?" In the passage I cited, Irigaray is quick to point out that this is not her question, but one that is constantly posed to her, one that has a tendency to repeat itself: all the other questions "lead right back to it." In response, she hands the question back. "It's *your* question," she replies, which is precisely what Lemoine-Luccioni does, in a gesture we will shortly be tempted to call not only analytic but ethical. To answer the question in this form, to say, "My dear sir, it's perfectly clear that I am a woman," and thus "to start from the certainty that I am a woman," she says, would be to remain within a certain discourse and its truth. We are accustomed to saying that the neutral subject of philosophy (the "cogito") is a metaphysical construction that obliterates the difference between men and women. Are we equally prepared to consider that *sexual difference*—"man *or* woman"—and with it the name of woman, *belongs to metaphysics*? The simple assertion of sexual difference is not endorsed by these writers, nor is the solution of "androgyny"; what is stressed is a certain *relation to the question,* in the face of a forced choice, a "having-to-choose" one or the other—a choice to which there is no alternative except the "no exit" taken, for example, by Anne-Marie.[18] Are we prepared, in other words, to think the question—not simply the proposition, "the *subject* is not neuter," but rather that woman *as such* is "this sex which is not one"? Irigaray is sometimes said to assert sexual difference, but what is not remembered is that this refers not simply to the difference between the sexes, but to difference within them—a point that is made by Lemoine-Luccioni as well.[19] It is a matter of universality: as I have tried to suggest above, the woman who takes the position of representing "all women," who is, in other words "La femme," cannot be *a woman.*[20] This is why Lacan says that "The Woman"—in taking the position of the universal—is one of the names of the Father.[21]

The Other Woman: The "One" and the "Other"

This brings us to the final point, which concerns Anne-Marie's relation to the other, the other woman, her analyst. From her very first interviews, Anne-Marie declared that she wanted to become an analyst.[22] This was her first demand, and her analyst refused. For Lemoine-Luccioni, the demand to assume this image, to become *like her analyst,* originates in the ego of her client, an ego that has been structured in accordance with an image that is maintained at the expense of Anne-Marie's desire. Irigaray writes of the hysteric: "She has left only two options—mutism and mimicry, and both of these at once" (134/137).[23] The demand to be an analyst is therefore linked to the other refusals of desire to which Anne-Marie has been subjected by the imaginary order to which her ego has been dedicated. The ego's demand to become an analyst is therefore referred by Lemoine-Luccioni to the amenorrhea that preceded it, and the pregnancy that followed. Anne-Marie, who has stopped bleeding and who has been anorexic *like her mother,* now demands to be a woman *like her analyst,* and when her analyst says, in effect, "I cannot ordain you as a woman in my image," Anne-Marie will try to bring the analysis to an end with her pregnancy.[24] In short, she plays out her history between a "no" and a "yes": having unconsciously refused to be a "woman," insofar as it appears to mean only "motherhood" (Lemoine-Luccioni calls her symptoms "a 'no' addressed to the mother" [62]), Anne-Marie now demands to be identifiable as a "woman," insofar as it will put an end to her question. These identifications, the "no" and the "yes," have determined her in her work, her marriage, her symptoms, her analysis, and most of her life; but at the level of desire, which is signified upon the flesh, in the form of symptoms, which she cannot articulate but which she suffers, Anne-Marie is silently asking, without knowing it, whether there is a place for her outside the imaginary positions she has been trying to assume at such great cost.[25]

That is the final point: for Lemoine-Luccioni, the properly analytic, and perhaps also the ethical response, is to recognize that this pregnancy must not be allowed to close the case, but should open again, in the dimension of speech, this question that Anne-Marie has been living in her flesh and silently repeating throughout her history ("like a good hysteric," Lemoine-Luccioni says), namely, whether she is a man or a woman. The kernel of the story, for her analyst, is that she is quite capable of being a little girl (anorexic and amenorrheic) or a mother (pregnant, or a child psychologist, or an analyst), but that between these two positions, neither of which is truly hers, "there is no place for the woman" and her desire (70). Irigaray, too, is guided by this relation to the other, which we see in the refusal, on the part of the analyst, to sanction the image of woman (*"La femme"*) which Anne-Marie would like to assume—an image she finds in her analyst, and which would certainly be a gratifying and even seductive role for the analyst to play, as the mother figure strong enough to rescue the lost daughter and serve as her benevolent role model. The analyst's refusal of her client's demand, therefore, is at the same time the refusal to gratify her own ego, in favor of the desire of the other woman, an other desire for which there has never been any place.

Let me pause again to cite the opening words of Irigaray's essay, "When Our Lips Speak Together":

> If we keep on speaking the same language together, we're going to reproduce the same history. . . . If we keep on speaking sameness, if we speak to each other as men have been doing for cen-

turies, as we have been taught to speak, we'll miss each other, fail ourselves. (205/205)

Another point should be added here concerning a certain "history" or "transmission." We have seen Anne-Marie's relation to an ego ideal that coincides with the relation to the mother and structures the history we are addressing—her passage, in other words, from being a *child* to being a *woman* (an analyst, a mother). Now this relation to the mother is *replayed* in the relation to the child, confirming our remarks on the problem of generations of women. One can see this with Anne-Marie, whose own pregnancy has the effect of *replacing* a relation she sought with her analyst: You must make me a "woman," Anne-Marie in effect demands, and when she is refused, "What I do not give her," Lemoine-Luccioni explains, "she takes from me with force" by her "proof" of womanhood. This attempt to resolve the question of femininity by using maternity as a solution is not only problematic for Anne-Marie insofar as it repeats, in an inverted form, the history that has bound her to maternity by way of a "no" (anorexia) and a "yes" (pregnancy). It also entails a problematic relation to her child, as yet unborn, who will be delivered into a world that is governed by the symbolic chain of inheritance linking its mother and grandmother. What is important, for Lemoine-Luccioni, is therefore that Anne-Marie work through her relation to her mother, not only for herself but for her child. This is what it means to speak of the birth of the subject, in a symbolic process that not only goes beyond the birth of the organism, but entails a historical transmission of the question of femininity across the generations.

There is a beautiful and rather disturbing account of the moment of giving birth, by Michèle Montrelay in *L'Ombre et le nom* [(Paris: Editions de Minuit, 1977), pp. 119–46], in which the delivery of the child is shown in its connection with our theme of *generations* of women. In this passage, it is not a question of biological birth, but of the obscure process by which the woman becomes a "symbolic" (rather than an imaginary) mother, thereby *allowing* her child to be born. The passage, then, not only shows how the "moment of becoming the mother" is *both* a relation to the child *and* a replaying of the new mother's relation to her own mother; it also marks the transition from "real" mother (at the level of physiological fact) to "symbolic mother," and it is this particular aspect that entails a distinction between the image and the signifier—which entails a relation to lack. I cite an excerpt of a passage that is worthy of more attention:

> The child coming into the world as the descendant of a lineage can do nothing other than describe the senses that are impressed upon him by a structure he knows nothing about. How does he make his *first move* into the order that manipulates him, an order that is Other and omnipotent? How does he learn the rules of the game? Does he grasp them like a parcel of knowledge? On the contrary, everything begins when *an index* of these rules, *through repetition*, is *detached and posed as an object* that can only signify itself. An example, borrowed from Freud: the cry, he says, inscribes a trait and brings a being to life. Freud detaches the infant's pleasure or pain from the organic night to take them outside: toward the ear and thus toward the other who hears. What we see there is a manifestation of the *Bejahung* [the primary affirmation], where the life drawn *from the shadows* is concretized into "good" and "bad" objects. However much the child is dependent on the sensation he experiences, this object is no longer confused with the stupidity of the body. It has henceforth become Other: not an object of reality, but a hallucinated object, which as such places a being.

One sees here the first constitution of an index, not an object of need such as the breast is sometimes taken to be, but a mark, constituted through repetition, and therefore strictly speaking not an empirical thing, but a first signifier, described by Freud in the child's play of the fort-da game. This, in Montrelay's words, is the moment that detaches the infant's pleasure from the organic night, and takes it toward the other, in a movement that will forever mix the substance of the flesh with the substantial shadows of hallucination and fantasy. Montrelay continues:

> This hallucinated matter, never again equal to living matter, is the breast: not the real breast, but the breast as part object, never possessed—woven of clouds of representation *lacking limits*, suspended out of time.

The question is, how can this index, this mute signifier, detached from the organic night, but in a fashion that is as yet without limit, "woven of clouds of representation"—how can this be referred to another signifier, taken up in articulation? How can this unspeakable displacement from the "organic night," this primordial anxiety of the speaking being, be given limits, through articulation? This is the question of the "relation to the mother." Montrelay continues:

> To permit the hallucinated breast to exist for the child is to open for him a place other than the one that concerns the satisfaction of need. His desire begins to take form, inseparable from an unspoken suffering. How can he support this suffering, which he can say nothing about? The love of a child is doubled with an anxiety that is much more difficult to sustain, in that it repeats another anxiety, obscure, ungraspable, lived by the mother with her mother during the first months of life. A woman is also impotent to say something at the moment of giving birth. The loss of the breast reproduces the loss of the placenta.

We see here, then, a repetition involving

> the way in which the mother lived the birth of her child and her own birth, which is replayed during that of her offspring, but not in the same way. It is as a speaking being that she experiences real loss this time. When she loses herself as *the substance of jouissance that exceeds, in containing them, the edges of the body and its objects*, seized by the infinity of the Other, who is "not whole"—at this moment a woman becomes a symbolic mother. We know the story by Hoffmansthal entitled "The Woman without a Shadow," and the truth that it postulates: the woman who does not have a shadow because her mother does not give her one cannot have children. In the Shadow where a woman gets lost, there is also her own mother, "absent" and real. At the moment of giving birth, the real mother is encountered. That is where we are, from mother to daughter, transported and lost in the Shadow. From mother to daughter, because one does not live the birth of a boy and a girl in the same way. (emphases mine)

I close this long quotation.

From the example given by Lemoine-Luccioni above, I underscore two points: first, a link between the body and history (personal history, family history, social history); and second, an effort by the analyst to give to the woman, Anne-Marie, a future that will be different from that history, another femininity, one linked, in this case, to the analyst's relentless and I would say ethical insistence upon difference—her refusal, in other words, to put in the place of her client's sexuality the image of Woman that her client would like to assume as her own. Let us now turn from this example to a more general statement of the relation between biology and sexuality.

SEXUALITY AND THE VITAL ORDER

In its impetus, source, object, and aim, human sexuality is unmoored from its grounding in the vital order.[26] To speak of the body in its sexuality is not to speak of an organism that is determined by anatomy and the functions of reproduction. Consider these four terms briefly. Clinical work on *the impetus or force* reveals that no "mechanical" account of energy, no "physics" of libido, will account for the difference between instinct and the sexual drive. Freud's discovery of the complications and "denatured" character of sexuality in the human— from "abnormal" to everyday instances, and including experiences of childhood, which, from the standpoint of "reproductive maturity," would be merely premature, whereas they are structuring in the psychic specificity of the child—provide a first indication of why he differentiated between *Trieb* and *Instinkt*. This should clarify a point taken up in the title of Irigaray's essay "The 'Mechanics' of Fluids," in which the word "Mechanics" appears in quotation marks (105–16/106–18). Is this a biological energetics of femininity? A *reductio a soma* that would produce on behalf of women just one more form of the maternal, prelinguistic, anatomy-is-destiny argument, while leaving out of bounds all politics, all history, all questions of speech and the symbolic order? Is this what Irigaray, the psychoanalyst and philosopher, would have recourse to as a "political solution"? This is the conclusion to which many of her readers have been drawn, precisely because her discussion of the body is completely isolated from its psychoanalytic context, taken to be purely physiological, and thereby separated altogether both from symbolic and linguistic questions, and also from questions of historical determination.[27] Her essay on the "mechanics" of fluids, far from being a precipitous celebration of female anatomy, is dedicated for the most part to a question concerning the history of scientific discourse. The same issue is present in the title of another essay, "When Our Lips Speak Together [*se parlent*]" (205–17/205–18). Here again, as the very title points out, anatomy is addressed in its primordial relation to speech, and not at all as an isolated, physiological, prelinguistic domain that would have no connection with history and the symbolic. This does not keep her readers from reducing her account to biomechanics.

However much Freud might initially have expected to provide a mechanics for the "energy" of libido, then, it immediately became clear that the biological principles of self-preservation, feeding, heat conservation and homeostasis—in short, the whole system of energy regulation—may very well account for the activity of the animal (discharge of tension, satisfaction of needs), but it cannot describe the peculiar investments of *psychic* energy in the human animal.[28] The principle of pleasure, which is initially linked to this model of "life" and "energy," in fact meets its limit in the peculiarly human "death drive," which characterizes, not instinct, but *sexuality* in its relation to the signifier. This is a sexuality that goes "beyond the pleasure" of the organism. This is why psychoanalysis distinguishes between the instinct and the drive, by demonstrating that the investments of energy in the drive are always bound up with representation. This is why Freud always saw sexuality as bound to questions of memory; and this is what it means to speak of sexuality in connection with mechanisms, not just of energy, but of psychic inscription. Finally, this is why Irigaray must take up simultaneously the question of our cultural memory (for instance, the history of philosophy) with the question of the feminine: one cannot simply leave behind or forget a patriarchal past in favor of some projected alternative, because one *is* one's past, as one seeks a future. Thus, when it is a question of historical change, "We do not escape so easily," Irigaray writes.

> We do not escape, in particular, by thinking we can dispense with
> a rigorous interpretation of phallogocratism. There is no simple

manageable leap outside it, *nor any possible way to situate one-self there, simply by the fact of being a woman.* (157/162, original italics)

As in analysis, then, it is a matter of re-engaging the past; and without this re-engagement, the past only repeats, and the future does not come:

> In order that woman might reach the place where she takes pleasure as a woman, a long detour by way of the analysis of various systems of oppression brought to bear upon her is assuredly necessary. And pretending to fall back upon the single solution of pleasure risks making her miss *what her enjoyment requires*—the retracing of an entire social practice. (30/31)

As for the second term, the relation to *the object,* investigation of the perversions, especially fetishism, showed that the "object-relation" is not fixed by nature and the reproductive function, but is highly variable. As always with Freud, the "exceptional" case turns out to be guiding for the interpretation of the "normal" case:

> Are we thus suggesting, since deviance is necessarily defined in relation to a norm, that Freud himself would rally to the notion of a sexual instinct [a biological norm]? Such is not the case. . . . The movement we sketched above, a movement of exposition, which is simultaneously the movement of a system of thought and, in the last analysis, the movement of the thing itself, is that the *exception*—i.e. perversion—ends up by *taking the rule along with it* . . . that exception ends up by undermining and destroying the very notion of a biological norm.[29]

The effort of the analyst is therefore hardly to *normalize* this variability, channeling it back into the canal of biology; such normalization is not the goal of analysis but, on the contrary, one of the sources of neurosis that psychoanalysis confronts, as the example of Anne-Marie is intended to suggest. With respect to its *aim,* the satisfaction of pleasure, the sexual drive can be satisfied in the most diverse and indirect ways, through eating (the pleasure of which is not exhausted by satisfaction of the need for nourishment), speaking (the pleasure of which is not exhausted by imparting a message), looking (the pleasure of which is not exhausted by seeing), and so on.[30] This is why we eat long after we have had our fill, and why the anorexic can find that the satisfaction of the oral drive can directly conflict with the biological need for food.[31] This is why we continue to *look* long after we have *seen*, with the fascination or captivation that characterizes our relation to works of art, to which we return long after we "know" what they "look like," as well as our relation to other forms of "the beautiful"— nature, the other person, and so on. There is a pleasure that *goes beyond* the information gathering of the organism that behaves in response to stimuli. This is the detachment of sexuality from its grounding in nature, sexuality's peculiar excess.[32]

In addition, as soon as the human subject enters into the world of others and has an image to uphold, pleasure will be henceforth referred not to the satisfaction of needs (which is a matter of material necessity, and not yet what is called a "relation to the object"), but rather to the satisfaction of a desire for recognition, attention, love, or even power, intellectual distinction, moral superiority—all of which shifts the order of things into a complex relation with words, since the thing, as Hegel points out, cannot give recognition or love, condescension or disdain. In short, the question of the aim of the drive (pleasure), far from being based upon bodily instincts, carries human sexuality beyond the functions of reproduction and self-preservation, and into the order of representation, intersubjectivity, and speech.[33] And finally, with regard to *the source* of the drive, which Freud at times took to be the somatic basis, the organ or part of the body that originates the drive, this concept too is always submitted to the order of representation: this is the meaning of the concept of erotogenic zones in the human animal.[34] As Monique David-Ménard writes:

> In these attempts to define the body that is at stake in hysteria, the reference to language makes it clear that the physiological body is not what is involved, even though the symptoms in question are not to be identified exclusively with discourse either. Instead, what is played out in the body takes the place of a discourse that cannot be uttered. Now this is the decisive turning-point; and when Freud speaks of thinking in terms of energy, when he speaks of pleasure in terms of energetistic [sic] or motor discharge, his formulations can no longer be accused of organicism.

Elsewhere she adds:

> If we are to arrive at an adequate conceptualization of what is "offered to view" in hysteria, we have to follow Freud . . . and free ourselves from what Gaston Bachelard called the substantialist obstacle, a realist approach to the body that grants ontological priority to physiological constructs.[35]

Analysis of the sexual drive, as distinguished from instinct, thus reveals the denaturalization of human desire. More precisely—since one cannot properly speak of an "originally natural" sexuality that would (later) be distorted by *external* and therefore merely *accidental* deformation by the particular conventions of a given culture—the analysis of the sexual drive should lead us to speak of its original emergence as unnatural, as intrinsically constituted through an organization that is beyond the "law" governing the organism alone. This is the "imperative" of culture, the "symbolic law" that is not to be mistaken for an "instituted law," along the lines of a "contractual agreement" produced in history by *already given subjects*. Rather, the symbol is constitutive for the human subject: without its relation to the symbol (a relation in which the subject is not master), the subject would not enter into history, and sexuality would be governed by the necessities of nature—it would not be susceptible to history. One must therefore distinguish between the *particular historical forms* that a given culture may institute for sexuality (this is its history), and that *inevitability* of symbolic inscription that is constitutive of the human animal. In the absence of an adequate recognition of this symbolic inscription as constitutive, one will always be tempted, even in the name of "liberating" it, to *return* sexuality to its purportedly "natural" (and indeed ahistorical) foundation—which is what some readers have mistaken Irigaray as claiming in her discussion of "the feminine."

This conflation of the symbolic, as organizing—in *every* culture and for *every* human society—human sexuality, on the one hand, and, on the other, the institutions of patriarchy that arise *in time,* for a given culture, is what has allowed Elizabeth Grosz to deal so harshly, and I think mistakenly, with Kristeva's work. With the collapse of the symbolic into the concept of a particular form of social organization, one will also immediately find a collapse of the "function" of the Mother and the Father, two positions which will be filled in, given a particular meaning in one way or another, for every infant born of two sexes, and, on the other hand, the meaning of the "woman" and the "man." In my account of Lemoine-Luccioni, I have been following the crucial distinction between the maternal and the feminine, a distinction that has been lost for this particular subject (there being only the place of the mother); but it would be possible also to distinguish between the paternal function and the meaning of masculinity. This is something Kristeva has in fact been exploring, but Grosz's reading tends, in my view, to *identify* the function of the third term, which is structural, with the position of the "man." There is no question that this identification is almost inevitable in our culture and may even be called one of our pathologies, but this does not mean that Kristeva herself should be seen as asserting it, when her work is one of the more eloquent and careful efforts at exploring alternatives to this quick collapse of the "man" into the "paternal function"—a collapse no less worrying than the equation of "woman" with "motherhood."[36]

One begins to see here what the link is between the symbolic and the category of history, and the erroneous claim that the "symbolic" is "ahistorical": in fact, it cannot be a question of "returning to history" *against* the notion of the symbolic, since it is the inevitability of the symbolic that makes history not only possible, but inescapable, for the human animal.[37] This is something that Kristeva has understood very clearly, and her assertion of the necessity of the symbolic can be construed as a "capitulation to patriarchy" only if one does not distinguish, as Kristeva does, between the inevitability of prohibition and taboo that seems to attend the animal that speaks, and the particular content that is given to this inevitability of historical inscription, in one or another society. The fact of the symbolic is therefore not to be identified with any particular institutional arrangement, so much as it is a concept used to resist naturalistic discussions of sexuality, to insist upon the susceptibility of human sexuality to history, and to underscore the fact that the inscription of the body in accordance with the symbolic law is not one that the human subject can master. The concept of the symbolic, then, stresses the essentially historical nature of sexuality while at the same time refusing to support the traditional thesis that the autonomous, conscious subject can be placed at the origin of this history as its cause or moving force. This should be compatible with those theories that recognize what we might call the *machinery* of language, the autonomous character of the technology that structures our bodies, alters our vision, our motion through space, our ways of perceiving and gathering information, the spaces we inhabit, the entire language and heraldry of our existence, in accordance with structures that are in no way the *products* of autonomous subjects, since each subject is as much an "effect" of this machinery, the logic of which is not in our hands.

This is why Irigaray takes so seriously women's relation to speech and writing (the "symbol")—an issue that might be thought to be secondary to material and economic change, or to the task of revising particular *institutions* (this is what we normally understand as working for "historical change"), but which is in fact the condition for the possibility of women having a history in the first place:

> The "liberation" of women requires a transformation of the economic, and thus necessarily passes through a transformation of culture, and its operative agency: language. Without this interpretation of the general grammar of culture, the feminine will never have a place in history. (151/155)

With regard to the question of history, then, insofar as it concerns the drive, the "development" of sexuality is not at all reducible to the "psychological" phenomenon of "adaptation," popular among some theorists of child development, according to whom the ideally autonomous person "learns" (consciously) to control his or her "natural" inclinations, and comes to accept the "cultural rules" of the game of civilization. Such a view starts with an *already given subject* that *subsequently* encounters the social order, whereas the psychoanalytic conception of the subject is very different, holding as it does that the subject is not originally given in an autonomous form, but begins in the symbolic. This is one reason why one cannot properly reduce the symbolic to historical conditions exterior to the individual, then; and it suggests why Irigaray insists upon that process of going back over the old ground, which is integral to the possibility of the future.

Thus, what Freud lays down as the peculiar and primordial organization of the human animal, in accordance with the unnatural law of the signifier, provides the basis for what Irigaray will discuss as the symbolic order, in which human sexuality is arranged through a configuration of desire and representation that places the subject beyond the system of instinctual need. Consequently, when Irigaray speaks of "the body of woman" and "feminine sexuality," she is always engaged with a highly variable, nonbiological, multivalent, culturally organized, and historically specific phenomenon.[38] This is not at all to say that there is no biological dimension to the human being, or that sexual difference is to be conceived without any reference to the biological difference between the sexes, as though it were purely a product of linguistic convention and sociohistorical determination. It is precisely this historicist notion that the concept of the symbolic puts in question, as a notion that *does not take history seriously enough,* insofar as it tends to maintain a faith in the ideally uninscribed or "free" subject as the agent of historical change. A purely "culturalist" position, then, would be as reductive and unconvincing as the idea that cultural practices have *no* effect upon the "natural" meaning of sexual difference.[39] Neither of these positions is taken by Irigaray, though both have been misleadingly attributed to her. It is not a question, therefore, of eliminating the biological in the conceptualization of the body, but of recognizing the peculiar organization of sexuality in the human being, its inscription and translation and distortion within the dimension of desire—a dimension that is not at all confined to the personal domain of psychology, but is thoroughly political, historically situated, and contingent.[40]

From this analysis I underscore two points: first, Irigaray's focus on sexuality cannot be understood as a reduction to the vital order of biology; second, because sexuality is always inscribed within an order of representation, the biological organism can never serve as an origin, a means of returning to a primordial or prehistoric source, on which the meaning of femininity might be constructed. Sexuality is always already marked by history.[41] It is clear that Irigaray's discussion of the body (and the feminine imaginary) is one that takes history seriously; and we can say, moreover, that to take history seriously is to recognize the difficulty of leaving it—either for a prehistoric *origin* (in the natural body, in the pre-Oedipal, or in a conception of matriarchal societies that would have preceded our history), or for a more attentive description of the *present,* a phenomenological attentiveness to the immediacy of so-called real experience, as though this could yield up a region unaffected by history, or, finally, for a *future* that one produces by willing it into existence. When it is a question of desire and of our historical determination, history is not so easily dispensed with, because the will that wills, that makes its demands, is produced by the history it wishes to contest, just as Anne-Marie's demand for a future as a mother or an analyst or a woman proves to be a *repetition* of the past, burdened by the very history she seeks to avoid. Her demand for a future that would go beyond the symptom, that would free her of anorexia and give her a new life, turns out to be a repetition of the past. That is precisely why she stands in need of the other woman. As the example of Anne-Marie is meant to suggest in a preliminary way, then, Irigaray's work confronts us with a question regarding the future, a future that does not appear simply because it is willed. Some writers on Irigaray have, as Margaret Whitford writes, seen her work as "a precipitate celebration of the female imaginary, which bypasses the problem of its existence (*whether* it exists and *what kind of existence* it might have)." There is a "sense in which the female imaginary," she suggests, "does not yet exist." This would be a non-essentialist thesis; the female imaginary would not be something lurking in the depths of women's unconscious, but a possible restructuring.[42]

Similarly, the term *body,* properly understood, is not reducible to a biological phenomenon, because it belongs within the field of sexuality. Obviously, this does not mean that the references to physiology are "only metaphors," with no relation to the flesh: it means that this physiology is *subject to* sexuality, in the sense of being differently structured, differently organized, than what would otherwise be its counterpart in nature. The body, therefore, this physical *and* sexualized field, is an *imaginary* body. Only the imaginary body can be subjected to the kinds of symptoms we find in Anne-Marie, symptoms that are physical and real but that cannot be reduced to the "organic disorders" treated by the medical community. This point is also stressed in my opening claim that what is at stake in the case discussed by Lemoine-Luccioni is a question of how to think together (A) a body that does not reduce to the organism, and (B) a history the specificity of which does not reduce to the general order of social conditions. This is the question of the relation between the signifier and the flesh.

THE PROBLEM OF TEMPORALITY

Once this concept of the imaginary body is understood as a physiological reality that is not to be reduced to the apolitical dimension of biology, then it becomes evident why Irigaray not only *can* but *must* speak of the body and the symbolic order at one and the same time. With the introduction of the symbolic, we pass more decisively into history—a connection that is, however, attended by additional complications, above all, complications of time that are central to Irigaray's work but almost universally neglected by her readers. The basic issue is to understand the juncture between the imaginary and the symbolic, and this will also be to raise the question of the relation between the body and history. This is one problem. Again, Margaret Whitford has suggested that this is an area of Irigaray's work that is in need of elaboration: readers who mistakenly see in her work an essentialism, psychic or biological, cannot rightly neglect—or pretend that Irigaray neglects—"the symbolic, linguistic dimension in which sexual identity may be constructed." This is certainly correct, and the relation between the body and history is clear enough; but an additional difficulty, for many of her readers, is to recognize that this sense of "symbolic" organization is not to be equated with the usual notion of *external* cultural conditions. This is a second and somewhat different problem, for it introduces the task of rethinking history itself. The basic difficulty here is to recognize that the symbolic is not a set of conditions external to the subject, and that, as a result, the subject who labors to change the world is already its product. The notion of a "change in the symbolic," understood as "outside" the subject, must therefore be supplemented by a "change in the subject" as well. How is this change to occur? And perhaps more pointedly, "who" is it that "makes" this change? This is where the theme of the relation to the other, so central to the analytic relation, and so closely linked to the question of ethics and difference, becomes important. Let us follow this issue through some specific passages.

From the psychoanalytic point of view, the symbolic is also a problem *within* the subject.[43] This is to say that Irigaray, as an analyst, is particularly attentive to the fact that the social conditions in which the subject is formed are precisely *formative* for the subject, so that one of the tasks Irigaray sees as crucial for feminism is recognizing that women, who must engage in the effort to obtain equal rights (her example), at the same time cannot suppose that this struggle will give them access to the identity they may have, or wish for, *as women*:

> Women must of course continue to struggle for equal wages and social rights. . . . But that is not enough: women "equal" to men would be "like them," therefore not women. Once more, the difference between the sexes would be canceled out, misunderstood, concealed. . . . That explains certain difficulties encountered by the liberation movements. If women allow themselves to be caught in the trap of power, the game of authority, if they let themselves be contaminated by the "paranoic" operations of masculine politics, they have nothing more to say or do *as women*. (160–61/165–66)

Thus, it is not only clear that Irigaray is fully engaged with questions of history; it is also apparent that as an analyst she is particularly wary of claiming to perform a critique of the "symbolic" understood as *exterior social conditions*, since there is the additional problem of determining "who is speaking" during this critique. Women must struggle for equality on behalf of historical change, but *where* and *who* "woman" is *in this struggle* remains unclear. Indeed, one might question whether "woman" even appears on this stage, since the particular female subject is not as such necessarily also in possession of what it means to be "a woman" ("a woman," since there is not *one* "Woman") given her historical determination. As Irigaray puts it in "This Sex":

> [T]he feminine keeps secret. *Without knowing it.* And if woman is asked to sustain or reanimate man's desire, the request neglects to spell out what it implies as to the value of her own desire. A desire *of which she is not aware*, moreover, at least not explicitly. (26/27, my italics)

And even if she were aware, Irigaray adds, the desire she might claim would still be "capable of nourishing at length all the masquerades of 'femininity' that are expected of her" (26/27). The same point is made in "Questions." There *may* be a sense in which "woman" remains uninscribed, excessive, somehow outside everything that has been made of her on the stage of history; but this does not automatically mean that actual women have access to it: "[D]oubtless she needs to *reenact it in order to remember* what that staging has probably metabolized so thoroughly that *she has forgotten it*: her own sex" (148/152, my italics). This task of "reenacting in order to remember" is the problem of "speaking as a woman."

One might argue that the *question* of woman—where or who woman is—coincides quite precisely with the question of "excess," in the sense that the question of woman's "freedom" from the culture in which she finds herself is this question: what, *of her*, if there is anything that escapes patriarchy, *presents itself*, yet without presenting itself as what has been made of her? One could follow, in other words, the *question* of the feminine in Irigaray, by taking up the more or less phenomenological question of presence and its relation to what exceeds presence. The theme runs throughout: despite her "exchange value," woman is also "supplementary" (*un en-plus*) to her position as she is circulated in the market (175/179); or again, Irigaray will "move back through the masculine imaginary," showing how woman appears "implicated in it and at the same time exceeding its limits" (157/162–63); and therefore it will be a matter of "analyzing not simply the double movement of appropriation and disappropriation in relation to the masculine subject, but also what remains silent" (156/161); woman has "fulfilled the role of *matter*," and she thereby "functions as the *resource* . . . but also as *waste*" (this is linked to the "divinity" of woman) (147/151); women's "gestures are often paralysed, or part of the masquerade," she writes, "except for what resists or subsists 'beyond'" (132/134). Finally:

> "And there you have it, gentlemen, that is why your daughters are dumb." . . . And interpreting them where they exhibit only muteness means subjecting them to a language that exiles them at an ever increasing distance from what perhaps they would have said to you, and were already whispering to you . . . *l'affemme. Zone de silence.* (111/112–13)

The symbolic, then, cannot be understood as an exterior social order that an *already available* subject named "woman" might seek to reform. And the sense of history must be complicated accordingly: far from neglecting history, Irigaray is providing a critique of our familiar conception of history, and posing the problem of change itself. The remarks made by Lemoine-Luccioni suggest that Anne-Marie's very desire to resolve the question of "woman" for herself only produces a repetition of the problem with which she began. In a similar way, metaphysics repeats in the very forms most designed to eradicate it. The logic of such repetition ("That explains certain difficulties encountered by the liberation movements") cannot go unconfronted. This is why the task for the analyst is to put her client in a position from which she can begin to speak differently. The conjunction of psychoanalysis and politics begins here.

Irigaray therefore does not claim to speak on behalf of the "essence" of woman. She writes: "I could not, I cannot install myself just like that, serenely and directly, in that other syntactic functioning—and I do not see how any woman could" (133/135). Any number of instances make this clear: The exploitation of women, she writes, is so much a part of our culture that even the critique of this culture has no way of beginning except *from within,* and with critical tools that are themselves formed by the cultural order they would contest. "Exploitation," she writes (in "Women on the Market"), "is so integral a part of our sociohistorical horizon that there is no way to interpret it except from within this horizon" (167–68/171). Elsewhere, with regard to the history of philosophy, which she reads critically, to be sure, but which at the same time she in no way simply claims to abandon or to provide an "alternative" to, Irigaray insists: "There is no simple manageable way to leap to the outside of phallogocentrism, *nor any possible way to situate oneself there, that would result from the simple fact of being a woman*" (157/162, her italics).

A Question of Method

Obviously, this attentiveness to historical determination will have consequences for her own method, insofar as it is psychoanalytic (see her skeptical remarks on the pre-Oedipal and its supposed analogy with the prehistoric, as a way of identifying "woman" prior to her social determination—a gesture toward prehistory that is attributed to Irigaray but profoundly foreign to her [46–48, 122–23/48–49, 123–25]). Far from claiming to articulate the truth of "woman as such," independent of her historical situatedness, by using what one might take to be the privileged method of psychoanalysis, she suggests that one begin with the difficulties *of psychoanalysis* in its effort to find the truth of woman. This hardly means repudiating psychoanalysis in favor of a "truer" method, untainted by history—one that would capture woman "in herself," apart from what has been made of her in time. Precisely *because* of history, she refuses to "leap" outside of metaphysics to the truth of woman, and instead is led to take up psychoanalysis all over again. Will psychoanalysis, then, yield up the "truth" of woman?

> Can I sketch the *content* of what that other unconscious, woman's, might be? No, of course not, since that presupposes disconnecting the feminine from the present-day economy of the unconscious. (123/124)

At this point she is asked whether, if psychoanalysis has no privileged access, another less tainted region might serve better, as a more authentic or uncontaminated point of access, namely, "the relation of women to the mother and the relation of women among themselves." She is asked whether this arena of "women among themselves" might provide access to "woman":

> Would that produce a sketch of the "content" of the "feminine" unconscious? No. It is only a question about the interpretation of the way the unconscious works. (124/125)

The link between the problem of history, the problem of her own specific historical determination, and her use of psychoanalysis should thus emerge clearly as one of her central concerns. She neither abandons all the techniques of patriarchy, because of their affiliations with a cultural order she questions (to do this would be to "leap outside," to neglect her own historical situatedness, as she is sometimes wrongly accused of doing), nor does she simply "take up the tools" of analysis in order to reveal the hidden truth of woman (to do so would be to claim an access to "woman" that is not possible, given her own symbolic determination, and it would be to take over the psychoanalytic method as unproblematic). "To do that," she writes, to present woman, to claim access through psychoanalysis to "woman,"

> would be to anticipate a certain historical process, and to slow down its interpretation and its evolution, by prescribing, as of now, themes and contents for the feminine unconscious. (123/124)

The relation of method to history could not be clearer: "The tool is not a feminine attribute. But woman may re-utilize its marks on her, in her" (147/150). Not only is her work profoundly engaged in history, but that engagement itself reflects upon the methods she uses, so that far from *simply* appealing to psychoanalysis or abandoning it for some "elsewhere," she takes its difficulty with the question of woman as calling for a revision of psychoanalysis—a revision she finds necessary in part *as an analyst*, as one who has learned to listen for what history has left in shadow:

> So long as psychoanalysis does not interpret its own entrapment within . . . a certain type of discourse (to simplify, let us say that of metaphysics) . . . it cannot raise the question of female sexuality. (124/125)

Elsewhere she makes unequivocal her relation to the methods she employs:

> [I]sn't it the method, the path to knowledge, that has always led us away, led us astray . . . from woman's path? In order to re-open woman's path, it was therefore necessary to note the way in which the method was never as simple as it purports to be. (146/150)

If, given her historical determination, there can be no immediate and unproblematic access to the feminine, what, then, is the significance of the phrase "speaking as a woman"? In her work, she cannot claim access to the essence of woman, in part because of her own historical determination, and in part because woman is not understood as a category with *one form*, but is internally differentiated, "not one."

Consequently:

> Speaking (as) woman is not speaking *of* woman. It is not a mat-
> ter of producing a discourse of which woman would be the
> *object*, or the *subject*. That said, speaking (as) woman, one may
> attempt to provide a place for the "other" as feminine. (133/135,
> my italics)

While the historical dimension of her work cannot be neglected, then
(and it has been), it is nevertheless important to recognize that Irigaray
does not simply speak of the *symbolic* as the order of cultural history
that *determines* the subject from without—again, the usual argument
that Copjec calls "the argument from construction," an argument that
takes the politics of feminism to be, along the lines of a rough analogy
to Marxism, an effort to change the historical order. This view of the
symbolic, taken (non-psychoanalytically) as a register of social conditions, too quickly leaves behind the problem of the *relation between*
the imaginary and the symbolic. We know that Lacan, to the infuria-
tion of many of his readers, insisted that the symbolic, strictly speaking, is not the equivalent of "the historical order," despite its being
popularly understood in this way. This view of the historical order as
a set of determinations that have been produced by humans *in the
course of time*, conditions that determine the subject but that also
promise a certain liberation, since after all they have been produced *by
human beings*, and are therefore subject to revision, however much
they may determine us—this anthropocentric view of history as something that structures us, but that we in turn have produced and can
therefore restructure (man as the maker of all things)—is precisely the
foundation of a powerful tradition of nineteenth-century historicism,
grounded in the thesis that "Man makes himself," a humanism that is
deeply troubled, as Hegel was, by the fact of historical determination,
but that promises, on the very basis of this determination, to provide
the human being with a way out, a way of putting himself (and the
masculine is intended), as a conscious subject, at the center of that history that would otherwise override him. This reduplication is the strategy of "modernity" that has been so brilliantly and exhaustively
described by Michel Foucault in *Les mots et les choses*. And Irigaray

is fully aware that one cannot provide a genuine interrogation of the *subject of metaphysics* without relinquishing, indeed giving an *analysis* of, and one might even say *mourning*, this humanistic understanding of history and historical change.[44]

As I suggested in the opening section in a concrete way, psychoanalytic feminism not only questions the idea that the "body" is biological; it also and simultaneously questions the idea that "history" can be put in the hands of the conscious subject, since it links Anne-Marie in her very historical determination to an unconscious subject who does not *know* what she *wants* (a position of ignorance that is not simply negative, as Irigaray suggests in her refusal to "start with the certainty that I am a woman"). This does not mean that someone else should speak for her (and Lemoine-Luccioni refuses this role, when it is offered to her). But it means that the question of finding her voice is made into a central problem, rather than being taken for granted as the starting point for historical change. The discontinuity between desire and knowledge—in particular the supposed "subject of knowing"—and between the trajectory of the subject of conscious actions and, in contrast to this, the history that repeats despite those actions, cannot easily be overcome. This is the reason why psychoanalysis, in its very structure and functioning, radically depends upon the other—not the "freedom" of the analysand to produce a new future, nor the "knowledge" of the analyst to provide a future on behalf of the client, but the radical experience of alterity that makes psychoanalysis into a relation we can call not scientific, not methodological, but ethical.

I am suggesting that there is in Irigaray's work a connection being developed between ethics and the concept of history, which is nothing other than the formation that develops between subjects, the "community," in which sameness and difference are articulated.[45] The problem is therefore how to understand historical change as the "time" of a community that is not the linear, narrated time that has been developed in the nineteenth-century forms of humanism. This is the context for approaching her discussion of the past, present, and future, and the possibility of a time in which sexual difference would appear differently.

With this focus on the relation between the imaginary and the symbolic, then, it becomes clear that, as Whitford says, "biological essentialism (in the form in which it is usually attributed to Irigaray) is a deterministic and often simplistic thesis which makes change impossible to explain." I think it should be possible to add at this point that the usual notion of "symbolic determination" (in the form in which it is often found in cultural theory) would also make change impossible to explain. The question, then, is truly one that involves a rethinking of time, of *how history happens*: it cannot be adequately ascribed to "developmental" theories that would argue along the lines of nature, but neither can it be convincingly understood as an unfolding produced by the willing subject of humanism.[46] Neither of these two points of orientation for sexual difference—neither the argument from biology nor the argument from construction—can give an adequate account of history and historical change, because neither of them has an adequate conception of subjectivity in its relation to the symbol.

The Evidence of the Present (Who Are We *Really*?)

We should now be in a position to elaborate the question of time more accurately. Can one say that historical change will be possible by focusing more carefully *on the present*, on what is available in the here and now of immediate experience, as a site of evidence for the femininity that has been passed over? This is a tempting line of thought, and Irigaray will certainly not rule it out altogether. But she does register some reservations. For to say that the feminine can be retrieved in the immediacy of experience is not to take history seriously enough. What presents itself here, in this or that example, which you may wish to see as an instance of the neglected feminine, Irigaray says in effect, is not as free of history as you might think. The most "nurturing," "positive," "empowering" and "supportive" images one can find (but none of these epithets comes close to Irigaray's vocabulary, or if they appear, it is under a burden of suspicion and wariness, for decisive reasons, as we shall see) will all, according to Irigaray, prove to be captivating "ruses," "capable of nurturing at length all the masquerades of 'femininity' that are expected of her" (see note 13). It is clear that, for Irigaray, whose doctoral training is in philosophy and linguistics, the question of what woman is, where woman is, how and whether woman presents herself, cannot be adequately addressed by the appeal to empirical evidence, which will only provide products that belong at least in part to patriarchy. The feminism that is engaged in a critique of science has a point of contact here, with respect to "evidence," in that the discourse of science is not automatically accepted by either as transcending its socially specific situation. I would also suggest that the reason her vocabulary excludes a whole series of words that are common fare in the Anglo-American traditions of feminism, which are largely not psychoanalytic—or, when psychoanalytic, dominated by models that work toward "empowering" the ego—is that these words all serve *a conception of group dynamics and identification* that too often effectively excludes difference and otherness, and demands "bonding" and "mutual support" in their place. Thus, the refusal we saw at the outset, by Lemoine-Luccioni, to play the role of the autonomous and powerful woman who might serve as the benevolent model for her client, is repeated by Irigaray in relation to her readers who might wish for her to speak on behalf of women, or to demonstrate and lay claim to a repressed femininity to which others might then equally lay claim. I would also add that the impatience, and often the rage, expressed in the reception of writings by Irigaray, and Kristeva as well, could very easily be shown to be aggression directed not so much at the supposed theoretical shortcomings of these writers as at the refusal of these writers to play the role of Woman that is demanded of them.

Irigaray does not claim to produce positive images of women on the basis of immediate evidence of the present, then; but neither would the idea of a femininity outside patriarchy be of interest to her. One of the principal reasons for "certain difficulties encountered by the liberation movements," she suggests, and the main reason she has not identified with any group, is that such groups too often purport "to determine the 'truth' of the feminine, to legislate as to what it means to 'be a woman'" (161/166). What is worse is that these efforts, in Irigaray's judgment, amount to precisely a *slowing down* of history—an impediment at precisely the point where one believes change is being produced. Accordingly, speaking of *Speculum*, she reminds us that it "is obviously not a book *about* woman; and still less a studied gynocentrism":

> Such naïve judgments overlook the fact that from a feminine locus nothing can be articulated without a questioning of the symbolic itself. (157/162)

It ought to be clear, therefore, that her work on the feminine imaginary is to be understood not as a claim to occupy "the feminine"—if such a project were even desirable—but as "a possible restructuring," in Whitford's phrase, "suspending and exploring," as Meghan Morris puts it.[47] Her refusal "to install [herself] just like that" in a femininity that would *present itself as such*, as *the* (essence of the) feminine, is the clearest possible evidence that Irigaray's interrogation of sexual difference goes hand in hand with her critique of the metaphysics of presence. The matter of taking history seriously, then, and recognizing that what one designates (or even imagines: fantasy is clearly no less prey to historical sedimentation) as the feminine is likely to be already bound to the structures one wishes to contest. The history of metaphysics does not come to an end upon demand; in fact, the demand for its end belongs to metaphysics as one of its basic features. Evidence of the feminine in the present, then, is not altogether ruled out by Irigaray, but it is met with considerable wariness.

When it comes to "affirming the feminine," therefore, Irigaray takes history very seriously indeed, to the extent that even the most immediate, empirical, private, intimate, or bodily experience gives only the most problematic access to a femininity that might show itself through the sedimentations of history. As Irigaray puts it: if "multiplicity" is now put forth *in the name of woman*, "must this multiplicity of feminine desire and language be understood as shards, scattered remnants of a violated sexuality?" Let me focus very closely on this question. Multiplicity, she suggests, may perhaps be put forth as a definition of "the feminine"—assuming (contrary to fact) that a definition is being sought; but if this multiplicity is put forth in the name of woman, are we to understand this as *her essence* or rather as an effect of *her historical position?* Are we to understand that "the feminine," when we look closely at the evidence of the present, shows itself as *essentially* multiple, or are we to understand that multiplicity is *what has been made of her* ("shards, scattered remnants")—multiplicity, marginality, waste, or excess, which, at the same time, can *now* be celebrated as somehow capable of contesting partriarchy? This is the question Irigaray is asking.

>1>

The Question of Origins

Let us proceed slowly here. This remark is put forth as a question, as if to say that perhaps we have no access to a femininity that would be pure, free of all historical determination. Perhaps even "femininity as excess" is only what has been made of woman, "scattered remnants" rather than her "nature." Perhaps it is therefore not a matter of returning to a pure but repressed origin (the pre-Oedipal or the semiotic), either, since it is not a question of a "prehistory" that one might aim to recover or liberate. Certainly this would be in keeping with the psychoanalytic understanding of repression, namely, that the *repressed* is not something which exists and then is subsequently covered over in such a way that one might then return to it and liberate it. (This may once have served for the notion of "oppression," but even this notion would oblige most writers currently to acknowledge that the oppressed cannot be simply liberated to their rightful "earlier" condition, since the experience of oppression is constitutive for them.) More basically still, the linear narratives we construct around the notion of repression take no account of the temporal complications by which the human psyche is constructed in a series of repetitions and retroactive constructions that disturb the familiar concept of time. This is what is at stake in the claim that the purportedly "original" bond with the mother, the nurturing unity that one might like to place at the origin, as a "stage" that is subsequently lost, is rather, from the psychoanalytic point of view, a "state" that comes into being for the child *only on the condition of being lost*. The "mother" of primary narcissism, which can represent for the subject a utopia that once was, did not exist as such at the time, but came into being as an "object that has already been lost." It can certainly function, like the Garden of Eden, in orienting the desire of the subject (or a culture) in a nostalgic direction, but the strictly mythological status of this purportedly "real object" must be confronted. This is one of the issues at stake in Irigaray's conception of history. Without going into this problem, we should be able to see that the repressed does not exist and then "suffer" repression, but is rather produced in the movement that separates it from itself: it does not predate that movement but is constituted by it. So we must say, with Irigaray, not that *there is* something original called "woman's pleasure," which is then repressed, but rather that woman's pleasure *is repressed*. This is what she means when, after speaking of woman as multiplicity, Irigaray asks, "Must this multiplicity of feminine desire and feminine language be understood *as shards*, scattered remnants of a violated sexuality?" In this case, feminine sexuality in its "scattered" and historical existence would not be simply a "fragmentation" to be overcome, a "fallen" state to be redeemed. "Multiplicity" would not be the prehistoric essence of the feminine, or even a definition put forth by Irigaray as an answer to the question of the feminine as such, but would rather be what the feminine has become historically, in its factical existence. Women cannot take refuge, she is suggesting, in the romanticism of origins that would seek an unrepressed zone of prehistoric femininity. This point is made rather directly by Jacqueline Rose, who writes (in regard to Kristeva) that "archaic images of the mother, for all their status as fantasy, are not without their effects . . . if we follow this through, we find ourselves having to relinquish an idealized vision of the lost maternal continent."[48] The problems of time that underlie these considerations have been all too little recognized by her readers.

Imagining (and Not Imagining) the Future

Irigaray's question at this point is therefore "must this multiplicity of feminine desire and language be understood as shards, scattered remnants of a violated sexuality?" The cultural order in which she lives, Irigaray adds, "certainly puts woman in the position of experiencing herself only fragmentarily . . . as waste, or excess" (29/30). I stress that this is stated in the form of a question: Isn't this what multiplicity means? Irigaray responds to this question by saying, "The question has no simple answer" (29/30). Certainly, on the one hand, if we look at every available piece of evidence, we do not find a true "femininity" that would reveal itself beneath the repression, but rather femininity as repressed, and this, as Irigaray says, "puts woman in the position of experiencing herself only fragmentarily." There is no simple answer, however, for on the other hand, one might ask what the feminine might actually be if it could be articulated apart from its existence as repressed, or what, in other words, might *remain* of woman, apart from what she has become.[49] The conditional and subjunctive verbs she often uses are important here, indicating, as the grammarians put it, "a condition contrary to fact."[50] Thus, after writing that the feminine is nothing other than what it has become, that the feminine is its history through and through, she adds, on the other hand, in the future subjunctive: "But if the feminine imaginary were able to deploy itself, if it could bring itself into play otherwise than as scraps . . . would it represent itself, even so, in the form of *one* universe?" (29/30) Would it present us with the original nature that has been lost, the "Mother" who has been abandoned, or the truth of the feminine as such? Irigaray's answer is "No." If the feminine *were* able to deploy itself otherwise than as scraps, any representation of itself as "*the* feminine" would amount to one more reinscription within patriarchy; it would amount, in Irigaray's words, to "*a privileging of the maternal over the feminine. Of a phallic maternal at that*" (29/30, my italics). I stress all this in detail in order to suggest just how vigilant and wary she is about the quest for origins, the privileging of the maternal, the identification of the feminine with maternity, and indeed about even the possibility or desirability of claiming to speak on behalf of the feminine, not only because she is taking history seriously (despite many critical misreadings), and not only because she is refusing to essentialize and universalize woman (despite many critical misreadings), but also because of the extreme difficulty of *access* to any theoretical position, any methodology, that would be free of historical sedimentation. This is a problem of method, which I have addressed in this section in its relation to the question of historical determination.

Once the severe difficulty of working, from within history, toward a critique of history, is appreciated, it is no longer possible to believe that Irigaray's work represents a "return to the female body," or an "expression of the feminine imaginary," or a "dangerous essentialism," or "a matter of purely linguistic indulgence" that has "no political relevance." If the sequence I have outlined from biology to the concept of the body as sexual, to the meaning of the imaginary as bound up with representation, and then finally to the dimension of history, is convincing, then it should be clear that Irigaray's purported elaboration of the feminine imaginary neither claims to identify, nor even wishes eventually to identify, an essential femininity, much less one that would be rooted in a presocial physiology.[51] I would like to stress that the sequence I have outlined is not an historical or genetic one, as though the biological were to be understood as an origin upon which human sexuality would be subsequently elaborated, this sexuality in turn being eventually repressed, and deferred or sublimated through representation, and thus, as a consequence, entering into history. The sequence is not temporal in this way but is rather a series of strata, which are always in play for Irigaray whenever she speaks of "the feminine" in order to interrogate its determinations, its specificity, its possibilities. From this standpoint it perhaps becomes clearer that the charges of essentialism and ahistoricism, if they are ever of use, would, from Irigaray's position, describe the work of those who believe they know (quite directly, and on the basis of real experience or historical "evidence") what women are, and who only wish to claim for this figure—woman—the same rights and privileges that other humans have, and that have been denied her. There is no prejudice whatsoever against the struggle for equality, the discourse of rights, and strategies of empowerment. There is only a question as to *who it is* that seeks these rights, and whether the rights themselves are, so to speak, the right rights. Especially in the area of legal studies, feminist theory has repeatedly confronted the disturbing fact that even if equal rights are accorded, they place women inside a network of determinations that do not accomplish what are at least arguably desirable ends. The "subject" who acquires rights is also given the sometimes dubious status of a neutral, or rather purportedly neutral but in fact masculine, position, so that, for example, the argument for pregnancy leave appears weak because it cannot be "distributed equally," without regard for gender. In short, the cause of equality is in no way repudiated, but is simply seen by Irigaray as being in some respects insufficient; and thus her work is brought to bear upon a questioning of the subject, and the philosophical tradition that has established it—not in order, as is sometimes said, to "deconstruct" subjectivity (as though that meant simply dispersing subjectivity in a random fashion, which is not at all the function of deconstruction), but rather in order to interrogate precisely what the social and historical meanings and dangers of "subjectivity" are, rather than taking for granted its innocence and desirability.[52]

What I am suggesting, then, is that the kinds of reservations expressed by some readers are due to a drastic misconception, according to which the biological body, or the so-called feminine imaginary, are abstracted from this set of historical and discursive problems, and then substantialized as autonomous entities ("the body" or "the imaginary"), with no sense of the cognitive models in which these terms are produced, discursive and historically precise models that Irigaray is *analyzing*. This premature isolation and substantializing of her terms produces a situation in which Irigaray's readers almost absurdly characterize her as endorsing precisely the kinds of notions Irigaray herself regards as symptomatic and in need of criticism. In short, the words she offers in order to analyze something like the feminine imaginary are problematic words that she scrutinizes as they emerge, words that, however much they might disclose, are always prey to the discursive order in which they arise—which is always likely to belong to patriarchy. She has no other words: that is her theoretical problem, and her very real, historical, experiential determination. It is the affliction about which, and out of which she writes, using words that she must continually be reluctant to endorse as her own, not finding herself in them, and yet not having any other resources. This is the question of *who woman is*—a question that her work is about, and which her writing enacts in the very movement of her thought.

2

Maternity and Femininity

RECEPTION THEORY

In recent psychoanalytic theory, two points have been particularly vexing and confused. The first concerns the mother, and specifically the question of whether the mother belongs to the imaginary or the symbolic. The second concerns the distinction between the mother and the woman. These two issues have been especially important, and perhaps especially divisive, for the interpretation of Kristeva, particularly for her reception by feminist readers whose relations to Lacanian theory are uneasy and complex. When we speak of the "otherness" of woman, or of "feminine alterity," at least in psychoanalysis, the meaning of this femininity can emerge only if the position of the mother is clearly situated, and only if the distinction between the mother and the woman has been understood.

Two schemas from Lacan can help to clarify these two points, and cast some light on the opening sentences of Kristeva's essay "Stabat Mater."[1] We will not develop the technical details of her divergence from Lacan, but will elucidate the elementary framework in which these two points are situated. The reason for proceeding this slowly, without immediately engaging the differences between these two thinkers, is that the question of their relation has been too abruptly foregrounded; as a result, the basic terminology of each has been trapped in a debate about allegiances that leaves the concepts undeveloped. This is especially so in regard to the "maternal." As we shall see, the debate as to whether Kristeva "follows" or "breaks with" Lacan has allowed a clear formulation of their differences, but only at the cost of misrepresenting both. One thus appears to settle the score as to whether Kristeva is a "heretic," who questions the "master doctrine," or is merely a "dutiful daughter," who should be regarded with suspicion, but this question is settled only at the cost of a reduction of both authors, a reading that puts a fantasy in place of the object it seeks to encounter. This is not an "external" issue insofar as Kristeva is thereby trapped within a fantasy of the mother to whom readers may address their demands in the form of love or hatred.

The result of this reception—which one might almost call a "repressive reading," regulated by the demand to settle accounts in relation to the Father—is of course a "return of the repressed," clearly evidenced in the fact that the reception of Kristeva has produced a symptomatic split, in which we are offered two contradictory images at the same time. For some readers, she is a radical voice who devotes her attention to China or Eastern Europe, to those avant-garde writers who are especially disturbing, or to depression, melancholy, and abjection—all those aberrations of normal discourse that are marked by suffering and marginality. For others, Kristeva is virtually a neoconservative, someone who rejected the women's movement, a "dutiful daughter" who follows Lacan too closely, and thereby seems to promote patriarchy as the only alternative to psychosis.[2]

Under these circumstances, it should be obvious that our obligation (it is an ethical question) in relation to her work is not to take sides in defending one of these images as correct while denouncing the other, but rather to recognize this "oppositional" reception as a symptomatic avoidance, a turning away from her work. These interpretations are well known, and I will not discuss them in detail. I mention them only in order to suggest that the dramatically conflicting accounts of Kristeva are not simply chaotic, incoherent, or merely "mistaken" representations; on the contrary, they have a clear logical relation to one another, like the oppositions generated in the face of the "uncanny" or unapproachable object. They are not "random" misreadings, but the clearest evidence of an impasse: they show us the precise point at which her terminology has been neglected, thereby giving rise not to mere confusion, but to the production of opposite readings—what psychoanalysis might call "conflicting" readings.

We thus find readers celebrating Kristeva's category of the "semiotic" as a return to a quasi-maternal language that offers an alternative to the "paternal language" of Lacan's symbolic order, while others simultaneously denounce her for apparently claiming that rational, coherent "subjectivity" is possible only through the renunciation of this maternal space, or for seeming to believe that this semiotic language is the special province of male writers like Joyce and Artaud, thereby perversely refusing to identify the semiotic with women. In both interpretations, however, the term *mother* is never truly clarified, but only secured in an imaginary form, as a pre-Oedipal figure to be endorsed or denounced.

This split in the reception of Kristeva is not surprising, and might even be expected, in that in bears on our relation to "our ancestors," who are inevitably entangled in mythological constructions. As Freud says in *Totem and Taboo*, speaking of "the subject's ambivalent attitude toward a single object" that is characteristic of the "totem ancestor":

> The conflict . . . cannot be promptly settled because . . . they [the two attitudes, hatred and love, the desire to touch and detestation] are localized in the subject's mind in such a way that they cannot come up against each other. (*SE*, 13:29)

Such ambivalence and splitting is characterized by the production of "uncanny" icons that one can fear or idolize; and such is the divided reception that protects the two readings from each other and keeps them separate and "incompatible." But Freud also notes that, though such a relation to the totem appears to localize conflict, thereby pacifying the subject, there is a further "result of the repression," for it also entails a "loss of memory," a form of "amnesia."

The academic reception of many other thinkers is marked by precisely the same structural conflict, in which two incompatible images are offered to our gaze. Often, the problem is resolved by appeal to a *historical narrative*, which allows us to split the author into two parts by locating one interpretation at an "early stage" of the writer's career, and the other at a "later stage."[3] In the case of Kristeva, we find a narrative according to which the early stage of her work elaborates the semiotic as a radical, disruptive, and revolutionary force that is linked to the maternal, while in her later work the semiotic is abandoned, repudiated, deprived of political efficacy, and regarded as dangerous, so that Kristeva is thought to turn away from the mother, taking refuge in the "father of individual prehistory." We thus have a strategy of what Freud, in *Totem and Taboo*, calls "localization," a process that ensures that the two ideas (the mother and the father?) "cannot come up against each other"—thereby leaving us with a forced choice between opposites, each governed by idolatry, and perpetuating all the passions of devotion and hatred.

Similar narratives have been constructed in order to pacify and regulate a number of contemporary thinkers, according to a logic or narrative that makes them similarly "self-contradictory." The canonical reception of Heidegger has even provided us with two separate *names*—Heidegger I and Heidegger II—thereby encouraging us to regard the existential analytic of Dasein as a "serious phenomenological investigation," while dismissing the later work as a kind of "poetic revery" in which the proper work of philosophy has disappeared. This narrative can of course be inverted, so that the "early" Heidegger is regarded as still trapped in metaphysics, while the "later" Heidegger is celebrated as a thinker who announces the end of philosophy; but this reversal, while endorsing and repudiating the opposite stages, does not change the fundamental arrangement of the story that takes the place of (or substitutes for) Heidegger's thought—and this despite the fact that Heidegger himself, when asked about these two stages of his work, issued a warning about how history is constituted through narrative:

> Instead of the groundless, endless prattle about the "reversal," it would be more advisable and fruitful if people would simply engage themselves in the matter. . . . [O]nly by way of what [Heidegger] I has thought does one gain access to what is to-be-thought by [Heidegger] II. But the thought of [Heidegger] I becomes possible only if it is contained in [Heidegger] II.[4]

Despite this warning about the reductive "staging" of thought—which relies on a linear, developmental chronology that neither Heidegger nor Freud was willing to accept—we must also acknowledge the inevitability, the peculiar "fate" or "destiny," by which human history is subject to such mythological investments. As Heidegger himself adds, not only the *reception* of his work, but even *that work itself* "inevitably remained captive to contemporary modes of (re)presentation and language" (xiv). "Every effort to bring what has been thought closer to the prevailing modes of (re)presentation must assimilate what-is-to-be-thought to those (re)presentations and thereby *invariably deform the matter*" (viii, emphasis added). This point is also made by psychoanalysis: human history departs from natural, sequential "chronology" precisely to the extent that it *invariably* "remains captive" to representation, without which there would be no time, no history, and thus no opportunity to return to the past, in order to reread.

A similar narrative has been constructed for Foucault, whose work has been quickly divided between a supposedly "structuralist phase," dependent upon linguistics, and a sudden, dramatic "return to history" (the two stages also having been baptized under the names "archaeology" and "genealogy"), and with similar disputes about which half of the work should be celebrated and which denounced. Psychoanalysis can only point out that if such narratives have a pacifying, regulatory, and normalizing function (assimilating thought to the "prevailing modes of representation"), these narratives nevertheless do not resolve the "matter," the "thing" these thinkers confront *at every stage* of their work, but only repress and allow us to forget the conflict that the narrative pretends to overcome. Psychoanalysis itself is not free of such difficulties. As Lacan wrote in *Television*, "The Oedipus myth is the attempt to give epic form to the operation of a structure."[5]

From the standpoint of psychoanalysis, then, the reception of many contemporary writers can be seen not simply as a "contested" or "diverse" set of interpretations, but as the organized resolution of a conflict by means of a type of splitting. Whenever conflicting or opposed readings are produced, we have the clearest evidence of the specific point at which something in the writer's work has been systematically avoided, on both sides of the debate.[6] I will not pursue this further, but it should suffice to suggest that I choose these two issues— the mother and the woman—because this is where clarification would allow us to break the conflicting, imaginary, oppositional readings of Kristeva, what one might call the canonical and repressive reception of her work, thereby allowing us to read her again.

LABOR OF LOVE: THE MOTHER AND THE IMAGE

Let us take first the question of the mother. It is often said that in the course of the Oedipal conflict, the child passes from the mother to the father. Entry into the symbolic order is thus taken to mean that the child has to give up its initial attachment to the mother and pass into the "law of the father." According to this view, it would seem that the *mother* is confined to the imaginary, and that *women* as such are thereby excluded from the symbolic order (except to the extent that they imitate men). Kristeva's work on the semiotic can thus be seen as an attempt to recover a pre-Oedipal, maternal language, or perhaps a "feminine discourse" that has been "abjected," or repressed by civilization. On the other hand—and in perfect keeping with this reading—she can be criticized for insisting that there is no "feminine language," that the semiotic belongs equally to male avant-garde writers, and that in any case the semiotic only appears from *within* the symbolic order, as a disturbance from within, a moment of rupture that has no autonomy. As Madelon Sprengnether puts it,

> There is no access either to the Imaginary or to the semiotic except through the route of the symbolic. In this respect, Kristeva follows Lacan's two-tiered system of development. . . . Kristeva's adherence to Lacan's (and Freud's) developmental scheme, in which the symbolic (or Oedipal phase) must supercede the Imaginary, means that she cannot endorse Irigaray's project for the recovery of a language unique to the Imaginary or to the mother-daughter relationship.[7]

This also affects the position of "women," since "the relegation of the mother to the realm of reproduction and her corresponding exclusion from the symbolic create a double-bind situation for the daughter, who, in the process of her own development, must choose between maternal and paternal identification."[8]

This discussion, however, presupposes that the semiotic and symbolic can be directly gendered, that the symbolic is "masculine" while the semiotic is "feminine" and "maternal" (so that if the semiotic is "occupied" by men, this amounts to a betrayal of "women," who have been identified with the semiotic, and excluded from the symbolic). But the semiotic and symbolic cannot be directly gendered in this way; in fact such an account *presupposes* a commonsense account of sexual difference, thereby circumventing the question psychoanalysis is seeking to address, namely, the question of how sexual difference in the human animal is subject to representation rather than being naturally given. Thus, the semiotic is not automatically a domain of maternal or feminine identity, but a domain in which sexual difference is not yet established, and consequently it cannot be gendered without *returning* to a pregiven sexual difference (based on common sense and anatomy) that avoids the very question Kristeva's categories seek to address.

What is more, the "feminine" and the "maternal" should not be so quickly identified with each other. On the contrary, it could be shown that the maternal is precisely a forgetting or concealment of the feminine, an imaginary or even symbolic mirage in which the woman does not appear. As Kristeva says in the opening of "Stabat Mater," "femininity is absorbed by motherhood." We must therefore distinguish between the woman and the mother. Kristeva begins her essay by saying that one cannot simply *identify* the semiotic with the feminine, thereby isolating an "essence" of femininity: "We cannot say of a *woman* what she *is*," for this form of identification would amount to a betrayal of the issue, and would "risk abolishing her difference" (161). Let us therefore leave the question of woman for the moment.

As for the mother, here too—as Kristeva writes in the same passage—"we are caught in a paradox" (the section is titled "mother or primary narcissism?").[9] For when we speak of the "mother," when we speak of the "maternal" in terms of this semiotic or pre-Oedipal region, we must recognize that *sexual difference does not appear there*, and that in this sense, the pre-Oedipal mother is not only distinct from the woman, but also not sexually marked, whenever she is viewed as belonging to the semiotic domain. We must therefore distinguish not only between the "mother" and the "woman," but also, within the figure of the mother, between *two forms* of maternity: the archaic maternal image, which is a phallic figure that cannot be understood in terms of sexual difference, and the mother as sexually marked. Only then will it be possible to raise in a clear way the question of how "feminine sexuality" is in turn distinct from the mother as sexed (the figure to which women are often reduced).

It should therefore be clear that to read the semiotic and symbolic as gendered is to *begin* with sexual difference as already given, and thereby to avoid the entire problematic of psychoanalysis, which is to explain that sexual difference in the human subject is not given with the birth of the organism, or distributed according to common sense and anatomy. Such is the opening gesture of "Stabat Mater": "If it is not possible to say of a *woman* what she *is*," if "femininity is absorbed by motherhood," so that we cannot easily speak of "woman," if we must therefore begin with a question "concerning the mother," we must nevertheless also recognize that this motherhood is itself a "fantasy," an idealized archaic mother, an imaginary figure that *conceals* the maternal by offering up an imaginary idealization, one which, according to Kristeva, is binding and narcissistic: it is not "motherhood," but the retroactive fantasy by which "the adult, man or woman," remains bound to primary narcissism.

In short, we must distinguish three terms—*image, mother,* and *woman*—recognizing that this archaic image represents neither the maternal nor the feminine. And even if the mother can be distinguished from this fantasy, this imaginary figure, we will still face the task of distinguishing the mother from the woman, who is too easily "absorbed" by motherhood. A temporal question also emerges here, since this "archaic" figure is not *chronologically* or *developmentally* archaic, and cannot accurately be regarded as a "pre-Oedipal stage," but is rather the *retroactive* fantasy of the adult: "It involves less an idealized archaic mother than the idealization of the *relationship* that binds us to her, *one that cannot be localized*—an idealization of primary narcissism" (161, emphasis added). For all these reasons, it would be a mistake to *identify* the semiotic with the maternal and the feminine (whether to celebrate or denounce it). Kristeva's work can in fact be read in precisely the opposite way—as an attempt to break these quick and reductive identifications, an effort to distinguish between the imaginary, the maternal, and the feminine. (A more technical discussion would have to add that the semiotic is in turn distinct from the imaginary since it is a linguistic category—distinct from the symbolic as the imaginary is, but yet concerned with the field of speech. It would also be necessary to distinguish between the terms *woman* and *the feminine*, but we will remain with these few basic terms.)

In Freud, these illusory identifications are easier to maintain. In his account of the Oedipus myth, Freud relies on an imaginary narrative, the "family romance" (or "family novel") in which the child of either sex passes from an initial, identificatory relation to the mother, to a later, secondary identification mediated by the intrusion of the father. Because of this little narrative in which the mother and the father are inscribed, it was not always easy to see that under the term *mother*, there were at least three separate questions that needed to be distinguished. This is why Lacan introduced the terms *imaginary, symbolic,* and *real.* They allowed a terminological clarification of different *elements* that were all collapsed together by Freud's *psychological* language, his use of the family romance. Thus, when contemporary readers believe that Kristeva's account of the semiotic is also an account of the maternal and the feminine, they are "psychologizing," collapsing together three different categories, refusing the distinctions with which Kristeva is working, and returning to the most imaginary aspect of Freud's theory (often to contest it), the popular but misleading narrative in which the child passes from the "mother" to the "father" in a psychological sense.

Lacan's account of the "paternal metaphor" is an attempt to break with this imaginary narrative.[10] This is why he insists upon distinguishing the symbolic father from the actual person, the "real father" (*E,* 557/200), and stresses "the signifying function that conditions paternity" (*E,* 555/198), claiming that it is not the presence or absence of an actual male person, but rather the intrusion of the signifier, the presence and absence revealed in the fort-da game, that opens the child to the mark of lack by which the "second birth" of the subject, the passage from organic life to being-toward-death, becomes possible.[11] This signifying relation to death is what Freud discussed in *Totem and Taboo,* which Lacan refers to when he writes: "The symbolic father is, insofar as he signifies this Law, the dead Father" (*E,* 556/199). And this is why the father who seeks to be the law, to *incarnate* the law, thereby confusing his living image with the symbolic function, is precisely a *perversion* of the law, a "père-version," a punishing form of tyranny, which coincides with "the present obscuring of this function of the phallus," a confusion of imaginary and symbolic, which, like Freud's little narrative, contributes to "the profound mystification in which culture maintains the symbol of it" (*E, 555/198*)—the same confusion of the imaginary and the symbolic that we find on the side of woman whenever the feminine is captured by maternity, itself reduced in turn to an archaic fantasy.[12]

Kristeva's account of the linguistic categories of the semiotic and symbolic, for all its differences from Lacan, can thus be seen as a similar attempt to distinguish between (among other things) the imaginary and symbolic mother. Let us look at this distinction more closely. The sentences cited from "Stabat Mater" distinguish the woman, the mother, and the retroactive fantasy of an archaic maternity, a fantasy that can take us in two directions—precisely those that have characterized Kristeva's reception—leading us, as she says, either to "identify motherhood with that idealized misconception" or "to reject the image and its misuse," but in either case leading us to "circumvent the real" (161). Before we take up the question of the woman, then, we must distinguish further between this image and the mother.

These terms can be clarified by reference to Lacan's schema R, taken from the essay on psychosis, which gives a visual form to the distinctions Kristeva is addressing. In place of the usual Oedipal triangle, with the "psychological" mother, father, and child, we now have two triangles, one imaginary and one symbolic (see Figure 1).[13] The imaginary triangle is defined by three points: the ego (e), the image (i), and the phallus (Φ). It is important to note, however, that in the original French version of this diagram, the position of the phallus is marked by a lower case phi (ϕ), which designates the phallus as an "imaginary object" (as André Green's elaboration indicates), and not as the "phallic signifier" (Φ). The English text of *Écrits* is therefore misleading, and in addition, Green's notes introduce further confusion by defining R as "the real," when it in fact corresponds to the field of "reality," and thus to Freud's "reality principle," as Lacan's own notes make clear. The symbolic triangle is defined by the ego ideal, the mother, and the father (or more precisely, the "signifier of the primordial object" [M] and the "name-of-the-father" [F]). We should note immediately that the mother (M) is not confined to the imaginary order (contrary to popular belief); in fact she cannot even appear there. Strictly speaking, the mother only emerges insofar as the "capture" of the image has been broken, that is,

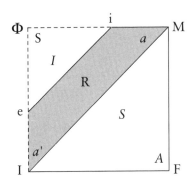

FIGURE 1   Schema R

A: the Other (*Autre*)

I: the Imaginary

I: ego ideal

M: signifier of the primordial object (mother)

F: position of the Name-of-the-Father in the locus of the Other

S: Subject

S: the Symbolic

R: the Real

Φ: phallus (Imaginary object)

i ⎫
e ⎭ :   the two Imaginary endpoints of all later narcissistic relationships, the ego (e) and the specular image (i)

segment iM: the axis of desires (object choice)

a: Objects—figure of the Imaginary other of the mirror stage

a':   the identification of the (child's) ego through the identification with the ideal of the ego (the paternal imago)

SOURCE: André Green, "Logic of Lacan's *objet(a)* and Freudian Theory: Convergences and Questions." In *Interpreting Lacan*, ed. Joseph H. Smith and William Kerrigan (New Haven, CT: Yale University Press, 1983), 161–91.

insofar as a distinction has been established that separates the mother (M) from the image (i)—that retroactive fantasy of which Kristeva speaks when she refers to the "idealization of primary narcissism." The mother is not "abjected" by, but rather emerges through, the "incest prohibition," the prohibition bearing precisely on the archaic image.

These remarks also bear on the object-relation. For in fact, in the upper-right corner of schema R, along the segment (iM), we can see that the field defined as R, the "field of reality"—which is not to be confused with the "real," as happens in André Green's discussion of this diagram—this field that appears between the imaginary and symbolic triangles comes into being only insofar as a distinction has been established between the mother and the image.[14] A structure in which (i) and (M) coincided would mean a "loss of reality."[15] In different language, we can say that the "object-relation," the possibility of objects in the "world" (which is not a "natural" world, as phenomenology has taught us long ago) emerges only if the child's relation to the mirror image has been broken, dialectized, submitted to the play of negativity, articulated, and thus brought into being, constituted by way of the symbolic order and language. "Where word breaks off," Heidegger says, "no thing can be."[16]

For Lacan, then, the "object-relation" is radically dependent upon language, as it is not for others who speak of a pre-Oedipal relation in which "good" and "bad" objects can be discussed without reference to the signifying network in which Lacan claims they are always implicated.[17] Here again, we can perhaps see why the temporality of language, its structuring effect, deprives us of the developmental sequence to which we might nostalgically appeal, as if seeking an archaic time. "This schema," Lacan writes,

> enables us to show the relations that refer, not to pre-Oedipal stages—which are not non-existent of course, but which cannot be conceived of in analytic terms— . . . but to the pregenital stages insofar as they are ordered in the retroaction of the Oedipus complex. (*E, 554/197*, slightly modified)

We might add that, for the human animal, who differs from other animals in this respect, it is not only being toward death, but also sexual difference, that emerges in its radical dependence on the word: "The subject is presented with the question of his existence, not . . . at the level of the ego . . . but as an *articulated question* . . . concerning his sex and his contingency in being, namely, that, on the one hand, he is a man or a woman, and, on the other, that he might not be" (*E, 549/194*, emphasis added). This suggests that, contrary to most phenomenology, there is no object, and no world, without sexual difference. Perhaps sexual difference is indeed as fundamental as ontological difference.[18]

To summarize: far from being confined to the imaginary order, the mother cannot even appear there, but in fact serves as one of the defining elements of the symbolic order—as Lacan says when he claims that it is only *through* the desire of the mother (which is not present in the plenitude of the image) that the "paternal function," the opening of reference, is possible. We thus see how the coordinates from Lacan's schema might cast light on Kristeva's text. Accordingly, in "Stabat Mater," Kristeva argues that "maternity" is a term that can be analyzed into distinct elements that should not be confused: the "mother" cannot be reduced to the biological function of giving birth, nor confined to the silent field of imaginary idealization, but has a crucial role in the symbolic order, one that is conceptually distinct from these other, highly invested definitions.

The mother's relation to the symbolic order, her role in opening a path for the child into the world of speech, has been beautifully expressed by Michèle Montrelay in "The Story of Louise," where the maternal labor of love is defined not in terms of "nurturing" or "care," but in terms of discourse and desire. As Montrelay says, the animal in nature gives birth but once, while the human mother has to give birth twice, once to bring the organism into the world, and again to give it *the gift* of that world, in a second labor, which is a labor of symbolization, a labor of speech that, by giving voice to her desire, also opens the world of "reality" in which the child's desire can find its place as well.[19] The labor of signification, Kristeva says, is "an ordeal of discourse, like love" (162). It is not only the famous "mirror stage," then, that gives the child its body, establishing the cut that distinguishes the body from the world, but also this discourse of love, through which the body (as distinct from the "organism") is born. "Let a body venture at last out of its shelter, take a chance with meaning under a veil of words" (162).

We can see this "second birth," the birth of the subject, in Freud's analysis of the child's cry, according to Montrelay. For there is a moment when *the cry passes from the organism to the subject*, a moment when the cry is no longer the expression of need—a cry for food, or warmth, or some organic necessity—but has become instead the expression of demand, the first emergence of demand in the field of the Other, a demand that cannot be reduced to need, since it does not ask *for an object* that would satisfy it, but is rather the first appeal *to the Other,* an emergent speech that asks for nothing, nothing but recognition, which is now everything.[20] Here too, object-relations theory is at issue, for there is no "real object," no "good enough mother" that can satisfy this demand by recourse to the objects of need, since the cry, this opening of demand, no longer comes from the organism, seeking the satisfaction of its appetite, but from the subject who seeks "something other."[21] As Lacan puts it in "The Signification of the Phallus":

> Demand thus bears on something other than the satisfactions which it calls for. . . . This is manifest in the primordial relation to the mother, pregnant as it is with that Other to be situated *some way short of* any needs which it might gratify. . . . This privilege of the Other thus sketches out *the radical form of the gift* of something which it does not have, namely, what is called love (latter emphasis added).[22]

It is thus by the "gift of speech" (passing from the breast to the voice) that the mother *substitutes,* in place of the object of need (which cannot serve as an answer to demand), the "gift of love," which is a gift of the nothing ("there, there now, it's ok, don't you worry").[23]

Should we not suspect, therefore, that the autistic child, the child who refuses to speak, who demands not to speak, is a child whose cry has not been heard (by the "ear of the other"), whose every cry was answered as if it were the expression of need, as if it were the cry of the organism? In Lacan's formulation, "The satisfaction of need appears only as the lure in which the demand for love is crushed, by sending the subject back to sleep, where he haunts the limbo regions of being" (*E*, 627/263). Should we not suspect that the silence of the autistic child is the only solution left for this subject waiting to be born, the only way of articulating to the other a demand that has been reduced to need, a demand for which there seemed to be no place? Is not this aggressive and stubborn silence, despite appearances, not a "refusal to speak," but precisely the reverse, a last-ditch attempt by the child to demand entrance to the symbolic order?

We may see here the importance of maternal *desire,* in the child's passage from the order of need to field of the Other: "In the final analysis, by refusing to satisfy the *mother's* demand, is not the child demanding that the mother should have a desire outside him, because the way to the desire that *he* lacks is to be found there?" (*E*, 628/264, emphasis added). This passage to *maternal desire* is what Kristeva articulates in the left-hand column of "Stabat Mater." (*E*, 628/264, emphasis added). The symbolic mother thus performs a second birth, a symbolic labor, which escorts the child out of the organic night, out of the imaginary world of blood and milk, out of the oceanic world of primary narcissism, and into the world of speech, where desire can be articulated.[24]

Let me develop one more observation about schema R before turning to the question of the woman. The difference between the image and the mother, between the imaginary mother and the symbolic mother, corresponds to a difference in the paternal function. In the imaginary triangle of schema R, the third term is the phallus. This corresponds to what Kristeva calls (following Freud) the "father of individual prehistory." In the symbolic triangle, the third term is the symbolic father (F). We can thereby see that the difference between the image and the mother corresponds to a distinction between the phallus and the symbolic father. This distinction between the "father" and the "phallus" has not been very clearly understood; the two terms have been equated, partly because the difference between them cannot be clarified as long as the position of the mother is reduced to the space of imaginary confinement in which so much commentary has left it (largely from reading Lacan through the lens of object-relations theory, where the imaginary and symbolic are not clearly distinct). Lacan's account of the "paternal metaphor" is basically an attempt to introduce this distinction between the phallus and the symbolic father in a methodical way.

We have seen that, contrary to popular belief, the mother is not confined to the imaginary; in fact she does not appear there at all. It is only in the symbolic order, where the desire of the mother emerges, that the mother appears as distinct, as an other who is freed from the reflection of the image. But the desire of the mother can only emerge, can only find its place, if some reference is possible for it, if her desire can be registered as directed elsewhere than the child—that is, if the child is not to remain dedicated to being the only object of maternal desire (thus occupying the position of the phallus and maintaining the imaginary triangle, foreclosing all absence, all gift and debt). This *referential* aspect of maternal desire ("M" being designated as the *"signifier* of the primordial object") explains why Lacan says that, contrary to Freud, the "father" is not "real," but is precisely a signifying function, a metaphor, a purely symbolic operation, a substitution by which the "void" or "enigma" of maternal desire is given a "sense," a symbolic orientation beyond the child, thereby allowing the child itself to find a place beyond what would otherwise be the overwhelming abyss of maternal desire.[25]

Perhaps one can thereby hear something more in the child's cry, the first demand, which is not only a demand for recognition, but also a demand that bears on the phallus, a demand that falls short of desire, a demand to be the "one and only" object of maternal desire—a demand, then, which cries for plenitude, and amounts to the abdication of desire. Thus, even as it reveals the difference between the cry of need and the first dimension of demand, the child's cry also shows that this demand for recognition, this radical dependence of the subject on the Other, is something *suffered*. Demand thus shows, but also aims at overcoming, its own birth into the world. It is a demand *to the mother* that provisionally recognizes her as another, but it is simultaneously a demand *for the mother*, a refusal of difference, a phallic demand to go back to sleep in the fullness of presence. As Aristophanes says, desire is only born with an incision, a cut of separation that is painful, and leaves something wanting. That cut is also a story of sexual difference, arising from a mythical origin in which, "once upon a time," it did not exist, and therefore had to be produced in a uniquely human suffering, a division that even in Aristophanes left its mark upon the flesh.

This allows us, furthermore, to clarify Lacan's distinction between desire and *jouissance*. The first manifestation of the lack in the Other, the fact that the maternal Other is wanting, appears initially as an enigma, an overwhelming emptiness that has no limit. For the child, who apprehends this lack in the Other, it is not yet "desire" in the sense that it has no "place," no symbolic limit, but appears only as a void, a void that is registered in the child's cry, a cry that not only expresses the child's own lack, which it seeks to overcome with this appeal for recognition, but also expresses the knowledge that this Other is not complete, is wanting. Maternal "desire" thus first appears, not as desire, but as an obscure incompleteness, which is manifested in the Other. This incompleteness has an overwhelming, overpowering effect, which Lacan calls the *jouissance* of the Other. The child will do anything to fill this void, to appease the *jouissance* of the Other, even to the point of sacrificing itself, throwing itself headlong into the abyss, as is sometimes the case with the sacrifice of the firstborn child. We know this devouring Other of *jouissance* has a place in religion, and that whole civilizations can dedicate themselves to feeding this fire of the sun, sacrificing their neighbors if not themselves, in an effort to appease this great Other, whose appetite appears to have no limit. Speaking of the holocaust at the end of *Seminar XI* (which replaced a seminar that was significantly to have been called "The Names of the Father"), Lacan writes that this "offering to obscure gods of an object of sacrifice is something to which few subjects can resist succumbing, as if under some monstrous spell" (*SXI*, 275). We know that Kristeva, too, has taken up the theme of sacrifice and religion at many points in her work. When the lack in the Other first shows itself, then, the child will be only too happy to offer itself up in sacrifice, as if to say, "let me be the one object that will satisfy this *jouissance* of the Other." In a similar way, Schreber sacrificed himself to becoming the object of divine *jouissance*, in a delirious unfolding of pleasure and suffering that entailed the foreclosure of sexual difference.

We can thus elaborate the cry of the child a little further here. When the child cries out, not from need, but in a manifestation of demand, an appeal for recognition *from* the Other, this cry is also a recognition *of* the Other, a recognition that the Other is lacking. We thus face an obscure *relation*: the emergence of demand indicates not simply a detachment of the subject from the order of need or the emergence of the "subject" as distinct from the "organism"; the cry also testifies to the fact that the Other now emerges as lacking, not yet in the sense of "desiring" however, but in the sense of emerging as a "devouring" and "phallic" *jouissance*.[26] We are faced, in other words, with a *correlation*—consuming, nondialectical, and timeless—between demand and *jouissance*, and we can see from this that the symbolic order, the order of desire, sets a limit to *jouissance*, providing a point of reference, localizing what will otherwise be the overwhelming and sacrificial cycle of *jouissance* and demand. This limit is what Lacan calls the paternal metaphor. And this is why *maternal desire is strictly opposed to the imaginary jouissance of the archaic mother*, which Kristeva calls "binding" and "absorbing."[27]

We thus see why Lacan insisted upon a structural account that would allow the psychological terms "mother" and "father" to be broken into elements (like the "image," "mother," and "woman"), together with a terminology (demand, desire, *jouissance*), that would allow a departure from the chronological, developmental model that Freud's imaginary narrative maintained. Freud, we might say, believed too much in the real father, the little narrative of the mother and father, maintained in their imaginary forms. By insisting on the paternal function as a symbolic one, a metaphorical substitution (like the lamb sacrificed in place of Isaac, to an Other that allowed this symbolic substitution), Lacan clarified how the *jouissance* of the Other is localized, given a symbolic reference, and thus articulated, translated from the order of *jouissance* into the order of desire, so that the child's cry might be freed from the static impasse of demand and emerge at the level of speech. In short, with the paternal metaphor, archaic maternal *jouissance* is reconfigured, symbolized, in order that it might appear as desire. Lacan's shorthand for this transformation is given as the shift in the status of the Other from omnipotence (Φ) to lack (F), from devouring *jouissance* to symbolic castration, the transformation of the Other from O to Ø, which is the opening of sexual difference.

SEXUATION

Thus far, I have tried to show that the mother is not confined to the imaginary, that she cannot properly be situated there, and that if we allow Freud's imaginary scenario to guide our reading, that is, if we "psychologically" condense all the terms, interpreting the "imaginary" as "maternal" and "feminine," while regarding the symbolic as "male," we will not understand how the work of Kristeva or Lacan amounts to a reconfiguration of Freud's account, instead of simply reproducing it. Let me now turn to the question of "woman."

Schema R, by distinguishing the imaginary and symbolic mother, does not address the question of "woman." Woman does not appear in the schema. In a similar way, Kristeva set aside the question of woman in order to begin with a critique of the archaic image, and a distinct elaboration of the maternal relation to the symbolic order. Woman does not appear on schema R, but the schema does show us that woman remains a question, that the *place* of woman is not sufficiently established by reference to the mother, either in imaginary or symbolic terms—unless, as Kristeva says, we allow woman to be "absorbed by motherhood." Thus, the woman remains in need of articulation.

Late in his career, Freud returned of course to the question of "femininity" in an effort to understand not only the sense in which the figure of maternity could not serve as an answer to the question of femininity, but also the sense in which "something" of woman appeared to remain outside castration, in a different relation to the law. These are the famous or notorious articles in which Freud announces, for example, that women have no superego, that "for women the sense of what is ethically normal is different from what it is in men," and so on.[28] These statements have produced precisely the same sort of "opposite" readings that we have seen elsewhere, in that some readers have taken them as the most obvious evidence of Freud's misogyny, while others have tried to build a "feminine ethic" on the basis of this difference. But perhaps the problem is not solved in this way.

In "Stabat Mater," Kristeva would seem to be exploring the distinction between the "archaic mother" and the "symbolic mother" (who appears in the figure of the Virgin Mary); but she also suggests that even this symbolic figure is in some way insufficient to articulate the question of sexual difference. Put differently, the "mother" and "father" do not give us the "man" and the "woman." The terms should not be taken as equivalent, even if popular beliefs offer them as substitutes for one another. "What is it then in this maternal representation that . . . goes against both of the two sexes, and was able to attract women's wishes for identification?" (180). How is it, Kristeva asks, that "[t]he Virgin assumes" a "feminine *denial* of the other sex," and does so "by setting up a third person: I do not conceive with *you* but with *Him*"?[29] More precisely, how is it that the dimension of maternal desire, insofar as it appears at all, remains oriented—in this figure of Immaculate Conception where sexual difference remains veiled—toward an omnipotent Other, with the result that she can conquer her own "megalomania" only by "putting it on its knees before the child-god" (180)? And with the further consequence that the relation to *other women* is also compromised ("The Virgin especially agrees with the repudiation of the other woman" [181])? We should see here that the question of the child, the child-god, which goes hand in hand with the Immaculate Conception, refers us not merely to the problematic divinization of the male child (discussed by Kristeva in her book on China, where restrictions on childbearing have historically led to infanticide when it comes to female children), but also to questions concerning the daughter and the mother-daughter relation: "Out of the virginal myth there is the war between mother and daughter" (183). The two points ("repudiation of the other woman" and the mother-daughter relation) can thus be linked: "A woman seldom (although not necessarily) experiences her passion (love and hatred) for another woman without having taken her own daughter's place" (184).

Thus, for Kristeva as for Lacan, it is not only necessary to distinguish between the imaginary and symbolic mother, insisting upon the mother's relation to discourse and desire; it is also necessary to take up Freud's late questions on femininity, particularly since the image of the Virgin Mother no longer serves its mythical purpose. "While that clever balanced architecture today appears to be crumbling, one is led to ask the following: what are the aspects of the feminine psyche for which that representation of motherhood does not provide a solution, or else provides one that is felt as too coercive by twentieth-century women?" (182).

We do not have time to treat all the complex issues raised toward the end of "Stabat Mater." I would simply like to suggest in closing that a second of Lacan's diagrams—the sexuation diagram from *Encore*—can help to orient future discussion and clarify some basic terms. The top portion of the diagram (see Figure 2) has been discussed several times. It provides us with what Lacan, thinking no doubt of Kant, calls an "antinomy." On the "masculine" side, we find the proposition $\forall x \Phi x$, which can be rendered "All men are castrated," or perhaps also "all men are mortal," as the familiar syllogism has it.

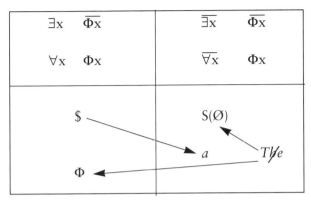

FIGURE 2

SOURCE: Juliet Mitchell and Jacqueline Rose (ed.), and Jacqueline
Rose (trans.). *Feminine Sexuality: Jacques Lacan and the école
freudienne* (New York: Norton, 1985).

If your name is Socrates, or if you have any other name, and if you are
also "a man," then you are mortal, subject not only to natural death
but to the law of death, the law of living as mortal. (The proper name,
as Derrida says, is always a name of death.[30]) But this group of "all
men"—what one might call the formation of the "universal," the
closed set of mortals to which "all" belong—is established only by a
paradoxical relation to its exception. Lacan thus produces a second
formula on the "masculine" side, $\exists x\ \overline{\Phi x}$, which can be rendered as the
exception to the law, "There is one who is not castrated." As Slavoj
Žižek has suggested, this formula, which locates the "Primal Father"
of *Totem and Taboo* (who like other mythical figures is the tyrannical
and "devouring" father), can also be seen as the father who "rises
from the grave," who perversely cannot be killed, like the vampires
who haunt the Gothic novel, arising at precisely the moment when
Kant formulates a law that would incorporate a universal or "cosmopolitan" community, or like the ghost of Hamlet's father who
returns after death to take vengeance on those who are living.[31] This
father can therefore be structurally equated with the position of the
phallus (Φ) on schema R, since it marks the place not of the symbolic
father (who is always the dead father) but of an absolute and unlim-
ited *jouissance*—the "père sévère."

   On the "feminine" side, we find a similar but not identical antin-
omy. The upper formula $\overline{\exists x}\ \overline{\Phi x}$, can be rendered "there is no woman

who is not castrated" (with the negation registered by a line above the symbol). This formula (because of the double negation) is logically equivalent to the one designating all men as castrated, except that, in place of the "universal" quantifier "all men" ($\forall$x), the "feminine" side states the "same" rule *in terms of the particular* (not "all are" but "there is none who is not"). The difference is therefore that there is no "set" of "all women." Put differently, one might say that the diagram provides no "essence" of woman, no universal definition in which "all women" could be included. One might also say that, when it comes to the castration of woman, there is only "this one" and "that one," which means, as Freud suggested in his late essays, that one cannot assume in advance that a given woman either is or is not subject to castration. The fact that the "rule" is stated using the particular ("there is no") thus provides a distinction between masculine and feminine castration, despite the "logical" equivalence of the formulae. As for the second formula on the "feminine" side ($\overline{\forall x}\ \Phi x$), the one that would correspond to the exception on the "masculine" side (the Primal Father), it can be rendered "not all of a woman is subject to castration." Here too, despite a logical equivalence, there is a difference from the masculine exception to the law. In this case, it is not that one figure *entirely* escapes castration and assumes the mythical, phallic position of the Primal Father (or Phallic Mother); it is rather that there is a partial escape from castration, a sense in which something of woman does not submit to castration. This is the sense in which femininity is "not all" inscribed within the law.

This diagram therefore is clearly intended as a way of returning to Freud's late essays in order to clarify the sense in which "femininity" does not submit to castration. It should be stressed, of course, that a given woman can perfectly well find herself on the "masculine" side of the diagram, and that some men will find themselves positioned on the "feminine" side (Lacan mentions certain writers in *Seminar XX*). This does not deprive the diagram of meaning or specificity, but simply indicates what we have said previously: that it is not possible to use the terms "man" and "woman" in the commonsense way, as if anatomical difference were the proper measure of sexual identity. The diagram thus designates structural positions that a given subject may come to occupy.

Let us turn to the bottom portion of the schema, which has been

treated less often. On the "masculine" side, we find the familiar formula for fantasy ($ ◊ a), which is composed of the divided subject ($)
in relation to the "objet (a)," in this case the object of fantasy. This is
the "normal" position, in the sense of "nor-mâle" ("normal male")
which Lacan often gave to this word. On the "feminine" side, we find
two possible positions, and it is here, I think, that the emphasis of the
diagram and its real contribution can be located. Insofar as this
schema returns to Freud's late work and the question of "femininity,"
we may say that these two positions are an attempt to formulate more
distinctly the aspects of femininity that an imaginary or "psychological" account will always tend to blur. It is also this "feminine side"
that has had such influence on the question of woman's "external"
relation to the symbolic order—the difference of "woman's language"
or woman's relation to language, often discussed under the rubric of
"*écriture féminine*." Let us therefore look in closing at these two possibilities on the "feminine" side.

The first formula (T\he → Φ) links The Woman to the Phallus. With
respect to the term "The Woman," it will be recalled that as distinct
from *women*, who obviously exist, *The Woman* does not exist, in the
sense that there is no essence, no "Woman as such" that might provide
a definition for "all women." Kristeva appears to have this refusal of
essence in mind when she stresses the verb "to be" in the opening
pages of "Stabat Mater," saying that we "cannot say of a *woman* what
she *is* (without running the risk of abolishing her difference)" (161).
With the term "The Woman," then, we appear to be addressing neither an "essence" of all women nor simply something that has "no
reality whatsoever," but rather those aspects of "femininity" that are
clinically related to the questions raised in Freud's late work. Now the
formula linking The Woman to the phallus can be read in two ways,
following Freud, namely, in terms of identification and in terms of the
object. Let us consider these more closely.

When it is a question of identification, we are concerned with a phallic identification that Lacan speaks of as *masquerade*. Lacan says that
this masquerade is a common counterpart of the "normal male": he
pretends, with a "fetishistic" trait of perversion that accompanies normal masculinity, to avoid castration through Woman as the object of
fantasy; and she plays the role of the phallus in relation to the gaze—

the scopic register that Freud spoke of in his remarks on "feminine narcissism"—thereby participating in a fiction of femininity that corresponds to the masculine fantasy.[32] As Eugénie Lemoine-Luccioni puts it: through her, he pretends to have what he does not, and through him, she pretends to be what she is not.[33] It should be noted here that this performance of the masquerade, despite being subjected to the mechanism of fantasy, remains consonant with desire, since desire is constituted in accordance with the lack that fantasy seeks to organize.[34]

When Freud spoke near the end of his life on the notorious topics of "frigidity," "feminine masochism," the "tendency to debasement" in women, and so on, it was because he had found that women *sacrifice* their desire for love, that often there appeared to be, if not a forced choice between love and desire, at least a complex relation that appears to go "against nature" in the sense that natural copulation does not call for such a "sacrifice" when it comes to the sexual relation. Thus, Lacan's discussion of "feminine *jouissance*" can be understood as a return to these clinical issues. Kristeva also addresses this issue of "feminine *jouissance*" as an "ethics of psychoanalysis" when she writes that "ethics is no longer seen as being the same as morality. . . . [E]thics amounts to not avoiding the embarrassing and inevitable problematics of the law but giving it flesh, language and *jouissance*" (185).

The second way of reading this first formula, the feminine relation to the phallus, is in terms of the object-relation. If the first relation, masquerade, consists in "being the phallus" (for man, who is castrated and does not have it), the second consists in "having the phallus." Thus, opposed to masquerade, we find *maternity*. We may therefore read Lacan's diagram as situating, at this point on the schema, what Freud means when he speaks of maternity as a way of obtaining the phallus from the father. (Freud, however, who does not distinguish *in explicit terminology* between the penis and the phallus, speaks of the "relation to the child" as one that resolves, or substitutes for, "penis envy.") Maternity in this aspect is thus, despite Freud's term "penis envy," not so much an avoidance of castration as it is a way of taking up or "registering" castration in a symbolic way (since the child, even when it serves as a phallic "substitute," is thereby understood from the standpoint of a symbolization of lack). But we should not neglect its "fetishistic" aspect (the child as maternal phallus) any more than we neglect the "trait of perversion" in the "normal" male (that is the similarity between $ ◊ a and T$\not{h}$e → Φ). We have explored this point in Kristeva's remarks on the Virgin Mother who subdues her "megalomania" by kneeling before the child, as well as the costs of this maternal position. Once again, this obviously cannot serve, nor is it meant to serve, as a description of "all mothers," but is rather a way of formalizing the particular relation to maternity that Kristeva regards as an investment in the "archaic image"—which schema R would situate in terms of the imaginary triangle, with the child-mother relation being dominated by a phallic identity. Here too, one might note that, despite appearances, the relation to the child as phallus is, like masquerade, a relation of desire. It does not so much refuse castration as take up castration (symbolic lack), but with the same fetishistic trait of perversion that appears, on the "masculine" side, in the formula for fantasy, where the divided subject veils its lack through a relation to the lost object.[35] This thesis would seem to be confirmed by Kristeva's remarks that even the Immaculate Conception of the Virgin, despite appearances, entails a symbolic aspect, a desire for the divine, that moderates what would otherwise be her megalomania. In other words, these two possibilities are in Lacan's view within the symbolic, masquerade and maternity being two forms in which The Woman is not only culturally validated in a sociological sense, but also, in a more clinical sense, subject to repression, to symbolization, and the law.

The second possibility on the "feminine" side—the formula linking The Woman to S(Ø)— takes up the extent to which "Woman" is outside the law. This is where the question of "feminine *jouissance*" is located (as opposed to the "phallic" *jouissance* described by the first formula, T$\not{h}$e → Φ. This is where Lacan situates the question of "femininity," of that "something" of woman which escapes castration, which stands as an exception to the law—the question addressed in Freud's late texts. It is also what Sarah Kofman treats as "women's madness," which is not too distant from the "enigmatic mysticism" that has been repeatedly figured in the form of the sylph, sphinx, or sibyl, who notoriously speak in a vatic language, inaccessible to the "human community," which for its part approaches this oracle at its own risk.[36]

Whereas the first formula, the relation to the phallus, moves "across the sexual divide," so to speak (just as the formula for fantasy on the "masculine side" moves across), we are dealing in this case with a form of "femininity" which is, as it were, "contained within itself." Accordingly, the formula in question here is not related to the phallus, but to S(Ø).[37] It thus concerns something that, as Freud said, makes the woman who occupies this position especially "intractable" for analysis—as if "she won't tell us, even when we beg her on our knees."[38] As Lacan says in his "Guiding Remarks for a Congress on Feminine Sexuality":

> We should also ask whether phallic mediation drains off everything that can be shown concerning the drives in woman. . . . Perhaps we should state here that the fact that everything that can be analysed is sexual does not entail that everything sexual is accessible to analysis. (*FS*, 92)

It should be clear that in speaking of this feminine *jouissance* that is in some way "outside language," it is no longer a question of that "*jouissance* of the Other*," which appears to the child as a devouring and limitless omnipotence, and corresponds to the phallic position that can be occupied equally by the phallic mother and by the father of *Totem and Taboo*. Here, by contrast, we are concerned not with the devouring "*jouissance* of the Other" in which sexual difference is lost, but with the "Other *jouissance*," that of Woman, a sense of *jouissance* that is not located in the imaginary triangle of schema R, but that concerns the woman, and is thus inscribed *within* sexual difference (hence the "question of femininity"). It should also be clear that since this "Other *jouissance*" concerns that aspect of "femininity" which does not follow castration, it is thus also distinguished from the "masculine" position, the "phallic *jouissance*" of the normal male.

Like the first formula, this one [T⫲e → S(Ø)] also admits of two readings. What is more, if the previous positions—maternity and masquerade—can be designated as "solutions by way of desire," as Marie-Hélène Brousse has argued, these next two possibilities can be understood as "solutions by way of love." Thus, "positions taken in regard to (Ø) . . . are clinically defined ways of giving an answer to the enigma of femininity."[39] As "ways of giving an answer," we are to understand these two possibilities, like the previous ones, not as *adequate* or *correct* answers to the question of sexual difference but, on the contrary, precisely as answers, as efforts *to close the question* of sexual difference, which, insofar as it is real in the Lacanian sense, *has no "adequate" representation.* This is what Lacan means when, in a strongly Heideggerian formulation, he says that the question of truth, which is in some cases the question of the truth of Woman, cannot be given in the traditional form of *truth as adequation.*[40] When Lacan defined hysteria *as a question,* namely, the question of sexual difference itself ("Am I a man or a woman?"), this suggests that the effort to *take refuge from the question*—"answering" the question of woman, for example, by "adequating" it to the figure of the mother— this refuge is a common but nevertheless problematic refusal of the real of sexual difference, a circumvention of the real through appeal to the maternal image that Kristeva calls a "binding" fantasy.

The two possibilities in this case are thus efforts to circumvent the real of sexual difference not in a phallic form (maternity or masquerade), but in another way. "There is," Lacan says, "a *jouissance* of the body which is, if the expression be allowed, *beyond the phallus*" (*FS,* 145). How then are these possibilities distinguished from the "answers" given by the first formula, in the relation to the phallus? One might say that while the first formula concerns the production of an answer to the "question of woman" that relies on symbolic means, but falls short of "castration proper" by seeking to incarnate The Woman (through masquerade or maternity), the second formula isolates subjective positions that fall outside "castration proper" by seeking, not a sort of imaginary incarnation (with all its corporeal effects), but rather a direct relation to the real.

According to Brousse, the first form of S(Ø) corresponds to the clinical category of erotomania. This may be defined as "the love of being loved," which is not to be taken in the "everyday" sense that might apply to virtually anyone, but in the more precise sense of that petrification or passivity in which the relation to the other (the other person) has become impossible, having been replaced with an idealized relation to "Man" in the universal, not another subject, but precisely the "idea" of Man, the idea of being loved not by another, but by "Man"—a position through which, moreover, a given woman seeks to occupy, for her own part, the position of The Woman, thereby losing herself in a perhaps masochistic labor of love. Thus, Lacan writes in *Television,* "Woman only encounters Man in psychosis," and Brousse comments, "This particular encounter with Man as Universal (and not a man, any man) is a way to affirm, in return, Woman as *La femme*" (125). In erotomania, "The absolute Other as Woman exists, but only as long as the subject devotes himself or herself to the *jouissance* of that Other which, therefore, ceases to be prohibited" (125). The second reading of this formula is equally concerned with clinical questions, which go beyond the limits of this discussion, but which can at least be indicated by the fact that when Lacan presents this diagram, he also discusses (as in "Guiding Remarks for a Congress") "the issue of so-called frigidity" (*FS,* 145) and "the problem of feminine masochism" (*FS,* 92).

These clinical disputes and their technical details are too complex to summarize in a few words, though one can begin to see from these remarks what is at issue in this diagram from a clinical perspective. My purpose here has been the more limited one of sketching out the basic structure, and some of the basic terminological distinctions, of a psychoanalytic theory that is still too often confused with "psychological" and "sociological" categories. I thereby hope to indicate that some of the issues Kristeva is addressing have remained obscure in the course of her reception, or confused with the imaginary narrative of Freud's Oedipal model. Let me simply stress in conclusion that, since the question of feminine *jouissance* in both these formulae is closely bound up with the topic of "love," and the complex, often incompatible relations in psychoanalytic theory between love and desire, it could well be that much of Kristeva's writing on this topic still remains to be read.

We know that Kristeva has often written on the problem of "love," not only in the text "Freud and Love: Treatment and Its Discontents," but also in virtually all her work on depression, melancholy, and abjection, as well as in her work on transference, and in the more recent *In the Beginning Was Love: Psychoanalysis and Faith.* The topic even plays a crucial role in her political writings, and in her relations to "feminism." For as we know, love takes many forms: in the imaginary it becomes entangled not only with identification, but with its attendant aggression; in the symbolic it entails what Lacan called "identification with signifiers," where, on the one hand, the "futural" potential of the ego ideal is formed (to be an "artist," an "athlete," and so on, beyond the entrapment of the imaginary), but where, on the other hand, we also find the most punishing effects of the superego (Freud speaks in *Group Psychology* of our investments in "ideas" such as national identity, race, and religion). Without elaborating these themes, we have nevertheless been able to suggest that, in "Stabat Mater," the "love" of a child is, from the point of view of psychoanalysis, a complex matter, entailing not only the child's own negotiations of need, demand, and desire, but also an important set of distinctions between the archaic mother, the symbolic mother, and the question of woman that arises in excess of these. Thus, it would seem that a more detailed elaboration of the clinical dimension of Kristeva's work, and of the specific conceptual terminology with which she is working, might allow us to cast some light on a body of writing that has thus far been to a large degree trapped within "conflicting" and oppositional readings.

3

The *Role* of Gender
and the *Imperative* of Sex

ROLE AND IMPERATIVE

In contemporary discourses on sexuality, the transsexual is sometimes referred to as the most radical example of the "malleability of gender." The distinction between the transvestite and the transsexual is often presented this way: if the *transvestite* is able to play with gender identity through the masquerade of clothing, demonstrating the "symbolic" character of identity through the mimetic adoption of behavior, the *transsexual* would assume the even more radical position of altering the body itself, changing the very material of the flesh, as if the body itself were another "constructed" phenomenon, subject to manipulation (displacement and substitution) in the same way that clothing is, as if it too were "fashionable." There would be a sort of continuum linking the transvestite and the transsexual, as two examples of the "construction of gender," one at the level of clothing, the other at the level of anatomy. The idea has been widely accepted today that "the subject," and thus "gender" as well, is historically produced; why should we not also expect that the *subject's embodiment*, like the *subject's role* in the symbolic order, would shift with the "fashions" of history? The power of modern technology would join hands here with the historicist thesis according to which "subjectivity" has no essential form, but is a "product" of history.

In her book *Horsexe*, a discussion of transsexuality, Catherine Millot argues on the contrary that we must not confuse the transvestite and the transsexual, as two examples of a common enterprise, two instances of a similar demonstration of the "constructed" character of gender.[1] Millot's book aims to introduce a Lacanian perspective to the specifically clinical literature on transsexuality. Despite its references linking transsexuality to religious practices of sacrifice, castration, and doctrines of divine *jouissance* (one recalls Schreber's conviction that God requires his transformation), as well as a few passing remarks—though important ones—on the legal questions raised by transsexuality (the right to change one's name, to keep one's previous identity private, to marry after an operation, to adopt children, and so on, and different national positions on these matters), *Horsexe* is fundamentally concerned with the clinical task of determining which subjects who seek an operation will in fact benefit from surgery, and which will not. Such a discussion may seem to some readers a rather marginal one, concerned either with a very specific and limited clinical problem, or else with "extreme cases" of identity, cases that will not shed much light on the more general theoretical issues of gender and sexuality. But although Millot's book is principally a contribution to a specific clinical issue, the theoretical implications of her work are in no way confined to the "exceptional" case.

As always with Freud, the "abnormal" instance, the "deviation," turns out to have a more decisive function, implicating the norm itself. In this sense, the categories of "normal and pathological" discussed by Canguilhem as fundamental to nineteenth-century thought, and taken up again by Foucault in *The Order of Things*, are displaced by Freudian thought.[2] This was already the case in the *Three Essays* for example, where Freud's analysis of "perversion," in which the purportedly "normal" sexual object was replaced by a substitute, eventually turned out to demonstrate that the sexual drive is intrinsically "perverted" (*SE*, 7:125–243, esp 135–60). Thus, as Freud's analysis proceeded, the model of a "normal" or "natural" sexual object with which he began had to be dropped, in view of the discovery that the sexual "drive" is *constitutively* denatured, that it does not follow the automatic machinery of the "instinct" in nature, passing through stages of adolescence and reproductive maturation, culminating in procreative sex through arriving at its "proper object."[3] The sexual "drive" in the human animal is thereby *originally detached* from what might otherwise be its natural foundation. Although the *Standard Edi-*

tion translates *"Trieb"* and *"Instinkt"* with the same Latinate word ("drive" does not appear in the index; see also 1:xxiv–vi), Lacan always insisted upon Freud's terminological distinction whereby the drive is distinguished from the instinct precisely insofar as sexuality in the human animal is *intrinsically bound to representation*. This link between the drive and representation is what separates human sexuality from the natural function of instinct—not only in the occasional or "perverse" instance, but in its very constitution. Will we not find, then, that if Millot refuses to regard transvestism and transsexuality as two instances of the malleability of gender, the question of the difference between them, despite its apparently esoteric or merely clinical character, will have consequences for the theory of sexuality as a whole?

The radicality of this distinction between the instinct and the drive has not been sufficiently grasped, as is clear from the fact that we still hear many commentators speak of a supposedly natural sexuality, an id that would be subjected to the constraints of civilization, like so many historical conventions or taboos imposed upon an original, organic "urge." That framework, as Slavoj Žižek has argued, provides the foundation for political theories (from Hobbes and Kant to the present, perhaps), which oppose "appetite" to "law," positing an innate human aggression or self-interest that must be ordered by the imposition of cultural convention (submission to the moral law)—that artifice by means of which humans transcend the "state of nature" and enter into "history."[4] But it is precisely this conceptual framework, in which nature and culture are opposed, that is refused by Freudian theory. Clearly, this point also amounts to rejecting the idea that a natural sexuality is constrained by the imposition of *external* taboos. In this sense, Freud's position coincides with Foucault's rejection of the "repressive hypothesis." This point is avoided by those who continue to read Freud as though "desire" were a natural fact regulated by cultural prohibitions, but the problem is not confined to that misreading. Insofar as current discourse is still organized around a cultural category of "gender" which we regard as "historical," opposing it to the "natural" category of "sex," do we not remain with the framework that Freud sought to contest?

We have indicated the most fundamental issue by distinguishing between the terms *role* and *imperative*. If we often hear today that gender is "constructed"—that it is a matter of convention, or in some way a "symbolic" phenomenon (I put the word in quotation marks to suggest that Lacan's use of the term is quite different from its use in cultural studies, where "the symbolic" simply designates those historically diverse conventions that various cultures produce)—it must nevertheless be acknowledged that *sexual embodiment* is not a purely "symbolic" phenomenon. In contrast to what we call "gender roles," sexual difference is not a human convention, like democracy or monarchy, a social form that was invented at some point *in historical time*, a contingent formation that one culture produced, but that might be replaced by another form, as socialism might be said to replace capitalism. Obviously, this is not to claim that sexual embodiment *escapes* historical inscription, as if it could be reduced to a simple "fact of nature." The distinction between the instinct and the drive already indicates that we are not concerned with a naturalistic conception of the body, or of sexual difference. The point is rather that we cannot treat embodiment as though it were simply one more human institution, another convention invented (in the course of time) by human beings, like agriculture or atomic weapons.

To speak of the drive as *constitutively* detached from nature ("always already") is thus to stress the *imperative of inscription*, the structural inevitability of representation that characterizes human sexuality in all its diversity—indeed, as the very condition for the possibility of this diversity, which would otherwise be reduced to the "natural diversity" discussed by evolutionary theory, in which the symbolic order is eliminated. Obviously, such an imperative does not contradict the idea that sexual difference has a history, despite the popular polemic according to which we are encouraged to choose "psychoanalysis or history." But it does suggest that we cannot (psychoanalysis does not) situate embodiment or sexual difference *in the same way* that we situate the human conventions that are developed historically, as particular responses to the "law" of inscription. This difference between the *contingent*, historically constituted forms of life, and the *inevitable* dimension of sexually marked embodiment, is what we have indicated by distinguishing between the "role" of gender and the "imperative" of sex.

PSYCHOANALYSIS AND HISTORY

The "law" of sexual difference, then, is not a human law; like death (that other imperative), it is not a human invention and should not be situated at the same level as the "social roles" that concern contemporary discussions of "gender." This imperative is, of course, taken up and "symbolized" differently by different cultures, and therefore enters into history, but it would be a mistake to reduce "sexual difference" to one more human convention, as though it were synonymous with what we usually mean by "gender." As Joan Copjec puts it, particular, contingent institutions, such as the family, are efforts to give some kind of consistency to a sexual division that is not organized in advance by the "laws of nature," or submitted to the regulative function of instinct.[5] Historicist accounts can describe the development of such institutions in their various forms, but what concerns psychoanalysis is a rather different problem, namely the fact that every construction such as the family is a "failed attempt," a symbolic integration that comes at a cost, and often at the expense of women, as Copjec points out.

> The problem with believing . . . that the subject can be conceived *as* all of those multiple, often conflicting, positions that social practices construct, is that the ex-centric, or equivocal, relation of the subject to these discourses is never made visible. (13)

Psychoanalysis is distinguished from historicism not only by "the insistence that the subject's essential conflict with itself cannot be reduced by any social arrangement" (as when "man and woman" are symbolically transformed into "man and wife"), but also by its recognition that "attempts at such a reduction are the source of some of the worst ethical misconduct." If feminist-oriented historicism needs to be "supplemented" (12) by psychoanalysis (not "replaced," for again this would engage in a superficial opposition that does not do justice to the complexity of the relation between psychoanalysis and history), this is because, "in the attempts to structure the relations between men and women as a resolution of conflict, as a cure for it . . . we will find the greatest injustices against women" (17).[6] The question of *the subject* in psychoanalysis is therefore distinct from the constructed *subjectivity* of historicism, understood as a discursive formation, precisely to the extent that the subject in psychoanalysis is conceived in relation to this "cost," this traumatic residue that remains, even in not belonging to the symbolization that seeks to pacify and regulate it.

It should therefore be clear that the "subject" is not to be understood as a sort of "ahistorical" foundation, a "pre-discursive *cogito*" that would supposedly underlie all cultural differences, any more than sexuality is a "natural urge" that would resist cultural inscription, according to a familiar schema (the id and the superego, as popularly conceived). The crucial point, repeatedly stressed by Slavoj Žižek, is that this residue "outside" symbolization, far from being a natural fact, or some sort of "reality" of the subject that underlies all historical forms, is on the contrary an effect of the symbolic order, a kind of by-product of symbolic inscription. We can see here why the "trauma" in psychoanalysis does not have the status of a "real event," an "event in reality," in the sense in which historical description usually employs this term.[7] The trauma is not an origin but rather a residue, a surplus effect of symbolization itself, which explains why, when a new interpretation appears, certain aspects of the past that were never previously noticed suddenly take on a traumatic status (as the wars over the literary canon should suggest). The trauma thus obliges us to distinguish ordinary, sequential time from the temporality of the signifier.[8] "When we spoke of the symbolic integration of the trauma," Žižek writes,

> we omitted a crucial detail: the logic of Freud's notion of the "deferred action" does not consist in the subsequent "gentrification" of a traumatic encounter [what we called a "real event"] by means of its transformation into a normal component of our symbolic universe, but in almost the exact opposite of it—something which was *at first* perceived as a meaningless, neutral event changes *retroactively*, after the advent of a new symbolic network . . . into a trauma that cannot be integrated. (221–22)

The difference between historicist accounts of various "symbolic" formations, and the psychoanalytic focus on the relation between the symbolic and this traumatic residue, this surplus effect of "the real" (understood, moreover, as a structural inevitability or "imperative"), should therefore be clear. When the term "symbolic" is used, not to describe the law of the signifier, the peculiar logic by which the human animal is detached from nature and subjected to symbolic regulation (at a cost), but rather to designate those social formations, the various "symbolizations," which this detachment from nature generates, then one is faced with a collapse, by which the specific questions of psychoanalysis concerning the *constitution of the subject* are lost, having been confused with the historicist task of describing the *historical formation of subjectivity.*

The further problem, which such a confusion entails, can now be clarified accordingly. Like death, sexual difference is not a human institution, and if in our theories we pretend that it is simply one more social construction, invented by a particular society (like democracy or Christianity), do we not unwittingly sustain the humanistic (narcissistic) notion that "man is the maker of all things"? Do we not remain committed to a familiar theory of "Man," the same conception of the "subject" in which sexual difference has always been foreclosed? As Constance Penley says, the effacement of sexual difference

> can be seen quite clearly in the recently renewed will to purge feminism of psychoanalysis [which] takes the form of a call to substitute "gender" for "sexual difference" as an analytic category for feminist theory—thus displacing the role of the unconscious in the formation of subjectivity and sexuality—or to substitute a theory of a socially divided and contradictory subject for one that is psychically split.[9]

What is more, this shift in terminology amounts to a return to certain aspects of humanism that the analysis of gender was intended to surpass (as Parveen Adams puts it, "the essentialism that is being attacked . . . often returns even if in a more sophisticated form").[10] Marjorie Garber, from a position well outside psychoanalysis, nevertheless observes that the idea of "Renaissance self-fashioning" may owe some of its popularity to the fact that it sustains a theory in which "gender" is discussed, while sexual difference quietly disappears, in favor of a *return* to a humanist historicism in which "man invents himself."[11] Is it possible that historicism, in treating the contingent formations of "gendered subjectivity," unwittingly obliterates the question of sexual difference?

Irigaray too, from a rather different perspective, sees precisely this erasure of sexual difference in our current appeal to categories of "gender," an appeal that, she says, unwittingly maintains a covert commitment to "the mastery of the subject." Her formulation also indicates that, in the current climate of opinion, any reference to "sexual difference"—as distinct from "gender"—will be immediately misconstrued as a return to "natural" categories (the so-called "essentialism").[12] In addition, she allows us to return to the question of technology, which is closely bound up with transsexuality:

> The human spirit already seems subjugated to the imperatives of technology to the point of believing it possible to deny the difference of the sexes. Anyone who stresses the importance of sexual difference is accused of living in the past, of being reactionary or naive. . . . Some men and women really do live in the past. But as long as we are still living, we are sexually differentiated. Otherwise, we are dead. The question of whether language has a sex could be subtitled: Are we still alive? alive enough to rise above the level of a machine, a mechanism, to exert an energy that escapes the mastery of the subject?[13]

The point we would add is that this effacement of sexual difference in favor of the category of gender is itself due to our commitment to a very specific, and perhaps inadequate, conception of history. Foucault saw very clearly that historicism is a recent invention, a nineteenth-century phenomenon, the central mechanism by which the theoretical edifice of post-Enlightenment "Man" was built. His thesis on the "death of man" was not just directed against a particular conception of the "subject," or aimed at exposing the contingent foundations upon which the "human sciences" had been built; it was clearly an argument regarding the collapse of nineteenth-century historicism. It is one of the ironies of our present theoretical moment that Foucault has been claimed by a "new historicism" that sustains the very conception of the subject that Foucault sought to dislodge. Could it be that, insofar as Foucault's work has been taken up as a renewal of historicism, this is strictly an indication of the *compulsion to repeat* (manifested in the term "*new* historicism")? The symptomatic cost of this compulsion to repeat (on the part of the concept "Man") would be clearly revealed in the fact that the "new historicism" easily coincides with the effort to demonstrate the social construction of gender, but in the process, the question of *sexual difference* has disappeared, having been replaced with forms of analysis inherited from the nineteenth century.[14]

One can see from this where a genuine encounter between Foucault and Lacan would have to begin—not with the familiar, polemical opposition between history and psychoanalysis, but with the following proposition: *To think sexual difference is to think the end of historicism.* It would therefore be a mistake to engage in the familiar polemic between "psychoanalysis and history"—not only because psychoanalysis is in no way simply opposed to history, as though psychoanalysis were simply "ahistorical," or as though there were a contradiction between them, obliging us to choose one or the other (one wonders what logic produces the popular, "economic" account, according to which it is always necessary simply to take sides, thereby confirming an opposition at the cost of recognizing the real complexity of the relation); but also because, in the absence of psychoanalysis, our concept of history itself remains truncated, conceptually impoverished, bound to nineteenth-century models that have lost their power without being reconceived, and are consequently condemned to repeat themselves, returning like the dead who have not been properly buried. (This is what Heidegger says too: at the "end of metaphysics," metaphysics does not come to an end—what it does is repeat.) Thus, in much of our current literature, there is no clear distinction between the constitution of the subject in psychoanalysis, and the social construction of subjectivity. As a result, "sexuality" is regarded as a "construction" at the same "historical" level as "gender," thus testifying to a difficulty that remains largely unconfronted by current discussions of history, like a traumatic element that remains to be encountered.

Having distinguished between the historicist *construction of subjectivity* and the psychoanalytic *constitution of the subject*, by reference to the terms "role" and "imperative," we must consider one final point. We have suggested that current accounts of the social construction of subjectivity replace "sexual difference" with the category of "gendered subjectivity," thereby confusing two different conceptions of the subject, while remaining bound to a specifically historicist conception of history, one which avoids the question of the body, and particularly the question of sexed embodiment, while treating subjectivity as a historical invention. According to the historicist view, however, any reference to sexual difference will be taken as an appeal to naturalism. Any reference to terms such as "imperative," or the "law," or "embodiment" will be regarded as a return to the ahistorical category of "sex"—a "natural" category that must then be resisted or denounced.

But the psychoanalytic emphasis on sexual difference is not a "return to nature," nor is it a refusal of history, as the distinction between the instinct and the drive should already indicate. To speak of embodiment and sexual difference as something other than a "social construction" is immediately to invite, in today's context, the misunderstanding that the body is being construed as a "biological fact," and that psychoanalysis amounts to a return to that essentialism of which it has so often been accused. But it is precisely this opposition between "biology and history," "nature and culture," "essentialism and historicism," that psychoanalysis rejects. It should be recognized that phenomenology, too, begins by rejecting precisely this conceptual framework.[15] In this respect, the appeal to historicism as a cure for the "universalist tendencies" of the tradition, remains bound to a conceptual network that psychoanalysis does not support. When commentaries debate whether psychoanalysis is "genuinely historical" or just "another essentialism," one has a clear indication that the most basic theoretical challenge of psychoanalysis has been obliterated.

Our final point is therefore clear: if contemporary discussions of sexual difference still tend to be split between two concepts, "sex" and "gender" (the biological argument and the argument for social construction), we may say that current discussions are strictly pre-Freudian. This is the great enigma, but also the theoretical interest, of psychoanalysis: sexual difference is neither sex nor gender. As we shall see, one consequence is that the body, from the point of view of psychoanalysis, is neither a natural fact, nor a cultural construction. One can see why French psychoanalytic feminism has had such a difficult and conflicted reception in the United States, where it is acclaimed as an argument on behalf of the symbolic or historical character of gender, and simultaneously denounced as another form of biological essentialism. Both views amount to a confusion whereby the question of "sexuality" is either collapsed into the historicist argument, or rejected for its purportedly biological determinism. In both cases, and whether it is affirmed or repudiated, the psychoanalytic dimension of this work is avoided, and the entire question of sexuality is displaced into a familiar paradigm, governed by the terms *sex* and *gender,* which are themselves inscribed in an opposition between nature and culture inherited from the nineteenth century. It is this entire configuration that psychoanalysis contests.

The larger stakes of this chapter will now be clear: insofar as contemporary French theorists who have taken up psychoanalysis are read as though they were engaged in a form of cultural studies, a form of new historicism, an argument about social construction—read, in other words, without an adequate sense of what is particular to the psychoanalytic conception of "the subject"—the distinction between the psychoanalytic argument and the argument for social construction will tend to disappear. Discussions of sexual difference as a biological phenomenon and arguments regarding the social construction of gender are both important and have many proponents today, as well as specific arenas within which they are illuminating. The theoretical specificity of psychoanalysis, however, consists in the fact that it coincides neither with biological accounts of sexual difference, nor with cultural accounts of gender construction. It is possible, and even necessary, to speak of the social construction of subjectivity, to show for example how sexuality is organized in the Renaissance or the nineteenth century, or how masculinity and femininity are historically produced in contingent and conventional forms. Psychoanalysis is not *opposed* to this view; it is not directly in conflict with this view, as though one had to choose between the *historical construction* of subjectivity and a supposedly *ahistorical* psychoanalysis. But there is a significant difference between the two, which perhaps becomes clear only when the specifically clinical dimension of psychoanalysis is recognized.

THE ORGANISM AND THE BODY

In order to clarify the particular way in which psychoanalysis situates "the body," as distinct from biological accounts and sociohistorical analyses, let us now consider the concept of the symptom, and the vocabulary (energy, force, cause, product, law) that such a concept entails. As we have seen, there is no doubt, from the point of view of psychoanalysis, that sexuality is subject to historical formation and deformation. If the constitution of the subject in relation to the signifier means anything, it means that the identity of the subject is not given at birth, but has to "come into being." Even "sexuality," which is still often understood as a biological substratum (something shaped by cultural prohibitions, but essentially a "natural force" or "biological urge") cannot be understood as natural, according to Freud—not because of "external" prohibitions (the "repressive hypothesis," which coincides with the sociohistorical account), but because of "internal" considerations, intrinsic to sexuality itself—what we have called its "original deformation." Thus, sexuality is not governed by *the laws of nature,* or reducible to an instinctual force; on the contrary, the sexual drive departs from the natural pathway of instinct precisely insofar as the drive is *subject to representation,* which Freud speaks of in terms of "displacement," "condensation," "substitution" and so on. The *energy* of human sexuality is therefore not a purely biological energy, a "physics of libido" governed by natural laws—chemistry or biology or fluid mechanics—but is rather an energy regulated by *the laws of language,* the laws of representation.

Let us consider this decisive point of departure for psychoanalysis, the very origin of psychoanalysis, the dramatic rupture that separates it from organic medicine. In an early paper (1888) titled "A Comparative Study of Traumatic and Hysterical Paralyses," Freud distinguishes between symptoms caused by an injury (what he calls here a "trauma," in the sense of a physical accident) and symptoms that are present in hysteria. Freud proceeds in this paper as a neurologist, whose training lay in the central nervous system. He expects to find a problem in the cerebral cortex, a "lesion" that will explain the hysterical paralysis according to the same mechanical principles that operate in traumatic paralysis (1:168).[16] But he finds that, in the hysterical paralysis, the model of natural science does not appear to function.[17] *The laws of cause and effect* do not explain the symptom. Instead, the hysterical symptom appears to confront us with what Freud calls "the force of an idea"—what Lacan will later call desire and its peculiar causality, which is governed not by nature but by another law, the law of the Other.

In this paper, Freud points out that the hysterical paralysis does not correspond to the anatomical organization of the nervous system. The arm, he says, is paralyzed "as far up as the shoulder." It is paralyzed not according to the organic structure of the body, but according to "the common idea of the arm," or in accordance with what we commonly designate by the word "arm." Hysterical paralysis, he writes, "takes the organs in the ordinary, popular sense of the names they bear: the leg is the leg as far as its insertion into the hip; the arm is the upper limb as it is visible under the clothing" (1:169).[18] There is an ambiguity here that Freud will only work out later, namely: when we speak of "the body" as organized beyond the laws of nature, when we speak of "the body" as subject to representation, *what is representation?* When Freud says that the arm is paralyzed *up to the point where one sees* it join up with the shoulder, or that the paralysis follows *the common idea* of the arm, *what we commonly designate by the word* "arm," are we dealing with a symptom governed by *the image or the word?* Is the "hysterical body" the visible body, or the body divided by the signifier?

Indeed, when Freud speaks of "the force of an idea" in order to explain the basic distinction between psychoanalysis and organic medicine, every reader of Heidegger will note that this ambiguity characterizes a long philosophical tradition, and is internal to the very term "idea": as many commentaries on Greek philosophy have pointed out, the classical term *eidos* means both the "concept" or "idea" and something "seen." Seeing and knowing are thus constitutively linked, and easily confused, but this should not conceal the fact that the logic of the concept has a very different structure from the logic of the image, understood as a supposedly immediate, "physiological" perception.[19] Where the image provides us with an illusion of immediacy and presence, supposedly available in a "physiological" perception, the symbolic confronts us with a play of presence and absence, a function of negativity by which the purportedly "immediate" reality (the "natural" world) is restructured. This is the difficulty Lacan takes up with the "imaginary" and the "symbolic." It's not such a mystery.

But this initial ambiguity in Freud should warn us against repeating familiar slogans about "Lacan's thesis on the imaginary body." We are often told that "the body," for Lacan, is constituted in the mirror stage as an "imaginary body," but this is clearly insufficient. For the closure of the body, the integration that comes with the establishment of a (perpetually unstable, but yet relatively secure) difference between inside and outside, is not given with the image, but only with the *first substitution*, the inscription of the void, the intrusion of nothingness, around which the "body" is structured.[20] Even in its earliest form, the concept of the symptom in Freud introduces a distinction between the imaginary and the symbolic. When Freud says the symptom behaves "as though anatomy did not exist" (1:169), this phrase is at first focused on the "imaginary" character of the symptom, its visual aspect, the fact that the symptom affects what Lacan will call "the imaginary body"; but Freud's remark will soon be linked with the claim that "hysterics suffer mainly from reminiscences" (2:7), which is to say, not "conscious ideas," but memories *that have not been remembered*, and are inscribed elsewhere (in symbolic form) upon the flesh. Freud is thus obliged to recognize that, in the course of an analysis, a discursive chain (a consciously spoken discourse) will intersect, at a particular point, with a bodily effect, as when a patient's "painful legs began to 'join in the conversation' during our analyses" (2:148), a thesis the "imaginary body" will not explain. The category of the real will complicate this picture further.

Kristeva addresses this problem in her discussion of the "father of individual prehistory," where orality is linked not simply to the breast, or to an "object" in the usual sense, but to the "thing" as a container of the void—an object she explicitly regards as foundational to the emergence of language. The various analytic conceptions of "introjection," "incorporation," and "internalization" thus entail a confrontation with the distinction between the "imaginary," "symbolic," and "real" aspects of the object, and the intrusion of absence is regarded as primordial, as the very opening of the symbolic. In the case of the oral object, she writes, "when the object that I incorporate is the speech of the other" (what Lacan calls the "voice as object"), we encounter the shift from the object as psychology usually conceives it—object of need or demand—to the object marked by lack, in relation to which the "body" finds its place: "Orality's function is the essential substratum of what constitutes man's being, namely, *language*."[21] Again, the link with Heidegger should be apparent insofar as, for Heidegger, the "thing" (the jug, to take Heidegger's example) comes into being only by virtue of its capacity to enclose the void and give it a place.[22] Although the body of *Dasein* is distinct from the thing, there is a general difficulty common to both, concerning the symbolic "containment" of the void, a problem of the relation between the symbolic and the real that is all too often confused with the imaginary. It is this "inscription" of the void which Lacan takes up with the "object a." The concept of the body, as it is understood in psychoanalysis, will therefore be completely misunderstood if it is taken for a purely "imaginary body," or (what amounts to the same thing) if the imaginary and symbolic are treated at the same level, according to the same logic.

The consequence should now be clear: when contemporary discussions speak of "the construction of the subject" and the "representation of sexuality" as if there were no difference between the imaginary and the symbolic—when the historicist thesis, in other words, is developed as though "images and words" both construct the subject in a similar fashion—then one of the most basic questions of psychoanalysis has been obscured from the very start. It is over elementary terminology, such as this, that an enormous gap still remains between historicism and psychoanalysis—a gap which is concealed whenever terms like "the symbolic" are used to designate "images and words" in more or less the same way.[23] It is no wonder that French psychoanalytic theory has had such a confused reception, according to which it is simultaneously accused of "biological essentialism" and of "reducing everything to language"—two readings which not only contradict each other, but also amount to a refusal of the very thing they pretend to discuss, collapsing the psychoanalytic "subject" into the "subject" of cultural studies, where the imaginary and symbolic are treated at the same level, and the question of the real is lost altogether.

In order to formulate the distinctive position of psychoanalysis, then, we may distinguish terminologically between the *organism* and the *body*. In contrast to the organism, the body is *constitutively* denatured, "organ-ized" (if I may use this term) by the image and the word. In this sense, psychoanalysis, far from being ahistorical, shows how human sexuality is *inevitably* historical, in that the body itself cannot take form without undergoing this subjection to representation. Born as an organism, the human animal nevertheless has to acquire a body, come into the possession of its body (to be "born again," as suggested by many rituals involving tattooing, circumcision, baptism, and so on), through the image and the signifier—the formative power of the Gestalt, and the radical dependence on the other, in the exchange of words. This is what it means to speak of *the constitution of the body* in psychoanalysis—that peculiar myth in which the little organism sets off in search of its body.

We have seen that Freud's early paper announces a radical separation between the symptom as it is understood by psychoanalysis, and the model of science that is used by organic medicine. One conclusion surely follows: insofar as psychiatry currently resorts to the methods of pharmacology and the model of natural science, it will no longer have anything to do with psychoanalysis. In other words, insofar as psychiatry seeks, like organic medicine, to intervene *directly upon the body*, as though the body were simply a natural fact, a bit of "extended substance" that could be technologically manipulated like nature, psychiatry will in effect seek a shortcut around the entire domain opened up by Freud, a shortcut that would return to the "natural body" and avoid the formative effect of the imaginary and the symbolic. The consequence, not only for our general account of the body, but for the discussion of transsexuality as well, should be clear: whereas sexual difference and the very concept of "embodiment" are understood by psychoanalysis to entail a confrontation with the imaginary and the symbolic, organic medicine is dedicated to a model of science in which *sexual difference is foreclosed*, and the body is reduced to a natural phenomenon.

TRANSSEXUALITY

One of Millot's most far-reaching arguments can be situated here: science offers the transsexual the possibility of transformation, based on the application of technological advances that are administered in silence, without asking too many questions *about the subject* (the "real work" begins with anesthetizing the patient). Concerning itself only with the manipulation of the "extended substance" of the organism (and perhaps, as Leslie Lothstein suggests, concerned with its own technical advancement, for which the subject is "raw material"), medical science operates by presupposing that it is dealing with the organism rather than the body, that the transsexual seeks an *anatomical change* rather than a *different embodiment*, a body that would reconfigure elements belonging to the categories of the imaginary, symbolic, and real.[24] Put differently, the surgeon works with a conception of anatomy that presupposes a natural version of sexual identity, thereby foreclosing the question of sexual difference. Since some of those who seek an operation also occupy a position which would foreclose sexual difference, we are obliged to recognize a clear homology: the very foreclosure of sexual difference that characterizes the transsexual position is also sustained by the medical community. Science, Millot says, participates in the transsexual demand, which is the demand for an exit from the question of sexual difference.

As striking as this conjunction between the transsexual and the surgeon may seem (as Millot says, the transsexual's demand, like all demand, is addressed *to the other*, and even shaped in advance *by the other*, demand being originally intersubjective), the link between sexual difference and the history of science will come as no surprise to those who have recognized in the metaphysical tradition a conception of the subject that forecloses sexual difference, and who see the history of technology as based on an interpretation of being as "presence-at-hand," according to which the body would be precisely a "fashionable" extended substance. In short, this focus on the body as material substance coincides with a short-circuit of the symbolic order, which brings the entire medical apparatus, despite its cultural centrality, into close proximity with psychosis. To the extent that a smooth machinery is established, making surgery *available upon demand* (as the vocabulary of commodification has it), science "may even constitute a symptom of our civilization" (16).

There is consequently a historical dimension to Millot's discussion, for although transsexuality has no doubt existed since ancient times, strictly speaking "there is no transsexuality without the surgeon and the endocrinologist; in this sense, it is an essentially modern phenomenon" (17). Here, technology seems to coincide with a certain, historically developed interpretation of the body as present-at-hand, a material substratum inhabited by a "spiritual substance," an animated "subjectivity" who—in keeping with certain tenets of liberal tradition—should be "free" and have the "right to choose." And after all, on what grounds would one argue that "the psychoanalyst knows best" and should stand as the gatekeeper of the law?[25] Paradoxically, however, Millot argues that the position of absolute mastery is in fact claimed not by the analyst but by the legal apparatus and the medical community, insofar as they, like the transsexual, seek to eliminate the imperative of sexual difference, to replace the real of embodiment with a fantasy body that would be fully manipulable, unmarked by the limit of the real, a body that would pose no limit to the mastery of the subject:

> Such, in any case, is the dream of doctors and jurists whose voca-
> tion it is to deal in the fantasy of seemingly unlimited power—the
> power to triumph over death (that other real), the power to make
> laws [laws that would demonstrate the superiority of human law
> over the imperatives of sex and death], the power to legislate
> human reality flawlessly, leaving nothing to chance. Transsexual-
> ity is a *response to* the dream of forcing back, and even abolish-
> ing, the frontiers of the real. (p. 15, emphasis added)

What then distinguishes, according to Millot, the position of the analyst from this position of mastery ascribed to the lawyer or scientist who would "legislate human reality . . . leaving nothing to chance"? What distinguishes the analyst from the "gatekeeper of the law," legislating who may enter, or stating (more democratically) that "anyone may enter freely," though the gate be narrow? We are faced here with the difference between knowledge and ignorance, between the certainty of the law that provides in advance the set of possibilities offered to a neutral (and neuter) subject, the anonymous "anyone," and the ignorance of the analyst who, not knowing who is speaking, finds it necessary (and obligatory: a different law) *to listen*. A distinction is thus drawn between the *question* posed by the analyst, or more precisely opened for the analysand in the analytic situation, and the *answer* that is *given in advance* by science and the law, a distinction that could also be stated by contrasting the *certainty* of the transsexual (which coincides with the mastery of the doctor), and the *doubt* that inheres in every symbolic formulation of sexual difference. This is a clue to Millot's claim that *the certainty of the subject who claims a transsexual position, like the certainty of science* (which, after a few words have been exchanged, has "nothing more to say"), is a sign that the symbolic order has been foreclosed.

Millot notes further that the preliminary interviews that prospective candidates undergo are organized by criteria which reinforce the most conformist sexual stereotypes. After hormonal treatments, a male-to-female transsexual is obliged to live "like a woman" (whatever that means) in order to demonstrate (and test out for herself) whether this identity truly "fits":

> Like the doctors, psychiatrists, endocrinologists, and surgeons whom they consult, transsexuals gauge femininity in terms of the conformity of roles. Hand in hand, they construct scales of femininity, and measure them with batteries of tests.[26] Permission to undergo sex-change surgery is contingent on the results of these tests, which also enable transsexuals to train for their future roles. (14)

Thus, Gender Identity Clinics, under the guise of freedom of choice, and admitting an apparent diversity (from the "exotic" to the "mundane," but all under the regulation of preordained "types") are in fact "in the process of becoming 'sex control centers'" (14)—a fact which is hardly surprising in a culture where standardization is essential for the regular administration of free trade and smooth international exchange.

> Transsexuality involves an appeal, and especially a demand, addressed to the Other. As a symptom it is completed with the help of this Other dimension—more especially, with that of the function of the Other's desire. Lacan said that the neurotic symptom is completed during the analytical treatment, due to the fact that the analyst lends consistency to the desire of the Other, an enigma with which the symptom is bound up. (141, translation modified)

If the Other takes the form of a science for which there are no limits, a form of omnipotence (or, in Millot's terms, if the desire of the Other is absolute, a position of omnipotent *jouissance*, outside the law), the subject who comes to this Other with a demand—a demand that is also a symptom—will find this demand "completed" by the Other. If, on the contrary, the Other takes the form of one who is lacking, one-who-wants-to-know (who desires, which is precisely the opposite of absolute *jouissance*), then the symptom will be completed only by a discursive articulation in which the subject, having run up against the limit in the Other, encounters the question of his or her desire—which the demand often seeks to evade.

In the context of these psychological measures and obligatory performances (a sort of "test drive" in which it is determined whether one can live "in" the new model body), it should be noted of course that candidates for surgery have often read as much of the "psychological profile" material as their clinicians, and are very well prepared for these tests (like candidates for the LSAT or GRE, they have taken "primer" courses in order to "pass"), and, as Lothstein points out, they often have a degree of expertise in the performance of their role that makes it difficult (for all parties) to discover *who they really are.* It would perhaps be fashionable to argue that there is no "real" subject there, no "authentic personality," but only the product of various performances, and in some respects this is precisely the case, given that "the subject" is not constituted at birth, but formed in the course of a singular historical experience. But again, the question arises of the *relation between* (on the one hand) the subject who performs for these trials of identity, who seeks to "correspond" to a given (or apparently "chosen") role, or who has somehow come to demand surgery as a solution to the enigma of sexual difference, and (on the other hand) those ideals, those images, those stereotypes or performances with which the subject has come to comply (like the prospective "lawyer" or "professor"). Truly a "correspondence theory" of (sexual) truth.

The difficulty Millot addresses here—it is the clinical difficulty, the diagnostic question, of distinguishing which candidates are likely to benefit from surgery and which will not—may be put in terms of *demand and desire*: when the "who" that chooses has been brought to this choice by the "mortifying exigency" (59) of a demand in which the future is shut down, a demand in which desire is lost, a demand that the subject appears to make, but which has come from the Other, and with which the subject has complied, then perhaps the analyst has a responsibility to open for the subject a passageway that would lead from absolute submission to this demand, to the possibility of desire, which also means the possibility of a future. This question of ethics is clearly *avoided* when the clinical machinery simply stands ready to operate upon demand in an economic circuit of "supply and demand" that presupposes the subject "knows what he or she desires," when in fact desire may be lacking altogether, having been eclipsed by compliance with a punishing identification, demanding the adoption of a role with which, however "mortifying" it may be, the subject has come to comply.

One sees here where the family structure, and the desire of the parents, would have to be considered, according to Millot.[27] But in focusing on the character of modern science, Millot's focus is different at this point: the readiness to answer all demands, on the part of the medical community, with indifference to "who comes," amounts to confusing desire and demand, a failure to make any distinction between them, whereas the task of the analyst is precisely to make such a distinction, neither to answer the demand nor simply to prescribe, to tell the client what is permissible, to lay down the law, but rather to listen, in order to discover whether, behind the demand addressed to the surgeon, there is a desire, or whether there is not rather an effort to escape desire, by complying with this "mortifying exigency" that compels the subject to "choose" a solution to embodiment that would in fact have the character of a punishing imprisonment, an exit from desire as such.

Insofar as medical technology and the transsexual coincide and "complete" each other, then, we may speak of a mutual relation between demand and *jouissance*, which Millot would contrast with the relation to desire. For Schreber too, it is the absolute *jouissance* of God that Schreber's transformation is supposed to satisfy, as though he himself were being offered up as a divine sacrifice, which has become necessary in order to fill the void that threatens to appear in the universe, and that Schreber alone is able to circumvent. The "opposition between desire and *jouissance*" (99) noted by Millot is also taken up by Lacan, at the end of *Seminar XI*, where he speaks of Freud's references to the specter of Nazism in his *Group Psychology*: there is always the possibility that a group will find a solution to the fracture of the symbolic order, the intrusion of lack within it, by offering up a sacrifice in hope of satisfying the *jouissance* of an obscure god, who has become incarnated in the figure of an Other. "That is why I wrote *Kant avec Sade*," Lacan says (*SXI*, 276).

The point may also be made in terms of identification: Millot argues that whereas *some* subjects who present themselves for surgery have a relation to sexual difference, are identified with "the other sex," and will consequently benefit from an operation, fashioning a future for themselves on the basis of this identification, *other* subjects, by contrast, are not in fact identified with "the other sex," but are rather *hor-sexe*, "outsidesex." *This* latter identification is not a symbolic, but a phallic identification, in which desire has become impossible. To celebrate the transsexual as a "free" subject, the most avant-garde instance of the "malleability of gender," is to disregard the virtually transfixed character of this identification, and the suffering it entails.[28] These latter subjects, as much of the secondary literature acknowledges, are structurally close to psychosis, and Millot argues that for them, it is not a question of identification with the other sex, but rather a fantasy of the other sex, in which *the "other sex" is regarded as not lacking.*[29] In short, within the group of those who present themselves for surgery, Millot distinguishes two forms of identification, one oriented in relation to sexual difference (identification as "a man" or "a woman," with all the ambiguity, uncertainty, and symbolic mobility this entails), and another oriented by a *simulacrum* of sexual difference, a fantasy of "otherness" that in fact amounts to the elimination of sexual difference, its replacement by the fantasy of a sex that would not be lacking. This identification is marked by *certainty*, by a demand to eliminate the symbolic ambiguity that accompanies sexual difference, replacing it with the immobility of a "perfected" body, one that would put an end to the difficulties of historical existence, and bring time itself to a halt, as it did in the case of Schreber's apocalyptic narrative.[30]

This distinction between two forms of identification may be expressed in three ways, according to three periods of Lacan's work. First, it is explained as the difference between the establishment of an ego ideal (which is always associated with the future in Freud's thought, and the temporality of language) and the position of primary narcissism, a position in which the differential structure of language, and the relation to the other, can be eliminated. These two positions are situated in schema R (see chapter 2), as point "I" (the ego ideal) and point Φ (a phallic identification, which amounts to a denial of sexual difference, a position outside the symbolic). The task of the analyst who conducts the clinical interview is thus to determine which of these positions the subject occupies in requesting surgery. This also means that the demand for surgery does not by itself automatically reveal the subjective position of the person who makes it. Here again, we see a division between those in the medical profession who take such a request at face value, and stand ready to operate on demand (asking only about insurance, perhaps), and the analyst, who will ask "who speaks" in this demand.

Second, these two identifications may be expressed in terms of the sexuation diagram from *Encore*: on the "masculine" side, as the difference between a man and the Primal Father, and on the "feminine" side, as the difference between a woman and *La femme*. As Millot points out, the true transsexual, in the case of the male-to-female transsexual, for example, is not properly defined as "a man who wishes to become a woman," but as "a woman born into a man's body that she wishes to be rid of." Such a formulation replaces anatomical classification (which would then be susceptible to "transformation"— from one to the other) with "identification." But in the case of a phallic identification, an identification with a simulacrum of the other sex (with "*La femme*" or "The Father"), which Millot calls an identification "outsidesex," the symbolic is short-circuited: "The subject is compelled to *incarnate* the phallus in the form of a narcissistic image, if nothing can show that this is impossible" (59). For these subjects, the demand to occupy the position of "the other sex" (which is not so much the "other" sex, in a relation to alterity, as a position outside sex, a "perfection" attributed to the other and then sought as a possibility to be obtained for oneself), is the demand, not for a sexed position, but for a position in which nothing would be lacking, a position that would be filled, in one case, by "*La femme*" and in the other case by the Primal Father—both of which amount equally to a foreclosure of sexual difference.

In short, what schema R designates as the phallus is later elaborated in the sexuation diagram as equally (A) the Primal Father, the "immortal" figure in *Totem and Taboo* who stands as the *exception to the law*, a position impossible to occupy (which does not keep it from being sought), and (B) "*La femme,*" the incarnation of "the woman who does not exist," the "spectacular" figure of a supposed "femininity" incarnated by some of the clients Millot discusses. "*La femme*" here occupies the position of "The Woman," the figure who would put an end to the question, "What is a woman?" (with emphasis on the *indefinite article*), by seeming to provide an answer for "the whole." Expressed in terms of set theory, the sexuation diagram distinguishes "women" in the plural as an open set (this one and that one and the next . . . without totality or essence), from "the one" ("*La femme*") who seems to incarnate the totality, to close the set of "all women" by representing "Woman" as such.

The crucial point here is the *contradictory relation* between "*La femme,*" who undertakes to represent the whole, and the open set of "women," which cannot be totalized by reference to a single essence. This contradiction between "women" and "*La femme*" (a contradiction that runs parallel to the opposition, on the masculine side, between the set "All men are castrated," and the exception to the law, "the one who escapes castration," the father of the primal horde) is crucial if we are to understand the peculiar (nondialectical) logic by which identification with "*La femme*" paradoxically amounts to a foreclosure of sexual difference, making it impossible to identify as "a woman." This paradox, by which an incarnation of "The Woman" amounts to an exclusion of "women," is clearly expressed by the subject cited by Janice Raymond who says,

> Genetic women cannot claim to possess the courage, compassion and breadth of vision acquired during the transsexual experience. Free from the burdens of menstruation and procreation, transsexuals are clearly superior to genetic women. The future is theirs: in the year 2000, when the world is exhausting its energies on the task of feeding six billion souls, procreation will no longer be held to be an asset. (13–14)

Sixty pages later, Millot quotes one of her own clients who says:

> The conviction [has come to me] that the nearest humanity
> approaches to perfection is in the persons of good women—and
> especially perhaps in the persons of the kind, intelligent and
> healthy women past their menopause, no longer shackled by the
> mechanisms of sex. . . . In all countries, among all races, on the
> whole these are the people I most admire; and it is into their
> ranks, I flatter myself, that I have now admitted myself. (70)

As Millot explains, such an identification is not only outside the symbolization of difference, but also an effort to circumvent desire; moreover, it is a demand that the subject *seems to make* (to "choose freely,"
etc.), but that in fact *comes from the Other*. This apparent "choice" of
identification is thus regarded as an "exigency" with which the subject
has agreed to comply:

> The Other's logical position, since unmarked by castration, can
> be replaced in the imaginary by the myth of the father of the
> horde as much as by the phantasy of the phallic woman. It is the
> place of absolute jouissance, which can be expressed by the for-
> mula $\exists x \, \overline{\Phi x}$. (58)

This is why Lacan writes that "The Woman" is one of the names of
the father. Thus, among those who request what in the United States
is called "sexual reassignment surgery," some are not identified with
the other sex, but hold together a precarious identity by means of a
fantasy of totalization, ascribed to the other sex. The subject who
seeks such a position is thus regarded as seeking to move, not to
another sexed position, but to a position in which his or her lack might
be eliminated.

This allows Millot to make a further clarification, distinguishing
these subjects in turn from psychotics. For in much of the clinical literature, debates hinge on the question of whether the transsexual is
psychotic. Millot enters this debate in the following way: having distinguished the "true transsexual," who is identified with the other sex
(as "a man" or "a woman," again, with all the uncertainty this
entails), from the subject who maintains (or rather seeks to occupy) a
phallic identification, she distinguishes further between *these* latter
subjects and psychotics. She argues that the subjects who maintain this

relation of fantasy to the "other sex" as not lacking, have their subjective consistency precisely on the basis of this relation, this quasi-
symbolic link, which is also a relation to alterity, difference, and lack.
The consequence is decisive: for these particular subjects, an operation
would deprive them of the one *point of reference* in relation to which
they have established a subjective consistency. For them, an operation
eliminates this point of reference, replacing a *relation to the other* (a
symbolic link), however precarious, with a *condition of "being"* that
is outside the symbolic, so that surgery, far from liberating them for a
future, will on the contrary imprison them once and for all in a position of foreclosure that has been kept at bay only by this fantasy of the
other sex. For these subjects, surgery will precipitate a psychotic break.

The third account of transsexuality in Millot's book formulates the
point we have just made in terms of knot theory. Arguing, on the basis
of Lacan's later work, that in some cases the three orders (imaginary,
real, and symbolic), are not truly knotted together but are nevertheless
kept in something like a semblance of consistency by means of a symptomatic formation, Millot suggests that the transsexual demand plays
the part of such a symptom. In other words, this demand provides a
consistency and a symbolic relation for the subject, such that if the
subject were *in fact* allowed to undergo surgery, the symptom would
be resolved, but in such a way that the three orders, the three rings of
the knot, would fall apart. The proper course of action in this case
would therefore be to work with the demand, rather than to answer it
directly with a "hands-on" operation.

TRANSVESTITE AND TRANSSEXUAL

How, then, are we to understand the difference between the transvestite and the transsexual, if it is not just a matter of degree, but a more
decisive difference? Cross-dressing and other instances of the malleability of the subject, its "constructed" character, have gone far
toward illuminating the symbolic mobility of gender, and the transsexual is sometimes enlisted to serve as a more radical example of this
mobility. But perhaps the question of the body cannot be situated at
precisely the same level as clothing, conceived as another fashionable,
"symbolic" phenomenon. Whereas the transvestite already "has" an
identity that is able to orchestrate and enjoy, the transsexual that con-

cerns Millot is in limbo, waiting for the operation that will one day make possible the assumption of an identity that has hitherto been lacking. Recent research on literary forms has shown us the great variety of functions that cross-dressing can perform (in comedy and farce, in romance and burlesque, a whole vocabulary can be found); but the transsexual we find in Lothstein and Millot does not play a role or adopt a disguise to seduce or deceive, or to appropriate the power and privileges of the other sex in a scheme that aims at someone's erotic gratification, or at obtaining social leverage (one thinks of *Dangerous Liaisons, M. Butterfly,* and *The Crying Game* as recent examples in film). In Millot's account, the transsexual does not have the same grounding, the same identity, or the same relation to sexuality, to "being sexed," that one sees in the transvestite. In some sense, the transvestite already "has" a body with which to perform, while the transsexual lives a time of suspension in which the body has not yet been constituted. The question of identity, as it arises at the level of sexed embodiment, is not equivalent to what we usually understand by the term "gender role."

There is a different relation to the social order, as a result. Cross-dressing can always be a technique of social criticism; it can organize the forces of laughter or defiance against the stultifying boredom and routine of heterosexuality; it can be enlisted to demonstrate the arbitrary, artificial conventionality of a social standard that tries to pass itself off as "natural," or to expose through parody the excess of a type that takes itself as the measure of all things. Millot would seem to suggest that the transvestite not only has a body to dress, but is an individual with a relation to society, as might be confirmed through the fact that so many precise names can be given to the figures of impersonation, all of them functional and socially located: the "vamp," the "sex goddess," the figure of "Elizabeth Taylor dressed as Cleopatra," the "dyke," the "amazon," or the "brother-at-arms," "one of the guys," or the woman who takes her place as a man on the factory line, and is in it not for sexual subterfuge but for wages. The diversity of this language is clear enough from the variety of genres that have been developed by literature: burlesque, satire, farce, travesty, and so on. In this sense, the great variety of forms of cross-dressing are all socially subversive acts and can function as critique, even if the dominant culture subjects them to criticism in turn, limits their visibility, and their recognition to controlled places—certain neighborhoods, houses, or cabarets. As a critical force, the transvestite is also subject to satire and victimization.

But the transsexual that Millot describes does not have this disruptive relation to society, this position of defiance. The transvestite has a position, however marginalized and oppressed, that would seem to be denied to the transsexual, who does not yet have, on Millot's account, what the transvestite takes for granted. The transsexual, one might say, has instead a relation primarily to his or her body: if *this* relation could be settled to some extent, then a relation to society could be more effectively mobilized. In some sense, the acquisition of a body—which is not automatically given with the "fact" of embodiment, but has to be accomplished—would seem to be a prerequisite to the subjective act of dressing or undressing. The constitution of the body, Lacan would say, is the condition for the possibility of the act of a subject. Perhaps we could say that cross-dressing is the act of a subject who plays with what we call "gender roles," while the transsexual is someone whose capacity to act (in the sense not only of "performance," but of speech-act theory) waits upon (an idea of) embodiment. There is perhaps a difference here between "gender role" and "embodiment" that remains to be understood, a difference that cannot be reduced to biological terms or answered by the shortcut of technology. If, among those who come to the clinic, hoping to be referred to a surgeon, some turn out not to be identified with the other sex, but to be confined to a punishing identification Millot calls phallic, a position from which (if it could only be occupied) nothing more would need to be said, we are perhaps led to encounter what Freud called "the silence" of the death drive: these individuals stand out, not as proof of the ultimate freedom of the subject (which is what many would like to see, in celebrating the figure of the transsexual, perhaps from the distance and safety of fantasy); rather, they articulate in their being that symptom of a social order in which it is possible to look for a solution to suffering in the most stereotypical fantasy of the other—a solution that amounts to a "no exit." According to Millot, these subjects are not in a position to take up a sexual body, because they are engaged in a fantasy of totalization regarding the "other sex." One can only wonder if the medical technology that comes to the supposed aid of these subjects, without asking them very much about who they are (time being a precious commodity), is not the partner of this refusal of embodiment. The medical solution, far from being a source of liberation, would serve on the contrary as the accomplice of a society that sustains this fantasy of "the other sex."

4

From *Oedipus Rex* to *Totem and Taboo*: Lacan's Revision of the Paternal Metaphor

> The voice of the Other should be considered an essential object. . . . Its various incarnations should be followed, as much in the realm of psychosis as at that extremity of normal functioning in the formation of the superego.
>
> Beyond he who speaks in the place of the Other, and who is the subject, what is it whose voice, each time the subject speaks, the subject takes?
>
> Lacan, *The Names-of-the-Father*

INTRODUCTION: TURNING TOWARD THE FATHER

In previous chapters we have explored the mother-daughter relation and the question of femininity; the status of the mother in relation to the imaginary and symbolic; and the structures that allow Lacan to distinguish between various forms or aspects of maternity, which a more "psychological" account of Freud will not as easily provide. We have argued, against the prevailing interpretation of Lacan, for the symbolic aspect of maternal desire, and for the necessity of distinguishing in turn between the mother and the woman—a point that, to some extent, distinguishes Lacan from Freud, and establishes a major link between Lacan's work and feminist theory. We have explored the consequences of these points by reference to some clinical material, not only in terms of anorexia, transsexuality, and identification, but also in terms of more general implications for the concept of embodiment, the status of the symptom, and the complex relation between psychoanalysis and bio-medical knowledge.

For the most part, we have addressed the Lacanian tradition in terms that are familiar to non-Lacanian analytic traditions, partly in the hope of generating dialogue between Lacan and other analytic orientations, and partly in order to suggest that there is a richer and more fruitful possibility of exchange between feminist theory and Lacanian psychoanalysis than some readers have supposed. But we have also tried to show how this broadly familiar vocabulary should intersect with some of the more technical terminology of Lacanian theory (demand and desire, the *jouissance* of the Other and the Other *jouissance*).

Thus far, however, we have said little about the "paternal function," which is not only one of the most familiar and most frequently stressed aspects of Lacanian theory, but also one of the points that has led readers to be most wary of Lacan, or to believe that his theoretical orientation is somehow tied to a particular form of the family, or to a doctrine of "paternal authority." It is this view, moreover, that has led readers to believe that a patriarchal and normalizing Lacan (who seems to promote a particular norm as if it were an ahistorical constant) can be opposed to a more transgressive Foucault, whose genealogical work would reveal the contingent nature of the family structure, and the historical malleability of sexuality in general. As we will see in chapter 5, the relation between Lacan and Foucault is far more intricate and interesting than this easy, polemical opposition would suggest. Before we turn to that discussion, however, let us consider more closely how the paternal function operates in Lacan's work. This will not only cast additional light on the questions we have already been asking about maternity and femininity, but will also allow us to pursue the clinical dimension of our argument, by introducing the problem of the superego, which, as we will see, is closely related to the Lacanian "object a," presented in our epigraphs in a form that is particularly close to the superego, namely, "the voice of the Other."

Lacan is famous—or notorious—for an interpretation of Freud that is mainly oriented by the symbolic order: according to the canonical interpretation, he gives us a psychoanalysis that is heavily influenced by the structural anthropology of Lèvi-Strauss and the linguistic theory of Saussure. Many well-known Lacanian aphorisms testify to his belief that the laws of language provide the fundamental groundwork of Freudian theory, giving us its logic and theoretical coherence. "The unconscious is structured like a language," he says. "The unconscious of the subject is the discourse of the Other," and "a signifier is what represents a subject for another signifier."[1] It is therefore no surprise that the paternal function in Lacanian theory has been interpreted as a matter of language, an essentially "symbolic" matter.

There are good reasons for such an account of the paternal function. The "paternal metaphor" is essentially an interpretation of the Oedipus complex that seeks to demonstrate the link between the institution of language and Freud's account of the father—a link that, according to Lacan, was not clearly articulated by Freud, because Freud did not have the tools of structural linguistics at his disposal. As we shall see, Lacan claims that Freud's discourse tended to remain attached to the "imaginary father," and failed to isolate the essentially symbolic aspect of paternity in a rigorous way. The interpretive force of the "paternal metaphor" was thus to establish the father as a distinctly symbolic operation, and as a result, the "law of the father" has often been understood—with good reason—as a matter of the symbolic order.

And yet, beginning in about 1960, Lacan became less and less convinced that the "symbolic father" could be established in any pure or unequivocal way. Thus, in *Seminar VII*, Lacan makes the following announcement: we can "no longer rely on the Father's guarantee" (*SVII*, 100). In fact, an entire series of terms begins to emerge in Lacanian theory—*jouissance, das Ding,* the *objet petit a,* and even the "real"—all of which bear on a certain inconsistency within the symbolic order, a dimension of transgression or malfunction that attends the very operation of the symbolic law. In a chapter of *Seminar VII* titled "On the Moral Law," for example, Lacan speaks of a peculiar void, an element that is excluded from the symbolic order, the "thing": "*das Ding* is at the center only in the sense that it is excluded" (71). And again in the chapter on "The Object and the Thing," he speaks of what is "excluded in the interior" (101), noting that this exclusion presents us with a "gap" in the symbolic order—something that escapes the law—"a gap once again at the level of *das Ding*," which indicates that we can "no longer rely on the Father's guarantee" (100). It could be shown that the "object a" emerges in Lacanian theory at the moment when the symbolic law no longer has the final word. We are thus led to what Jacques-Alain Miller calls "the formula of the second paternal metaphor," which "corresponds point by point to the formula of the name-of-the-father," but which adds a twist that "forces us to operate with the inexistence and the inconsistency of the Other."[2] In fact, Miller locates this moment in the development of Lacan's thought between seminars VII and VIII (the ethics and transference seminars). In the former, we find "the opposition between *das Ding*, the Thing, and the Other," but it is "worked out enigmatically" and remains "wrapped in mystery"; in the transference seminar, however, "this opposition is transformed into a relation," giving us "a revolution in Lacan's teaching."[3]

Other commentators have addressed this development, locating it at different moments in Lacan's work.[4] But however one may date this shift, the question it entails is clear enough. The paternal metaphor, which was supposed to guarantee the symbolic order, establishing "castration," setting a limit to the aggressive rivalry of narcissism, and providing a degree of mediation and difference, is now attended by a peculiar return of the "unlawful" *jouissance* it was intended to eliminate. The symbolic law which was said to eliminate incest and institute desire is now supplemented by a perverse and punishing underside—not the return of a natural state, a libidinal urge, or biological "id," which refuses to abide by the law, but another face *of the law itself*, which Freud develops through the concept of the death drive. Lacan thus begins to speak of *"le père sévère"* and *"le père jouissant,"* and even of *"père-version,"* a perversion of the father, an aspect of the paternal function that does not secure the order of law and symbolic mediation, but rather introduces a trait of perversion *within* the paternal function (with the word *version* [*turning*], Lacan plays on Freud's remarks in "Female Sexuality" on "turning towards the father") (*SE*, 21:221–46).

It is not a question of perversion as a distinct clinical category here—perversion as opposed to neurosis or psychosis—but of a perverse feature within the very constitution of the normal subject, a constitutive perversion that would thus belong to the very operation of the symbolic law.[5] The "turning toward the father," which Freud describes as a part of the "normal" Oedipal structure, is thus at the same time a "père-version." I stress this because it is not a question of identifying a bad father that one can eliminate, a false version of the father who might be replaced by the true father, the true and proper law. It is rather a question of a perverse feature *within* paternity, an element of transgression that is not opposed to the law, but belongs to the law itself.[6] In different language, we might say that the symbolic order begins to reveal itself as incomplete, insufficient, as a structure that not only constitutes the subject and leads desire to move along the signifying chain, but also "contains" (in every sense of the word) a pathological remainder. The theory of the *objet petit a* is designed in part to address this difficulty—to mark a certain excess generated by the symbolic order itself. Russell Grigg has noted the connection between this development and a shift in the paternal function:

> The development from the Oedipus complex to the myth of *Totem and Taboo* and later of *Moses and Monotheism* is very striking indeed. At the outset the father's function is clearly to pacify, regulate, and sublimate the omnipotence of the figure of the mother, called by Freud "the obscure power of the feminine sex." But by the end the father himself has assumed the power, obscurity, and cruelty of the omnipotence his function was supposed to dissipate.[7]

As we shall see, this development is closely tied to the problem of the superego, as Lacan suggests in the *Names-of-the-Father* seminar, where he describes the various forms taken by the "object a" (breast, feces, gaze, phallus, etc.). Noting that "the voice of the Other should be taken as an essential object," he adds that this object presents itself as a pathological trait "as much in the realm of psychosis as at that extremity of normal functioning in the formation of the superego" (*T*, 87).

This is where Lacan's remarks on the "ethics of psychoanalysis" (as an ethics of desire) should be situated. As he writes in *Seminar VII*:

> Freud brought to the question of the *source* of morality the invaluable significance implied in the phrase: *Civilization and Its Dis-*

contents, or, in other words, the breakdown by means of which a certain psychic function, the superego, seems to find in itself its own exacerbation, as a result of a kind of malfunctioning of the brakes which should limit its proper authority. (*SVII*, 143)

This chapter explores that malfunctioning, elaborating it in terms of two different accounts of the paternal function.

Jacques-Alain Miller has summarized this development with the following formulae:

$$\frac{F}{M} \to \frac{\Phi}{x} \to \frac{A}{J} \to a$$

This sequence of formulae can be explained as follows.

The paternal metaphor establishes a relation in which the name-of-the-father (F) serves as the symbolic reference for the desire-of-the-mother (M). This can be expressed as a substitution of the phallus as a signifier (Φ) for the unknown object of maternal desire (x). We can also interpret this substitution as a "prohibition" encountered by the child, the institution of a principal of symbolic mediation which separates the child from the "oceanic" plenitude of primary narcissism, and thus distinguishes the symbolic field of desire (the Other—*l'Autre*, A), from the domain of incestuous *jouissance* (J). This substitution, which splits desire and *jouissance*, is what the "paternal metaphor" was intended to express when Lacan formulated it in the 1950s.

But around the time of *Seminar VII*, Lacan begins to observe that this substitution does not take place without leaving a residue, a remainder of the very *jouissance* it was intended to transcend. A "trace" of the lost *jouissance* thus remains *within the symbolic order* (designated above by *a*). This development leads Lacan to speak of the object a as a sort of surplus-effect that the initial formulation of the paternal metaphor did not adequately confront: "That is precisely what Lacan called small *a*, that is the *plus de jouir* as the difference between the libido and language which produces this small *a* as a residue, $J - A = a$."[8]

To anticipate, let us say that we are thereby faced with a correlation between the object a and the superego. As Catherine Millot notes, "the superego is the representative of lost *jouissance.*"[9] Although I will not develop the point here (I will come back to it at the end), it is important to note that this "remainder" designated as the "*objet petit a*" is not, strictly speaking, left over from an original state, a "lost *jouissance*" that once existed. On the contrary, as the very term "superego" (so closely related to the familiar "conscience") suggests, it is a *product* of symbolization, and comes into being only *through* the symbolic law. As Miller suggests, "What supports the superego is the object a which *takes the place* of the lost object" (emphasis added).[10] The object a is thus not the residue of a presymbolic state, the fragment of a biological past that refuses to sign the social contract (what remains of the "state of nature"), a "libido" that transgresses the cultural law (the "repressive hypothesis"), but is rather a surplus effect of symbolization itself. This can also be put in temporal terms, for although the production of this object is (like the superego) a result of the law, it nevertheless generates a "mythical past" which it then claims to represent. As a retroactive effect of symbolization, the object a thus has the temporal structure of the "trace," in the sense that it is the "remainder" of *a past that was never present*—a past that comes into being only through the symbolic operation that constitutes it as "always already lost."[11]

Miller's formulae thus provide a rough outline, a schematic representation of the problem that leads Lacan to a revision of the paternal metaphor. This revision means that the symbolic law can no longer be simply *opposed* to *jouissance*, and that in place of a simple opposition, we have a more complex and tangled relation: far from simply eliminating *jouissance* in the name of desire, the very operation of the law now produces a peculiar surplus effect, a trait of perversion that is intrinsic to the law itself.[12] We will try to develop this transformation in Lacan's account of the paternal function, and show that it corresponds to a similar development in Freud's own work, a difference between the father in the Oedipal narrative and the father in *Totem and Taboo.*

THE OEDIPAL STRUCTURE

Let us first turn to the Oedipus complex in Freud, in order to see more clearly what the "paternal metaphor" was initially intended to accom-

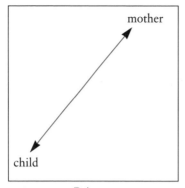

FIGURE 1   Primary
Identification

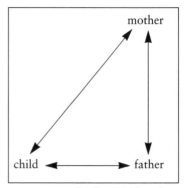

FIGURE 2   Oedipal Triangle

plish. The Oedipus complex is traditionally regarded as the centerpiece of Freudian theory. It explains the process by which the child is individuated, and addresses the peculiar logic of certain basic human emotions, such as anxiety and guilt, jealousy, aggression, and love, while also throwing light on the enigma of sexual difference.

Freud's account of these three issues—the formation of the subject, the logic of affects, and the question of sexual difference—is often represented in the following way: in the beginning, the child is not a distinct individual, and has no explicit self-consciousness or consciousness of others; its affective life is not yet developed, and the question of sexual identity has not yet become an issue. This stage is often described as a state of immediacy and fusion with the mother, an undifferentiated stage characterized as a dual relation in which two parties are not yet clearly distinguished (Figure 1). Through the mechanism of the Oedipus complex, however, this initial state is reconfigured, and a new set of relations begins to take shape: the child gives up its initial, "incestuous" attachment to the mother and accepts a certain degree of mediation or difference, beginning a process of separation that not only allows the mother to emerge as a distinct individual, but also allows the child to develop a certain degree of autonomy.[13]

In Freud's account, this process of differentiation depends upon the paternal figure. As we shall see, the same is not exactly the case with Lacan. For Freud, however, the father intervenes as a third party, introducing a principle of difference, claiming a right to the mother's attentions, and disrupting the child's sole possession of the maternal object

(Figure 2). The Oedipal conflict then begins: the child experiences the father as a threat to its happiness, as a rival or competitor; it feels a certain hatred and fear in relation to the father, to the point of entertaining murderous fantasies toward the father, which Freud regards as the logical correlate of incestuous desire for the mother (murder and incest thus being linked together). In the first stages of the Oedipus complex, this account holds true for both sexes: for both sexes, the mother is the object, and the father is a rival. As Freud says in *Totem and Taboo*, speaking of little Hans,

> He regarded his father (as he made all too clear) as a competitor for the favors of his mother. . . . He was thus situated in the typical attitude of a male child toward his parents to which we have given the name of the "Oedipus complex" and which we regard in general as the nuclear complex of the neuroses. (*SE,* 13:129)

Freud speaks here of the male child, as he often does, but we should recognize that the girl is in the very same position, according to Freud, during the initial phase of the Oedipus complex. As he says in his late essay on "Female Sexuality" (1931), "during that phase a little girl's father is not much else for her than a troublesome rival" (*SE,* 21:226).

One could therefore say that sexual difference has not yet entered the scene. The father has appeared as a third party in some sense, and the immediacy of the relation to the mother has been disrupted, but the position of the boy is not different from that of the girl (Figure 2 thus uses the term *child*). Correlatively (and for our present purposes this is the more important point), we may conclude that the difference between the mother and the father is not yet sexually marked. We thus face a very basic enigma, a "triangulation" that is somehow prior to sexual difference, an initial instance of the "law" of mediation that disrupts the relation to the mother, but which is nevertheless prior to the "symbolic law" in which sexual difference comes to be inscribed. There would thus be a "law before the law," a proto-mediation prior to the symbolic order, which somehow comes to be "translated" into properly symbolic law: an initial relation to the Other, Lacan would say, that is not yet castration, not yet a relation in which sexual difference has been articulated.[14]

We thereby arrive at a first difficulty with respect to the usual

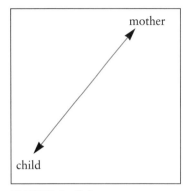

FIGURE 1 Primary Identification

account of the Oedipus complex (a difficulty that is perpetuated by our initial diagrams). For we commonly speak of the "mother" and the "father," and yet analytic terminology clearly requires a more precise vocabulary, for it suggests that we are dealing with a "primary object" and a "rival" or "threat" of some kind, and that the terms *mother* and *father* are profoundly misleading insofar as normal usage of these terms implies a difference between the sexes that is not, strictly speaking, appropriate or descriptively accurate with respect to the subjective position of the child.

This could be confirmed by a number of obscure and intriguing remarks in Freud, who, as many writers have pointed out, speaks of the child's first identification sometimes as paternal, and sometimes as maternal identification. Thus, while Figure 1 presents the child's primary identification as a relation to the "mother," the situation is not so simple. One can see here why Lacan's term "the Other," while more obscure in some respects, is also more precise, insofar as it refuses to insert a commonsense clarity where it does not exist. As Laplanche and Pontalis note in their definition of "primary identification":

> This modality of the infant's tie to another person has been described in the main as the first relationship to the *mother* . . . [but] it is interesting to note that Freud, on the rare occasions when he in fact uses the expression "primary identification," does so in order to designate an identification with the *father* in the individual's "own personal prehistory."[15]

From Lacan's point of view, this obscurity in regard to the mother and father is not a matter of confusion or indecision as to which parent is really the object of "primary identification," nor is it evidence that Freud is unwilling to give the archaic maternal figure enough consideration, and prefers to impose paternal authority even at the "pre-Oedipal" level where the priority of the mother would seem incontestable. The obscurity is rather due to the fact that the difference between the mother and the father is not yet clear, even if the child is aware that two parents are present.

Freud's remarks on the "father of individual pre-history" occur in *The Ego and the Id*. He speaks there of "the *origin* of the ego ideal" (*SE*, 19:31, emphasis added), not of the ego ideal itself, but of its "origin," its conditions of possibility. It is a question of the identification that would precede and make possible the "properly symbolic" identification in which sexual difference is also established. This is what Lacan, in "The Meaning of the Phallus," calls "the installation in the subject of an unconscious position without which he would be unable to identify himself with the ideal type of his sex" (*E*, 685/281).[16] Thus, Freud notes that behind the ego ideal, as its foundation, there lies a more primordial identification:

> This leads us back to the origin of the ego ideal; for behind it there lies hidden an individual's first and most important identification, his identification with the father in his own individual pre-history. (*SE*, 19:31)

This remark has received a great deal of interest recently, largely because of the attention it has been given by Kristeva.[17] The debates have almost invariably involved the question as to whether Freud (and Kristeva as well) wish to circumvent the pre-Oedipal mother and institute "paternal authority" at an even earlier period than psychoanalytic theory usually appears to do.[18] Our remarks would suggest, however, that this discussion is misguided, insofar as it imposes sexual difference at a level of analysis where it does not properly speaking belong, and thereby takes for granted precisely what needs to be explained. The debate *presupposes* sexual difference (reducing it to a more or less commonsense conception of biological difference, when it is rather more obscure what the terms *mother* and *father* mean), and then puts a "battle between the sexes" in place of the very different issue that ought to be at stake here, namely, the *constitution* of sexual difference, the question of its emergence, its enigmatic genesis, in a moment or a place that must be situated not only beyond the initial relation to the "mother" (primary identification), but also beyond the *initial* triangulation of the Oedipal structure, in which there would seem to be a difference without sexual difference, a presymbolic difference that is somehow translated into sexual difference.

We should therefore note that at precisely this point, when Freud speaks of the initial relation to the "mother" and its disruption by the "father," he interrupts his discussion (immediately following the quotation above), and adds a footnote regarding this primary "identification with the father in his own individual prehistory":

> Perhaps it would be better to say "with the parents"; for before a child has arrived at a definite knowledge of the difference between the sexes, the lack of a penis, it does not distinguish in value between its father and its mother. (*SE*, 19:31)

To speak of the "phallic mother" is to approach the same difficulty, as Lacan suggests in "The Meaning of the Phallus" when he writes that "the mother is considered, by both sexes, as possessing the phallus" (*E*, 686/282). At this point, then, and despite a degree of triangulation, the "symbolic order" is not yet established: the mother (if we can still use this term) is a locus of "primary identification," and the father (if we can still use this term) is a "threat" and a "rival" (an imaginary other), with the consequence that the "third party" has not been properly registered as law, in the sense that the promise of a return to the maternal dyad appears to remain open, if only the child can win the struggle to the death against this rival.

As the Oedipal conflict unfolds toward a tentative resolution, however, the child is obliged to recognize that it is not the exclusive focus of maternal desire. Maternal desire goes *elsewhere*, opening the field of the Other beyond the child, who thus encounters the "traumatic" fact that it is not her immediate and sole object. This allows us not only to grasp more clearly the symbolic aspect of the paternal function, apart from its imaginary investments, but also to locate the mother more precisely. It is often said that in Lacan's theory, the mother is *replaced* by the father, or that the father is substituted in place of the mother. This account, however, can only be maintained as long as the terms "mother" and "father" are used unproblematically, with the meaning they have in ordinary language—a meaning that psychoanalysis is intended to analyze and not simply repeat. In this psychological narrative, maternity would thus be denigrated by Lacan, confined to the imaginary, and regarded as something that must be transcended. In fact, the very opposite is the case: the name-of-the-father function is strictly the *correlate* of the desire-of-the-mother, and not something that could possibly supersede it. Maternal *desire*—as distinct from the fantasy of plenitude in which desire and lack have no place—emerges as such only insofar as it has a symbolic point of reference *beyond the child*.[19] The "father" is thus a metaphor, in the sense of being that which the child *substitutes* as an answer to the enigma of maternal desire. Faced with the lack in the Other (the gap opened by the question "What does the Other want?"), the child produces an answer in the form of the "father," whose essential function is to provide a symbolic point of reference, a localization, a grounding point that will give the lack in the Other a limit and a place.[20]

Without this symbolic limitation, Lacan argues, the child's own desire will be compromised, and the constitution of the subject will be in jeopardy.[21] For without this symbolic point of reference, which allows the child to locate maternal desire *elsewhere*, beyond itself, the child will *offer itself up as the object*, in a sacrificial effort to fill the lack in the Other.[22] This is the function of the "paternal metaphor," the signifying substitution that transforms the *enigma* of the lack in the Other into a *relation* between the "mother" and the "father," or more precisely, into a relation between maternal desire and the symbolic function, for as Lacan insists, it is "the signifying function that essentially conditions paternity" (*E*, 555/198).

We can see here a crucial difference between Freud and Lacan, which we will address momentarily: namely, that whereas Freud routinely speaks of the father as a *presence*, an agent who "deprives" or "frustrates" the child, claiming the mother's attention, or threatening the child with "castration," for Lacan, by contrast, it is not the power of the imaginary father—his authority or presence as a threat—which opens the field of the Other, but rather the signifying aspect of maternal desire, its indication of a domain beyond the child, which introduces a law of mediation that is irreducible to the imaginary rival. Maternal desire thus opens a third dimension apart from the child, who is thus forced to renounce the maternal object, and to accept the father as a third party, not as a rival who might be defeated, but as an irrevocable law, a principle of mediation and difference, by virtue of which not only maternal desire, but also the child's desire, will come to find its place.[23] On the basis of this difference, the child's autonomy is secured, and the possibility of a new object choice is opened— indeed, an entire series of objects, in place of the unique and irre- placeable mother. At the same time, Freud says, feelings of hostility toward the father are moderated by feelings of respect, acceptance, and love, which complement, even if they do not altogether eliminate, the initial hostility (we recall here the many passages in *Totem and Taboo* and elsewhere in which Freud speaks of *ambivalence*, the uncanny coincidence of opposite emotions, such as love and hatred). Finally, we may note that in addition to its mediating function, and its role in transforming the child's emotional life, the Oedipal conflict also has a decisive impact on the question of sexual difference. For the child's initial attachment to the mother is such that the mother has no sexual identity; it is only with the appearance of the father, and the child's emerging sense that the mother and father are anatomically dis- tinct, that the question of sexual difference begins to arise; and it is only on this basis that the question of the child's own sexual identity can begin to be posed. We thus have an initial grasp of (1) the forma- tion of the subject, (2) the logic of affective life, and (3) the peculiar articulation of sexual difference.

IDENTIFICATION AND OBJECT-CHOICE

We can clarify some aspects of the argument—particularly the ques- tion of sexual difference—if we restate the account in terms of two basic Freudian concepts, identification and object-choice. This will allow us to see not only that the Oedipus complex introduces the father as a principle of symbolic mediation (a point which Freud sees, and which Lacan isolates with greater specificity by distinguishing between the imaginary and symbolic), but also that the *resolution* of the Oedipal conflict (the phase specified as the "castration complex") usually takes a different form for boys and girls.[24]

In the beginning, the child of either sex takes the mother as an object. This object not only concerns a "mother" who is not yet sexu- ally marked (as we have just seen), but one who is moreover not even an "object," strictly speaking, since the mother is not yet clearly differentiated from the child. Freud therefore speaks of the initial relation to the mother as an identification without an object, a relation in which *identification and object-choice have not yet become distinct.* In *Group Psychology,* he claims that this earliest relation is the "original form of emotional tie with an object," adding that it is situated "before any sexual object-choice has been made" (*SE*, 18:106–7).[25] In different language, we might speak of an "oral" phase in which the "object" is consumed and loses its alterity in a movement of "identification with the object." As Freud puts this point in *The Ego and the Id,*

> At the very beginning, in the individual's primitive oral stage, object-cathexis and identification are no doubt indistinguishable from each other. (*SE*, 19:31)

As Laplanche and Pontalis also say,

> Primary identification is opposed to the secondary identifications that are superimposed on it, not only because of its chronological priority, but also because its establishment does not wait upon an object-relation proper.[26]

Because it is prior to the "object-relation proper," they note, it also concerns a relation "before the differentiation between ego and *alter ego* has been firmly established"—what one might call an imaginary relation that falls short of the alterity proper to intersubjectivity.

FIGURE 1   Primary Identification

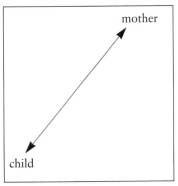

FIGURE 3   Identification and Object-Choice

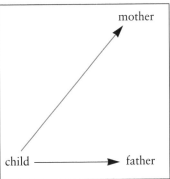

With the appearance of the father, however, the initial attachment to the mother is broken (or reconfigured), and mediation is introduced, opening an initial difference, in such a way that identification and object-choice now come to be distinguished (see Figure 3). In addition, the "destiny" of the little girl now takes a course different from that of the little boy: usually, Freud says, each child gradually comes to identify with the parent of the same sex, taking the other parent as an object (and initiating the Oedipal rivalry). The little girl thus identifies with her mother and takes her father as an object, while the little boy identifies with his father, taking his mother as an object (Figures 3a and 3b). On this account, sexual difference is obviously not reducible to biology, or *automatically* determined by anatomical difference, as it is in the case of the animal, which simply "is" its biological sex. For as Freud regularly points out, the little girl can identify with her father, and the boy can have a maternal identification; either sex, moreover, can take someone of the same sex as an object. But the *question* of sexual difference, and the law that obliges the child to take up a position *with respect to* sexual difference (understood not as a biological fact, but as a matter of identification), is opened by the appearance of the paternal figure. Let us stress that we remain here within Freud's account, and more precisely, within Freud as he is usually read (since it is an open question as to what "Freud's position" is), and that Lacan's account of the paternal metaphor (which will itself be revised) does not treat matters in quite the same way, even though it covers much of the same ground.

Let us venture a final point with respect to these diagrams—which, as we have already suggested, conceal as much as they show. For it should also be clear from this description that the two sexes are not only *distinguished* at this point (Figures 3a and 3b), but that the difference between them is *not symmetrical* (despite the apparent symmetry of the diagrams). It might seem that the formal structure is "the same" for each sex, identification and object-choice being distinguished following the reconfiguration of "primary identification." On this view, even if we recognize the malleability of identification, and the possibility of diverse object-choices, the basic formal structure appears to be "the same" for both sexes, which thereby pass from an initial identification-without-object, to a phase in which object-choice

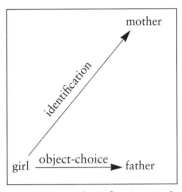

FIGURE 3a Identification and
Object-Choice

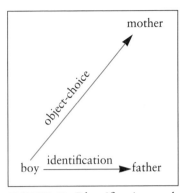

FIGURE 3b Identification and
Object-Choice

occurs, together with a reconfigured, "secondary" identification.[27] And yet, this illusion of symmetry is highly misleading. It is therefore insufficient to say that the two sexes are distinguished by this simple division between the "boy" and the "girl." As Freud himself says, "We have, after all, long given up any expectation of a neat parallelism between male and female sexual development" (*SE*, 21:226).

For each of the sexes is now confronted with a difficulty that the other does not face. In the case of the girl, she is obliged to form her "feminine" identity in relation to the mother, who was her original object, her point of primary identification.[28] As Jessica Benjamin and many others have pointed out, the girl, because she usually elaborates her "secondary" identification in relation to the maternal figure, is faced with a task of identification in which she is constantly at risk. Her "secondary" identification, and thus "femininity" itself, are haunted by the specter of primary identification, and the girl is thus faced with the perpetual task of differentiating herself from the mother, who often appears suffocating and overbearing, excessive in her presence.[29] The very process which is intended to secure a secondary identification (and with it, her "feminine" identity) threatens to take her back to a "regressive" identification with a pre-Oedipal mother (and thus to a position in which sexual difference is not readily registered).[30] In slightly different language, one could say that the girl appears to be faced with the insufficient choice of being a "mother" or a "man," which is to say that the position of the "woman" is not sufficiently clear (in psychic reality, and in psychoanalytic theory). As for the boy, in one sense it is easier for him to separate from the mother. He is not threatened with "regression" in this respect, insofar as he does not have to identify with the person who was his initial object of attachment. Unlike the girl, he relinquishes his primary identification by identifying with the paternal figure. But when it comes to his choice of an object, he will constantly present us with the comedy of confusing every purportedly "mature" object with his mother.

We will not pursue the question of sexual difference further here, but only stress that the process of identification, as Freud describes it, not only detaches sexual difference from any direct biological or anatomical determination; it also initiates a peculiar reflection on the *asymmetry of sexual difference*. A cursory glance might suggest the opposite: one might easily be led to conclude that "girls love their fathers" and "boys love their mothers," with identification and object-choice lining up according to a neat and mirrorlike dichotomy. Even the proviso that "girls" can assume the position of "boys" and *vice versa* does not change this symmetry between the "same" and the "other." Our remarks suggest, however, that one of the theoretical interests of contemporary psychoanalysis lies in the fact that it does not sustain this imaginary symmetry. Lacan has something like this in mind when he says that "there is no sexual relation"—no "Yin" and "Yang," no cosmic "male" and "female" principles (as Jung, according to Lacan, would claim), no order of the "same," which could allow us to divide the universe into two complementary halves, open to various and malleable "identifications." Sexual division in the symbolic order does not produce two halves of a whole, but an asymmetrical fracture that leaves a remainder. In different language, one might say that—contrary to what the diagrams suggest—the question of what a "man" and a "woman" are ("masculine" and "feminine" identification) cannot be resolved by appeal to the "mother" and the "father." This means that the question of "masculinity" and "femininity" is not in fact answered in the way that our diagrams would seem to suggest, namely, by the process in which the child comes to form a secondary identification with the "mother" or "father." The latter are, of course, often proposed as a solution to the enigma of sexual difference (within psychoanalysis, as well as in media, advertising, and in political speeches about "the family"), but according to Lacan, the difference between the mother and the father, even when it is sexually marked, cannot be "translated" into the difference between the man and the woman. Every attempt at such a symbolic translation leaves a "remainder," which is the real of sexual difference. As Lacan says in *Television*,

> The familial order is nothing but the translation of the fact that the Father is not the progenitor, and that the Mother remains the contaminator of woman for man's offspring; the remainder follows from that. (*T*, 30)

THE "SYMBOLIC FATHER"

This account of the Oedipus complex is extremely condensed and reductive. Problems arise at almost every point, and an enormous literature has been produced on the topic. In addition, different schools of thought have stressed different aspects of Freud's account. We know that ego psychology has not focused on the same questions that the object-relations school has emphasized, and Freud's own text provides several different treatments of the Oedipus complex, opening a number of different possibilities. Without entering into all these difficulties, we may nevertheless explore Lacan's treatment of the Oedipus complex, in order to distinguish two different formulations of the paternal function.

These two formulations correspond to two different presentations by Freud: the first is given in the myth of Oedipus, while the second appears in his great anthropological treatise of 1914, *Totem and Taboo*. We know that these two presentations have a great deal in common. In Oedipus, of course, we have the story of someone who unwittingly murders his father and commits incest with his mother. In *Totem and Taboo*, we find a second myth, taken (as Freud himself points out) from the work of Charles Darwin, a myth concerning the origin of culture and the moral law, Freud's two main themes being (1) the institution of totemism (a cultural grouping by nomenclature—identification with an animal ancestor—which distinguishes clan identity from biological lineage), and (2) the principles of incest and exogamy, which serve as an initial "law" distinguishing nature and culture. In this case, too, we find a murder of the father, a myth concerning the prehistory of the human race, in which the primal father, who keeps all the women to himself in an excess of devouring appetite, is killed by his sons, who band together in an act of collective murder, which allows marriage to occur, and establishes the lawful order of exchange and the structure of kinship relations. There is thus a certain obvious similarity between the two accounts, both of which center on murder and incest: in each case, the father is killed, and in each case the murder of the father allows access to the sexual object.

It might be pointed out, of course, that in the case of Oedipus, murder leads to an incestuous object, while in *Totem and Taboo*, murder puts an end to incest and establishes the order of law. The two stories would thus be not merely different, but precisely opposed to one another, as if they led to an explicit contradiction. This difference, however, is not as significant as it might appear. In fact, in *Seminar VII*, when he speaks of Lèvi-Strauss and the symbolic law, Lacan points out that this symbolic law is not reducible to the famous structure of diacritical differences found in Saussure, or the closed economy of symbolic exchange based on a finite totality of elements. On the contrary: on the very page where Lacan speaks of the "malfunctioning of the brakes," which ought to "limit the proper authority" of "a certain psychic function, the superego," he writes:

> As I pointed out in citing Lèvi-Strauss and especially in referring to that which buttresses his own formulation of the issue, myth is always a signifying system or scheme, if you like, which is articulated so as to support the *antinomies of certain psychic relations*. (*SVII*, 143, emphasis added)

The two stories would thus be, not merely different, nor even simply opposed, but rather the expression of a single structure in which the "law" gives rise to what Kant called "antinomies."[31] Freud himself insists that the two stories do not in fact differ (in one case, incest, in the other, the elimination of incest), and in *Totem and Taboo* he draws explicit parallels between the two accounts of the father, as if there were no difference at this level. But this only leads us back to the question of whether *Totem and Taboo* does indeed introduce, or respond to, difficulties that the Oedipal narrative fails to address. We will come back to this problem. For the moment, let us focus more closely on the status of the father.

For on this point, the two stories would be parallel to one another: they both present us with a murder of the father, and thus with a fundamental link between the father and death, a fact which is so crucial that, as Lacan observes, the father is in his very essence nothing other than a certain relation to death. "What is a father?" Lacan asks in "Subversion of the Subject." "'It is the dead Father,' Freud replies, but no one listens" (*E*, 812/310). Both stories would thus reveal this truth: the father is essentially the dead father.

In fact, when Lacan speaks of the paternal metaphor, when he interprets the Freudian account of the Oedipal conflict by claiming that it is essentially a symbolic matter, an act of substitution, a metaphorical operation—emphasizing the connection between the paternal function and language—it is precisely in order to stress this relation to death, to distinguish between the father as an actual person, the living individual who may or may not be present in a particular child's life, and the symbolic operation, the primordial metaphoric substitution, by which the symbolic order of difference and mediation is established. One could thus say that when readers of Lacan claim that his theory "asserts paternal power" or somehow gives "males" access to the symbolic order while confining the mother (and by implication "women") to the imaginary, they are following Freud (or certain aspects of Freud) and not Lacan—following, in other words, the tendency to *identify* the symbolic and imaginary father (the figure who threatens, prohibits, castrates, or frustrates the child), instead of distinguishing them. As Jacqueline Rose puts it, the conceptual isolation of the "symbolic father" represents "an insistence that the father stands for a place and a function which is not reducible to the presence or absence of the real father as such." The concept

> is used to separate the father's function from the idealized or imaginary father with which it is so easily confused *and which is exactly the figure to be got round, or past.* (*FS*, 39, emphasis added)

This also means that "when Lacan calls for a return to the place of the father he is crucially distinguishing himself from any sociological conception of role" (*FS*, 39). This is what it means to insist upon the symbolic father as "dead": there is a link between death and metaphor—between the dead father and the institution of the symbolic order.[32] This is the essential contribution of the "paternal metaphor": we must not confuse the actual living person with the symbolic operation that constitutes the paternal function.

The conceptual independence of the "symbolic father" from the imaginary or real father can be easily recognized if we simply note that, as Lacan points out, (1) the paternal function can be perfectly well *fulfilled* even for a child whose real father is absent, while conversely, (2) the presence of a father is in itself *no guarantee* of the paternal function, and can even amount to its distortion. In the essay on psychosis, this distinction is explicit, and it carries a clinical importance, for we find here

> the reason for the paradox, by which *the ravaging effects of the paternal figure are to be observed with particular frequency in cases where the father really has the function of a legislator* . . . whether . . . he is one of those fathers who make the laws or whether he poses as the pillar of faith, as a paragon of integrity and devotion . . . all ideals that provide him with too many opportunities of being in the posture of undeserving, inadequacy, even of fraud . . . in short, of *excluding the Name-of-the-Father from its position in the signifier.* (*E*, 579/219, emphasis added)

We could therefore say that in formulating the paternal metaphor, Lacan distinguishes between the imaginary and symbolic father, insisting that the crucial aspect of paternity is symbolic, and that certain clinical issues can be described as a collapse of the symbolic and imaginary, or in terms of a deficient distinction between them.[33] In the "Rome Discourse," Lacan puts the point as follows:

> Even when it is in fact represented by a single person, the paternal function concentrates in itself both imaginary and real relations, always more or less inadequate to the symbolic relation that essentially constitutes it. (*E*, 278/67)

In "Subversion of the Subject," we find the same point: the symbolic order introduces a gap, and "when the Legislator (he who claims to lay down the Law) presents himself to fill that gap, he does so as an imposter" (*E*, 813/311).

The Lacanian vocabulary thus has a certain advantage over Freud's own terminology, and allows us to see why the paternal metaphor is a useful interpretation of the Oedipus complex. Freud does not distinguish between the imaginary, symbolic, and real, and as a result, it is not as easy to distinguish these different aspects of paternity. Freud's language (like our ordinary language) remains more or less psychological, more or less bound to the family romance, the developmental narrative in which the child encounters the mother and father, and gradually enters the domain of intersubjectivity and language. In this "psychological" perspective, the essentially symbolic character of the paternal function is not as easily distinguished from the imaginary and real relations that are so readily confused with it. In short, we must distinguish between the father as a psychological individual, and the father as a symbolic function: "[T]he father can only be the effect of a pure signifier, of a recognition, not of a real father, but of what religion has taught us to refer to as the Name-of-the-Father" (*E*, 556/199).

This is shown very clearly in schema R, a structure that distinguishes several elements which are more easily confused in the usual Freudian model (I say "Freudian" because it is possible to argue that Freud himself was more careful about these differences than "the usual Freudian model" would suggest). For in place of the usual account

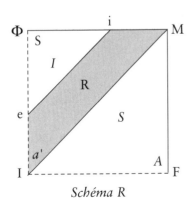

Schéma R

suggested by our initial diagrams, which present us with two "stages"—a dyadic relation to the "mother," followed by a triangulation introduced by the "father"—Lacan gives us two distinct triangles, one imaginary, and another symbolic.[34] The imaginary triangle is defined by three points, the "ego" (e), the "image" (i), and the "phallus" (Φ), the last of which, as we saw in chapter 2, represents an imaginary object, as distinct from the phallic signifier. The second triangle is defined by the ego ideal (I), the "mother" (M), which Lacan's notes define more precisely as the "signifier of the primordial object," and the "father" (F), or rather, the *symbolic father*, which Lacan again specifies as the "dead father." We thus have a series of distinctions: just as the "symbolic father" (F) is conceptually distinct from the "imaginary father" (Φ, as "imaginary object"), so also the "mother" (M) only emerges beyond the horizon of the "image" (i). These distinctions in turn correspond to a difference, on the part of the ego, between points (e) and (I), the ego of "primary identification" (which is situated "before the differentiation between ego and *alter ego* has been firmly established"), and the ego ideal (in which symbolic identification is located).

If one takes Freud (or indeed Lacan) to claim that the "mother" is confined to an imaginary, "pre-Oedipal" stage of fusion in which difference is not yet established and "proper subjectivity" remains impossible, while also claiming that the "father" is the agent whose presence and authority disrupt this "immediacy" (as our initial diagrams suggest), so that all proper subjectivity is grounded in the male figure, it is clear that schema R introduces a more highly differentiated structure, with three related shifts (for the child, from "e" to "I," for the mother, from "i" to "M," and for the father, from "Φ" to "F"). One can see here that the mother is not confined to the imaginary, as is often said, and that in fact the very opposite is the case, since *she only appears in the symbolic order*, where she serves as one apex of the symbolic triangle. The "mother" would thus appear only insofar as the "immediacy" of the relation to the image (i) has been broken (this is the meaning of "maternal *desire*" as a symbolic phenomenon). As for the father, if one maintains the notion that the "actual person" (as opposed to the symbolic function) is the "agent" or "presence" who introduces the law, one will be confusing Φ and F, and "excluding the Name-of-the-Father from its position in the signifier" (*E, 579/219*).

Finally, we should note that schema R casts light on a problem raised earlier. It is often said that the dyadic relation of primary narcissicm is always and only a relation to the "mother," and yet, as we have seen, Freud also speaks on occasion of the "father of individual prehistory," suggesting that this primordial relation is neither simply "dyadic" nor unequivocally a relation to the "mother." Freud's remark that, in discussing the first identification, we should perhaps speak of the "parents," would seem to stress both the quasi-triangular aspect of the "first" relation, and the fact that it appears to be a relation in which sexual difference does not yet clearly appear. This is what the imaginary triangle in schema R would appear to suggest. As Lacan says in "The Meaning of the Phallus," this initial triangulation "demonstrates a relation of the subject to the phallus that is established without regard to the anatomical difference between the sexes" (*E*, 686/282).

Thus, if we return to the question of whether the "first identification" is with the "mother" or the "father," and the correlative question of how to articulate a triangulation in which sexual difference is not yet present (a "law before the law"), we can see that Lacan proposes a solution to both these problems in schema R, which we can read as a correction of the diagrams given thus far. For "primary identification" would seem to correspond to the initial triangulation in which a degree of difference or mediation has been established, yet without sexual difference (the phallus corresponding to Freud's "father of individual pre-history," with the caveat that we cannot rightly speak of "mother" and "father" at this point, but would do better to speak of the "parents"). This is the "primary identification" which Freud presents as the *origin* of the ego ideal. We will not elaborate this schema further here (we have completely ignored the "real"), but only wish to suggest that it distinguishes the imaginary and symbolic from one another (to the point of separating the "phallus" and the "symbolic father") in a way that Freud's more "psychological" narrative does not. It can thus be regarded as providing an analysis—a breakdown into smaller elements—of features that are too easily condensed in the words *mother* and *father*.

We thus have a clearer sense of the "paternal metaphor," as a thesis that aims to clarify matters that remain confused in Freud. In Freud's account, it often seems that the paternal function depends on the presence of the male person (the imaginary father), and critics of Lacan have often claimed on this basis that Lacanian psychoanalysis and the entire theory of the Oedipus complex presuppose a traditional, patri-archal, Victorian family structure, and cannot be extended to other social arrangements. And yet, Freud explicitly deals in *Totem and Taboo* with the aboriginal tribes of Australia and the tradition of group marriage (the totemic clan), a "family" that is not only far removed from the Victorian world, but is also matrilinear. These cultures, Freud says, already revealed the true function of the father as symbolic: the child, he says, will call by the name of "father" anyone who might have lawfully married her or his mother, anyone with the right clan name, the right totemic affiliation, and will address as "mother" any woman who might lawfully have born her or him. This marks an explicit separation between biological origin and symbolic identity. One might even say that these "primitive" institutions reveal more clearly the true structure of culture, whereas our "modern" family retains a confused and misleading resemblance to the "biological unit," thereby sustaining an illusion of "nature" that *conceals the true function of the family* as a cultural institution. In fact, even the apparent "relation to nature," which the Australian clans maintain—the *animal ancestor* that gives the totem clan its name—is at the same time already a *substitute*, a passage beyond the "real father" of biology. As Lacan points out in the *Names-of-the-Father* seminar, the animal is my ancestor precisely because my biological origin has always already been lost, because I am always already no longer in the order of natural lineage: "Mythically, the father ... can only be an animal" (*T*, 88).

PÈRE-VERSION

We thus have a link between the father and death, between the symbolic order and the murder of the father, which distinguishes the "paternal function" from the "imaginary father" that is so often fore-grounded (idealized or denounced) in accounts of the Oedipus complex. And the "paternal metaphor" insists upon this link, by noting that the father is a principle of mediation and difference, a "law" that not only subjects the child to symbolic mediation, but also entails a connection with death: "The symbolic Father is, insofar as he signifies this Law, the dead Father" (*E*, 556/199). Both the Oedipus myth and the Darwinian story of the primal horde confirm this point: in both cases, the father is killed, and the essential link between the father and death is thus confirmed.

And yet the two presentations are not identical: for as we have seen, murder *transgresses* the law in the case of Oedipus, whereas in *Totem and Taboo*, the murder of the father *establishes* the law and the structure of kinship relations. The murder in *Oedipus* leads to criminal incest, while the murder in *Totem and Taboo* puts an end to incest and permits symbolic exchange. We seem to be dealing with two conflicting results: in one case, we have a "transgressive" murder that *makes incest possible*, and in the other case we have a "lawful" murder with precisely the opposite effect, since it *makes incest impossible* (for the sons, as a collectivity, will never occupy the singular position of the father, which is now located in an inaccessible "prehistory").[35] What is the reason for this difference, and why is Freud led from one account to the other? Is it in fact a genuine difference, or could it be in fact that we are still dealing with the same story, and that we are only misled if we draw the parallel in the wrong way?

According to Freud, we may indeed speak of a "murder of the father" in each case, but we should not think of the primal father and King Laius as two fathers who are killed, nor should we claim that there is a parallel between the murderers—Oedipus and the "primal horde." The crucial link is rather between the primal father and Oedipus himself, who is not the murderer, but another version of the father. This would make sense of the Sophoclean drama as a whole, since all three plays present Oedipus as "father Oedipus," father not only to his sons (Eteocles and Polyneices) and daughters (Antigone and Ismene), who inherit the paternal fate, but also father to the city of Thebes, which he "saves" from the Sphinx, the plague, and finally from himself, when he goes into his blind exile, taking his pollution with him (in a gesture that Freud regards as an explicit parallel with the figure of Christ, whose death cleanses the community of their sins).[36] Like the father in *Totem and Taboo*, Oedipus would thus be the murdered father, whose death brings order to the community: it is this primal father-figure who commits incest, who (consciously or not) remains outside the law and refuses castration, who must be blinded, killed, or expelled if the community is to be possible.

This would be why, in the first (and only) session of the seminar on *The Names-of-the-Father* (1963), Lacan draws an explicit connection between the blinding of Oedipus and the murder of the primal father, speaking of "that eye which, in the myth of Oedipus, fulfills so well the role of equivalent for the organ to be castrated" (*T*, 86). In this sense, if we understand the relation between the two stories in the correct way, our parallel would remain intact: both stories present us with the death of the father, the blinding, castration, expulsion, and death that stand at the origin of symbolic law and make possible the civilized order of exchange.

Freud himself reaches the same conclusion. In the fourth and last essay of *Totem and Taboo*, when he finally introduces the Darwinian myth, Freud points directly to a parallel between this myth and the tragedy of Oedipus. As he concludes his discussion of the primal father who suffers death at the hands of his own sons, Freud turns from this figure to Oedipus, the hero of tragic drama:

> Why had the Hero of tragedy to suffer? and what was his "tragic guilt"? I will cut the discussion short and give a quick reply. He had to suffer because he was the primal father, the Hero of the great primeval tragedy. (*SE*, 13:156)

He then draws a more general conclusion regarding the "law" of culture itself. Reflecting back on the course of his entire argument, which concerns not only the Oedipal structure but the origin of culture in general (totemism, religion, moral law, the prohibition of incest, etc.), and the initial passage beyond nature, Freud again turns from the murder of the primal father and draws an explicit link with Oedipus:

> At the conclusion, then, of this exceedingly condensed inquiry, I should like to insist that its outcome shows that the beginnings of religion, morals, society and art converge in the Oedipus complex. (*SE*, 13:156)

We thus return to the essential link between the father and death (the killing of the primal father and the blinding and exile of Oedipus). One can see here why it is misleading to say that in the case of Oedipus, murder leads to an incestuous object, whereas in *Totem and Taboo*, murder puts an end to incest and establishes the order of law. For if

Freud is correct, it is not the death of King Laius and the incest that follows, but the "murder" of Oedipus—his blinding and exile—that occupies center stage, and provides a parallel with the primal father. In both cases, then, incestuous *jouissance* is eliminated by the law. If we accept this connection between the Oedipal myth and the myth of the primal father, however, we are brought back to our initial parallel. The question therefore remains as to how the two stories are different, and why Lacan insists that something new emerges in *Totem and Taboo*.

According to Lacan, it is misleading to reduce the two versions of the father to a simple opposition. It is not the case that one story presents a case of incest while the other describes its termination, or that one murder transgresses the law while the other establishes the law and brings it into being. The two stories are indeed more intimately related than such an opposition would suggest. But this does not mean that they are identical. If Freud is correct in saying that both stories present us with a murder of the father, and that the primal father and Oedipus are one and the same, we must go on to note the crucial difference in the status of the "law" that follows this murder. For with Oedipus, we have a case of the dead father, a father (Oedipus himself) who is killed, and who gives us an instance of the law, an example of the symbolic function of mediation that restores peace to the community. Incest is punished with blindness and expulsion. The gods have their way, and the transcendence of the Other is demonstrated, together with the finitude and mortality of the human being. This is also what the Oedipal complex is meant to suggest, as a relinquishing of "incestuous *jouissance*" that allows the subject enter the community of others, where desire can move beyond its infantile "fixation."[37] In *Totem and Taboo*, however, things are quite different: here too, murder puts an end to incest and brings order to the community, instituting the laws of kinship exchange, but it also has another effect, for in *Totem and Taboo*, murder leads to guilt, a collective unconscious sense of guilt, which the sons retain from the act of parricide. Following the murder of the primal father, the sons are prohibited from occupying the position of the father (Φ), and incest is in this sense expelled; but in addition, we face the surplus effect of the law, namely, the phenomenon of guilt. Let us recall here that Freud's writings on the superego are all subsequent to *Totem and Taboo*.[38]

According to Lacan, then, *Totem and Taboo* does not simply repeat the story of Oedipus in another form: on the contrary, Freud turned to the myth of the "primal father" in *Totem and Taboo* precisely because of difficulties that arose in the Oedipal story. Something remained unresolved in the Oedipal narrative, according to which the child eventually accepted the "third term" and established itself apart from the mother with a degree of independence and autonomy, relinquishing its "incestuous desire." Freud discovered that this "civilizing" function of the father is not unequivocally established. Even in the purportedly successful resolution of the Oedipus complex, there was something left over, a pathological remainder (*"le reste"*) that appeared at the very heart of the normal subject. In Freudian language, we can say that a difference begins to emerge between the "ego ideal" and the "superego"—a term that, one will note, does not find a place in schema R, or indeed within the "paternal metaphor" in its initial formulation. Thus, if the ego ideal is the result of a *resolution* of the Oedipus complex, the superego is the *malfunctioning* of the brakes, the paradoxical effect by which the law gives rise to its own contradiction. In Lacanian terms, the distinction between the ego ideal and the superego is formulated as the distinction between I (ego ideal) and *a* (object a). This is the crucial point on which Lacan concludes the entire course of exposition in *The Four Fundamental Concepts of Psychoanalysis*: "the fundamental mainspring of the analytic operation is the maintenance of the distance between the I—identification—and the *a*" (*SXI*, 273).

In *Totem and Taboo*, then, the murder of the father gives rise not only to law and kinship ties, but to guilt. This is the "paradox" or "contradiction" of *Totem and Taboo*, the peculiar, nonoppositional logic that Freud elaborates in 1914. If, in the Oedipus myth, guilt would seem to attach to the party who commits incest, in *Totem and Taboo* it is precisely the reverse: the renunciation of incest has the surplus effect of producing guilt—as if the very subjects who follow the law are thereby guilty. In the Oedipus myth, we have an order of justice, for incest is followed by punishment and exile; but in *Totem and Taboo* we find a more paradoxical result, for precisely when you follow the law, you are guilty. It is not the primal father, but those who remain within the law, who are marked by the stain of guilt, the "pound of flesh" that the subject owes, the debt that cannot be paid, but that attends the very constitution of the subject. We often hear today that the "law" is simply a "social construction," a contingent historical formation, the "arbitrary" construction of an institutional apparatus that has no "necessity," no fateful relation to human being as such. It would thus be a contingent historical formation, invented *in historical time*, and destined to pass away again, like democracy or television or national identity, as though it had no ontological status. As Heidegger says, however, "The idea of guilt is not one which could be thought up arbitrarily and forced upon Dasein"; thus "'Guilty!' turns up as a predicate for the 'I am'."[39] This is also the conclusion of *Totem and Taboo*: we no longer have an *opposition* between incestuous *jouissance* and the law, but a more tangled relation, a *contradiction internal to the law itself*, such that the constitution of the subject is attended by a trait of perversion, a pathological *jouissance*, a primordial guilt that marks the very birth of the "I am."

We would thus arrive at a clearer grasp of the difference between the two versions of the father. In the Oedipus myth, the expulsion of the criminal restores order to the community: the murder or death of the father *coincides with the law*. This is precisely what the "paternal metaphor" was intended to demonstrate, by insisting on the "symbolic" aspect of the father, as opposed to what one might call his imaginary *incarnation*. And this is what schema R proposes, by separating the "dead father" from the phallic apex of the imaginary triangle. As we have seen, moreover, the symbolic father (F) is the correlate of the ego ideal (I). But in *Totem and Taboo*, the murder of the father not only establishes the law of symbolic exchange, but is attended by primordial guilt—as if the father somehow remained after his death, to haunt those who come after him.[40] In short, we now have *a perverse return of the father beyond the law of death*. As Freud puts it, after his death, the father does not pass away, but *returns* stronger than ever: for once he is dead, he can no longer be killed. Thus, where the paternal metaphor initially presented us with an *opposition* between "incestuous *jouissance*" and symbolic law, we now have a peculiar twist in which the very operation of the law keeps the father alive in the form of the superego—which is not simply the "positive" function of conscience, but a pathological "retention" of the very *jouissance* that the law was intended to eliminate. As Millot says, "the superego is the representative of lost *jouissance*."[41]

If *Totem and Taboo* exhibits a more radical logic than the Oedipal narrative, then, it is for both structural and temporal reasons, which are closely related but can be stated in two distinct ways. The structural point is easily grasped. The Oedipal narrative tends to suggest an *opposition* (either/or) between "incestuous *jouissance*" and the "desire" that is proper to the subject—an opposition, in other words, between the child's initial attachment to the "mother," in which mediation, difference, and the possibilities of intersubjective life remain undeveloped, and the later emergence of "desire" in the symbolic order. *Totem and Taboo*, by contrast, presents us with a *relation* (both/and) in which the very constitution of desire produces a pathological surplus effect, a dimension of *jouissance* that takes the form of guilt. The term "*jouissance*" can therefore no longer have the same meaning, for in the first case, it appears to designate an "early," presymbolic "pleasure" that the symbolic order is expected to transcend or overcome, while in the second case, it designates a product of the symbolic order itself. We thus see why the initial account of the "Oedipus complex" appears deficient, from the perspective of *Totem and Taboo*: it is no longer a matter of going "beyond" a supposedly "infantile" sexuality, in the name of a mature and "civilizing" law, but of a contradiction *internal to the law itself.*

CONCLUSION: LOGICAL AND TEMPORAL CONSEQUENCES

We are familiar with accounts of Freud that speak of the "id" and the "superego" as two opposed functions—on the one hand, a "libidinal force" or "biological urge" that seeks to discharge itself, and on the other hand a sense of the "requirements of culture" and a "conscience" that would resist this "natural" force, "repressing" the libido and subjecting it to the moral law. The Oedipal narrative tends to be read in just these terms, in perfect keeping with what Foucault has called "the repressive hypothesis," in which "law" and "transgression" are opposed to one another. But the "logic" of *Totem and Taboo* is such that we can no longer speak of the id as a "natural force," or indeed of the superego as a purely civilizing agency, simply *opposed* to the pressure of the id. For if, as Millot suggests, "the superego is the

146

representative of the lost *jouissance,*" this would mean that the super-ego is not simply the representative of the law, or the voice of moral restraint that is necessary for culture. On the contrary, the superego would be *the means by which the id continues to live,* within the symbolic order, and after its purported "transcendence." If we take this logical relation between "law" and "transgression" seriously, more-over, and insist upon the structural link between the superego and the "lost *jouissance,*" then we can no longer regard *jouissance* as a "nat-ural libido," but must rather see it as a *product of the law*—not some-thing that "follows" the law, but something within the law that nevertheless contradicts the law. This is why the concept of guilt is cru-cial in *Totem and Taboo*: it captures the paradoxical aspect of *jouis-sance,* as a phenomenon that cannot be regarded as "natural," but can exist only for those who are under the law, and thus attaches itself to the law *as such*—while simultaneously disrupting the law, since guilt is attributed not to the "father" who refuses castration, but to the very subjects who accept the law and seek to maintain it.

The temporal issue is thereby also clarified, for in the Oedipal myth, we have the illusion of *narrative*—the suggestion that a crime occurred one day, and was then punished, so that the law was then restored. Accounts of the Oedipus complex sustain a similar illusion, in which the child passes from an "uncivilized" stage of undifferentiated nar-cissism to a stage of maturity and authenticity. As a narrative, a story which unfolds through a series of chronological stages (following a more or less developmental model), the Oedipal myth tends to conceal the "logical" or "structural" operation that is the core of the "per-verse" father for Lacan (in which "law" and its "pathological remain-der" go together). Like our initial diagrams, which pass from "stage one" to "stage two," the Oedipal narrative allows us to imagine a pre-Oedipal period of incestuous *jouissance* which is transcended with the advent of the symbolic function, chronologically replaced when the child "relinquishes" the mother and passes through "castration."

Lacan already took his distance from these developmental narra-tives when he insisted that the "paternal metaphor" is a "symbolic structure." As a signifying substitution, the paternal function is essen-tially a structuring principle, and the question of its "chronological position" in a developmental narrative fades into the background. In the essay on psychosis, Lacan makes this point as follows: in the Oedipal structure, it is a question of

> relations that refer not to pre-Oedipal stages, which are not of course non-existent, but which cannot be conceived in analytic terms . . . but to the pre-genital stages *insofar as they are ordered in the retroaction* of the Oedipus complex. (*E*, 554/197)

"In analytic terms," therefore, the pre-Oedipal "period" is not a chronological stage, but is closer to a retroactive construction, which the subject, moreover, does not entirely abandon. It is precisely the "return" of a phallic identification that the Oedipal narrative tends to conceal.

This is where *Totem and Taboo* has a certain conceptual advantage over the Oedipal narrative, for with the thesis of a "prehistoric" father, and a "primordially lost" *jouissance*, the prohibition or "law" is not regarded as an imposition that arrives one day, in chronological time; rather, the law is viewed as an origin, a constitutive structure that retroactively *produces* the myth of a primordial state of "plenitude." If, in the Oedipal narrative, there is a time in which the father is still a rival, a time when the father might be killed so that *jouissance* could be restored, *Totem and Taboo* presents us with the peculiar thesis of a father who was killed "in the beginning," and whose death made possible the time of the community, the historical time of the symbolic order. With its "aboriginal" research into "prehistory," *Totem and Taboo* would thus seem to isolate with greater theoretical rigor the difference between *developmental time* (the chronologically sequential time of the Oedipal narrative) and *the temporality of the subject* (the time of retroaction and mythical "origins").[42] As Lacan says in *Television*, "the Oedipal myth is an attempt to give epic form to the operation of a structure" (*T*, 30).

This also casts light on the apparent "contradiction" we encountered earlier—the fact that in *Oedipus*, murder leads to incest, while in *Totem and Taboo*, murder puts an end to incest and establishes the order of law. Freud refuses this simple opposition, arguing that Oedipus is another version of the father. And yet, if the two versions are not identical, we are now in a better position to see why. For as Michel Sylvestre says, the Oedipal myth corresponds to the neurotic fantasy in which a *merely external and contingent prohibition* (the imaginary father) stands in the way of a *possible jouissance*, while *Totem and Taboo*, by locating *jouissance* in prehistory, in a past that is always already lost, presents the prohibition as *constitutive* or *necessary*, and *jouissance* as *impossible*. As a result, the "return" of this impossible *jouissance* can no longer be understood as an original, natural "pleasure," and we are forced to confront it as a symbolic effect, and thus to elaborate its punishing, sadistic, "superegoic" character.

We began with remarks on the "voice," with Lacan's observation on the "object," and his claim that "the voice of the Other should be taken as an essential object," a pathological trait that presents itself "as much in the realm of psychosis as at that extremity of normal functioning in the formation of the superego" (*T*, 87). We can now see more clearly what this means: the "voice of the father" returns from beyond the grave, as a "commandment," a "demand of the Other," which is not "conscience," but its very opposite, for in it, the subject's own voice is lost. This is why analysis asks the question, "Who speaks?" As Lacan says: "Beyond he who speaks in the place of the Other, and who is the subject, what is it whose voice, each time the subject speaks, the subject takes?" (*T*, 87). Do we not hear the paternal voice in Shakespeare's *Hamlet*, in the mandate of the father's ghost, who returns from the grave, unable to die, and driven by the command "remember me," in response to which Hamlet, bound by love, dedicates nothing less than himself, in this sacrificial response:

> *Remember thee!*
> *Yea, from the very table of my memory*
> *I'll wipe away all trivial and fond records,*
> *All saws of books, all forms, all pressures past*
> *That youth and observation copied there:*
> *And thy commandment all alone shall live*
> *Within the book and volume of my brain.*

> (Act I, scene v)

It is worth noting the lines on "woman" that result from this. As Lacan says, "Woman" is one of the Names-of-the-Father.

We thus reach our final observation, on the peculiar division within "conscience," a division that leads Freud to distinguish between the ego ideal and the superego. One might venture a reference here to the "call of conscience" in Heidegger's work, the call that appears to announce the radical individuation of Dasein's "authenticity," but also remains vulnerable to appropriation, open to the substitution by which "the Other" (sometimes a truly death-dealing Other) speaks in Dasein's place. Lacan might thus be read as observing that the "authenticity" of the call of conscience can always be compromised by a pathological attachment, which Freud theorized in terms of the superego.

It is well known that Lacan concludes *Seminar XI* with remarks on the question of "sacrifice." He speaks there of the "resurgence" of "the most monstrous and supposedly superseded forms of the holocaust." Returning to the question of the "object," the "gaze" and the "voice," he speaks of something close to conscience, which nevertheless amounts to the very opposite, a subversion of conscience, "the offering to obscure gods of an object of sacrifice" (*SXI*, 275). We are thus led to a relation between the "object a" and the superego, for Lacan claims here that the "voice" and the "gaze" (*SXI*, 274) are not attributes of the subject, but "objects" by means of which the subject is able to "identify" with the Other, to reply to the demand of the Other in such a way that desire is sacrificed.

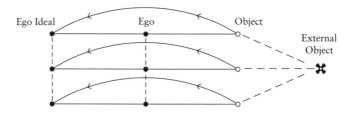

FIGURE 4   Freud's schema, *Group Psychology*

The same conclusion is reached by Freud himself. In the final pages of the seminar where these remarks occur, Lacan recalls Freud's schema from *Group Psychology*, and points out that it describes precisely the collapse of the ego ideal, the substitution by which the place of the ego ideal (a place of purely symbolic identification—what Freud calls "devotion to an abstract idea") is "occupied" by a real, external object. Freud's schema (see Figure 4), according to Lacan, shows us the relations between the ego, the ego ideal, and the object:

> In it he [Freud] designates what he calls the object—in which you must recognize what I call the *a*—the ego and the ego ideal. As for the curves, they are made to mark the conjunction of the *a* with the ego ideal . . . by superimposing at the same place the *objet a* as such and this signifying mapping that is called the ego ideal. (*SXI*, 272)

Freud's own remarks on this schema, given in a chapter on "hypnosis" and "love," suggest that we are dealing here with an overlapping between the ego ideal and the superego, insofar as the "critical" function of the ego ideal (its resemblance to "conscience"), is paradoxically silenced by another ideal that is very similar, but that takes the form of an *external object* to which the ego is now devoted, and for which the subject is now prepared to make great sacrifices. Thus, Freud writes of this schema in 1921:

> Contemporaneously with this "devotion" of the ego to the object, *which is no longer to be distinguished from a sublimated devotion to an abstract idea*, the functions allotted to the ego ideal entirely cease to operate. The criticism exercised by that agency is silent; everything that the object does and asks for is right and blameless. Conscience has no application to anything that is done for the sake of the object; in the blindness of love remorselessness is carried to the pitch of crime. The whole situation can be completely summarized in a formula: *The object has been put in the place of the ego ideal.* (*SE*, 18:113, first emphasis added)

In the course of his work on the paternal function, understood as a matter of "the symbolic order," Lacan would also come to negotiate the delicate relation between the "ideal" and its pathological "objectification," the unstable proximity of conscience to its very opposite, a punishing abdication of conscience which the subject has come to enjoy.[43]

5

History and the Real:
Foucault with Lacan

The entrance into world by beings is primal history [*Urgeschichte*] pure and simple. From this
primal history a region of problems must be
developed which we today are beginning to
approach with greater clarity, the region of the
mythic.

Heidegger, *The Metaphysical
Foundations of Logic*

The Oedipus myth is an attempt to give epic
form to the operation of a structure.

Lacan, *Television*

By the madness which interrupts it, a work of art
opens a void, a moment of silence, a question
without answer, provokes a breach without
reconciliation where the world is forced to
question itself.

Foucault, *Madness and Civilization*

The historicity proper to philosophy is located
and constituted in the transition, the dialogue
between hyperbole and finite structure, between
that which exceeds the totality and the closed
totality, in the difference between history and
historicity.

Derrida, "Cogito and the History of Madness"

SATIRE

Despite the difference between English and Continental philosophy, there is a link between Foucault and writers like Jonathan Swift, as there was between Nietzsche and Paul Reé: "The first impulse to publish something of my hypotheses *concerning the origin* of morality," Nietzsche says, "was given to me by a clear, tidy and shrewd—also precocious—little book in which I encountered for the first time an *upside-down and perverse* species of genealogical hypothesis, the genuinely *English* type. . . . *The Origin of the Moral Sensations*; its author Dr. Paul Rée" (emphasis mine).[1] Taking this upside-down and perverse English type as a starting point, let us begin with the strange tale by Swift.[2]

At the end of *Gulliver's Travels*, after returning from his exotic and rather unexpected voyage to the land of the Houyhnhnms, where the horses are so wise and eloquent in their speech, while humans sit in the trees throwing food at each other and defecating on themselves, our poor traveler goes back to his homeland, where he is so dislocated that he cannot even embrace his wife or laugh with his friends at the local pub (being "ready to faint at the very smell" of such a creature, though finally able "to treat him like an animal which had some little portion of reason"); and in this state of distress, he goes out to the stable and sits down with the horses, thinking that maybe he will calm down a bit, if only he can learn to whinny and neigh.

In Swift, how is it that this voyage to the land of the Houyhnhnms and Yahoos is not simply an amusing story about some ridiculous foreign land? How is it that this "topsy-turvy world"—this inverted world (*die verkehrte Welt*) where horses display the highest virtue and humans are regarded with disgust because they are so filthy and inarticulate—is not merely an amusing departure from reality, an entertaining fiction, but also a revelation of the fact that our own world, the world of reality, is itself inverted, already an absurd fiction, a place where human beings are already disgusting, irrational, filthy, inarticulate, and comical creatures worthy only of satirical derision? How is it that the inverted image turns out to reflect back upon the real one—that what begins as the very reverse of our normal world, an absurd, excessive, and foreign place, a world of science fiction, where madmen wander freely in the streets and objects in nature are inscribed with strange insignias, written on their surfaces by God, turns out to be both foreign and yet also a picture, both exotic and yet precisely a mirroring of our own world, by which we are brought to see ourselves?

This is a question of fiction and truth, but it is also a question of history, a question concerning genealogy. How is it that genealogy, which wanders around in what is most distant and unfamiliar—not the old world in which we recognize ourselves, finding continuity with our ancestors, but a strange and unfamiliar land—turns out to be, at the same time, an account of our own world, a history of the exotic that is also *our own* history?

Before we turn to the historical aspect of the question, let us stay a moment with the problem of fiction. For the exotic tale told by Swift captures the problem art posed for Plato: the problem is not that art produces an illusion, that it is merely a copy of what already exists in reality, or even a deranged, imaginary substitute; the problem is rather that art rebounds upon the world, that it discloses a dimension of truth beyond immediate reality, a truth that competes with what Plato regarded as the proper object of philosophy. As Lacan says, "The picture does not compete with the appearance, it competes with what Plato designates as beyond appearance, as the Idea" (*SXI*, 112). In the artistic competition, it is not the still life of Zeuxis that wins the prize, a work so accomplished that even the birds come down to peck at the imaginary grapes; it is rather the veil of Parrhasios, the illusion painted so perfectly that Zeuxis, upon seeing it, asks Parrhasios to remove this veil so that he may see the painting of his competitor. This is the difference between the level of the imaginary and the level of desire. The function of art is to incite its viewer to ask what is *beyond*. Art is the essence of truth: it leads us not "to see," as Lacan would put it, but "to look." For the human animal is blind in this respect, that it *cannot simply see*, but is *compelled to look* behind the veil, *driven*, Freud would say, beyond the pleasure of seeing. This is where we find the split between the eye and the gaze that Lacan takes from Merleau-Ponty. This is where the symbolic aspect of art emerges, as distinct from its imaginary dimension. And it is here that the question of true and false images must be replaced with a question about language.

If we return now to satire, it is clear that at one level, the satirical, inverted picture of the world, in which everything is rendered in an excessive form, may well evoke our laughter and entertain us, but the true function of satire, as a form of art that is also a political act, must be situated at another level, where the inverted image rebounds upon the so-called normal world, and shows us that *this* world is itself already inverted. At the first level, we have an illusion, the false reality of art that distracts us from the truth, like a distorted mirror image that captivates us while alienating us from reality; at the second level, we have an image that, precisely because of its unreal character, shows us that there is no reality, that reality itself is already an inverted image in which we are not at home. This is where the image goes beyond a picture, true or false, mimetically accurate or surrealistically bizarre; this is where art has to be understood, not in terms of the imaginary and reality, but in its symbolic function, its function as representation. The implication is that as long as we remain content with a discussion of the image and reality, fiction and truth, we will in effect repress the question of language.

THE PLACE OF ENUNCIATION

Let us now pass from satire to consider the historical issue, the problem of how these stories that Foucault constructs for us (the strange laboratory of Doctor Caligari or the fantastic clinic of Boissier de Sauvages), however distant and unfamiliar, operate neither as "mere" fiction, nor simply as truth, neither as an entertaining disclosure of strange practices long ago forgotten, nor as a compilation of facts about the past, but rather by rebounding upon us, to show us who we are for the first time, as if despite everything these bizarre images were portraits of ourselves. In an interview from 1984, François Ewald asks, "Why turn your attention to those periods, which, some will say, are so very far from our own?" Foucault replies: "I set out from a problem expressed *in current terms today*, and I try to work out *its* genealogy. Genealogy means that I begin my analysis from a question posed in the present" (emphasis mine).[3]

With this remark, Foucault stresses the fact that the position of enunciation, the point from which he speaks, is always explicitly thematized in his works. This feature gives his writings a dimension that can only be obscured if one views them as a neutral, descriptive documentation of the past (history), or as an attempt to construct a grand methodological edifice (theory). This is the point at which Foucault's work touches on something that does not belong to history, or even to philosophy, something we might speak of as fiction. "If philosophy is memory, or a return of the origin," Foucault writes, "what I am doing cannot, in any way, be regarded as philosophy; and if the history of thought consists in giving life to half-effaced figures, what I am doing is not history either."[4] This is also the point at which we may understand his work as a kind of action, what Foucault calls a "making of differences."

The New Historicism, which often views Foucault's work as revealing the specificity of various historical formations, without appealing to grand narratives of continuous emergence, or to universal notions (of "humanity" or "sex" or "justice"), nevertheless also regards his work as an effort at knowledge (rather than as a practice). If Foucault's work is taken as a form of historicism, by which the real strangeness and diversity of historical formations is revealed (and, to be sure, this captures *one aspect* of his work), such a view nevertheless subscribes to the idea that his work is a variety of *historical knowledge*, which aims at *the truth about the past*: which is to say (A) *a truth* that is partial, no doubt, and elaborated from within a historical perspective, but that still *shows us* what was previously hidden, like any form of hermeneutics (the secret normalization being installed under the guise of "liberal" institutions such as psychiatry, or the modern judicial system), and at the same time (B) a truth *about the past*, since it is always a question, in this perspective, of rereading the archive, a question of *historical* knowledge, knowledge that is bound to the past since, according to the often-quoted position, the archaeologist can by definition have no knowledge of his own archive, and thus cannot address the truth about his own discursive arrangement. Given this virtually canonical stress upon the "historicist" aspect of Foucault's work, which is thought to reveal the contingent moment in which things are given a historically specific form, one might take pause at Foucault's remarks in *The Archaeology of Knowledge*: "My discourse," he writes, does not aim

> to dissipate oblivion, to rediscover, in the depths of things . . . the
> moment of their birth (whether this is seen as their empirical cre-

ation, or the transcendental act that gives them origin); it does
not set out to be a recollection of the original or a memory of
truth. On the contrary, its task is to *make* differences. (205, original emphasis)

There are in fact two separate questions here. First, how are we to con-
strue the relation between the present and the past? For if history traditionally represents itself as a neutral recounting of the past, at the
level of knowledge, Foucault by contrast, however much he may insist
upon the documentary and empirical nature of his work, nevertheless
also emphasizes that the work is not written from the standpoint of
eternity, as a knowledge or representation that would have no place of
birth, but rather has an origin of its own, in the present. What is the
function of memory in genealogy, if it is not simply the recollection of
the past, in the name of information or knowledge? With this question, we come close to the psychoanalytic problem of memory: what
does it mean to say that in dredging up the past, repeating it, going
back across the river to where the ancestors lie buried, one is concerned, not so much with what really happened—with what Leopold
von Ranke called "the past as it really was in itself"—but rather with
intervening, rewriting the past, producing a shift in the symbolic structure of the narrative that has brought us to the point where we are
now?[5] As is often said, Freud's discovery concerning the symbolic
nature of the symptom also meant that he had to shift his focus—to
abandon his initial and "realist" interest in getting the patient to
remember exactly what had happened, and to recognize instead that
fantasy was every bit as real as reality. This is why it is correct to say
that psychoanalysis begins with the displacement of the theory of
trauma. With this displacement, Freud abandons the idea that the primal scene is a real event that took place in historical time, and recognizes instead that the trauma has the structure of myth, and that
human history as such differs from natural, chronological time, precisely to the extent that it is subject to myth.

This first question about genealogical memory and the relation
between the present and the past is consequently linked to a second
question about truth and fiction. How are we to understand the peculiar duality in Foucault's work—the patient archival research, the
empiricist dedication, and on the other hand his continual assertion

that he has never written anything but fictions? Can we genuinely accept both of these features without eliminating one? In fact Foucault believes that the standard histories are the product of institutions that write grand narratives culminating in the discoveries of the present, tales of the gradual emergence of truth and reason. These histories, according to Foucault, are false, and can be replaced with a more accurate account by the genealogist, who is not seduced by the mythology of a prevailing narrative.

But what are we then to make of his claim that he has never written anything but fiction? Is it simply a stylish French gesture that forms part of Foucault's public image, a rhetorical aside that has no serious philosophical weight? To say this would be to refuse the statement, reducing all such remarks (and there are many in Foucault) to a matter of style that would have no impact on the truth of his discourse. Or does the remark simply mean that he knows he might not have all his facts straight, and that one day someone may find it necessary to improve his account, in short, that his account is true but contingent, or true but written from a perspective? To say this would be to endorse a relativism that maintains the very commitment to truth that it seems to overcome, by admitting that it is "only a perspective," while simultaneously insisting upon a rigorous adherence to documentary evidence that tells the truth better than the grand narratives of the received history. What is this vacillation that makes genealogy neither an operation of knowledge, a true (or at least "truer") account of the past, nor simply a fable, a distorted image, an entertaining but bizarre representation of a time that is foreign to us? If we ask about the nature of genealogical knowledge, the fiction that genealogy is, how can we distinguish it from this dichotomy between the imaginary and the true? Once again, it is a question of language, a question that cannot be resolved at the imaginary level, by appeal to the dialectical interplay of image and reality.

Foucault touches here on the very structure we find in Swift, whereby the function of satire is not simply to create a strange and unfamiliar world, but rather to return, to rebound upon the present, such that the real world is shown to be itself a parody. Slavoj Žižek explains the shift from the imaginary to the symbolic in the following way, arguing that we will only misconstrue the relation between the image and reality if we attempt to resolve it dialectically (by showing that the image and reality are interwoven, that the image is a fiction that nevertheless rebounds upon the true world with formative effects, as Hegel shows in his *Aesthetics*). For there is a point at which the relation between the distorted image and the real thing becomes unstable, beyond all dialectical mediation, a point at which, moreover, it loses the *generative* force that is given in the concept of productive negation. The fact that the inverted image turns out not to be an inversion, but to reveal that the normal world is itself already inverted, calls into question the very standard of "normality" by which one might measure invertedness.[6] Freud says something similar about hallucination when he elaborates the concept of "the reality principle": if the patient were able to respond to the analyst's advice to be less narcissistic and "adapt to reality," the hallucination could be "reasoned away." This is why Lacan stresses that, contrary to the usual interpretation, Freud's "reality principle" is not simply *opposed* to the pleasure principle, but is its strict counterpart, constituted *through* the formation of the pleasure principle; consequently, as Freud himself discovered, it is not by means of shock therapy or behavior modification or any other adaptive technique (which are all governed by a *certain conception* of reality), nor through any "reality testing," that one modifies a hallucination or fantasy; on the contrary, it is only through a symbolic action that the relation between the "imaginary" and "reality" can be realigned.[7] This is why Lacan spoke of analysis as a way of working on the real by symbolic means.

To understand the relation between the imaginary and reality when it is regarded from the standpoint of the symbolic, consider the example of Adorno's remarks on totalitarian authority. How does the liberal individual, the free, authentic moral subject, stand in relation to the oppressive totalitarian dictator (the figure parodied by Charlie Chaplin)? Adorno described the typical authoritarian personality by *reversing* all the features of the bourgeois individual: as Žižek puts it, "instead of tolerating difference and accepting nonviolent dialogue as the only means to arrive at a common decision, the [totalitarian] subject advocates violent intolerance and distrust in free dialogue; instead of critically examining every authority, this subject advocates uncritical obedience to those in power" (Žižek, *For They Know Not*, 14). From one standpoint—what one might call the standpoint of "realism," the imaginary level where reality is brought face to face with its distorted image—these two are in complete opposition, mutually opposed ideals charged with all the pathos and investment of realist urgency; but from the standpoint of satire, from the standpoint of fiction, which asks about representation itself, the authoritarian personality reflects its image back onto the bourgeois democratic subject, and is revealed as already contained there, as the truth of the liberal individual, its constitutive other—or, to put it differently, *its common origin.*

This common origin is at play in *Madness and Civilization*, when Foucault speaks of the peculiar moment when madness and reason first come to be separated from one another, and are shown to have a common birth. This raises a question about history, for Foucault seems to suggest that the common origin of madness and reason is always *concealed by historical narrative.* The usual history of madness is a discourse of reason on madness, a discourse in which reason has already established itself as the measure, the arena within which madness will appear; it is therefore a history in which madness is relegated to silence. As a result, the standard history, according to Foucault, is one in which a separation between madness and reason has already occurred, thereby concealing their original relation or common birth. Derrida stresses this point when he cites Foucault's own remark that "the necessity of madness is linked to the *possibility* of history": history itself would seem to arise only insofar as a separation has been made between madness and reason. To go back to their common origin would thus be not *simply* to aim at writing history, *but also* to raise a question concerning the very possibility of history.[8] This would be, as Derrida puts it, "the maddest aspect of Foucault's work."[9]

Thus, the peculiar identity that links the liberal individual with the obscene and tyrannical force of fascism *must be disavowed*, and the best form of disavowal is narrative: what is in fact an original unity, a structural relation linking the Reign of Terror with the rise of free democracy and the Rights of Man, is best concealed by a *genetic* narrative, in which the original condition is said to be one of pure freedom, liberty, fraternity, and equality, an ideal that eventually comes to be corrupted by a degenerate or perverted form. In this case—what we might call the case of realism, the imaginary level where the true reality is set over against its distorted image—we would be *tempted to denounce* the authoritarian personality as an extreme distortion of the natural order of things, by measuring this degenerate form against the liberal, democratic individual; we would seek a return to the origin, before it was contaminated by the tyrannical violence that corrupts it; but in the second case, when we see with the eye of the satirist who recognizes that the natural order of things is already a parody, we have to recognize that the supposedly natural state of things, the normal, liberal individual who has "natural rights" and a native capacity for moral reflection, is itself already inverted, that it contains the totalitarian authority in its origins, not as its opposite, not as its contradiction, not as its degenerate or perverted form, but as its repressed foundation, its internal "other."[10] In Lacanian terms, the first relation of aggressive, mirroring opposition (in which the communist and the democrat face off) is imaginary, whereas the second relation (in which they are mutually constitutive) is symbolic, which means that it can be grasped only at the level of language, and not by a return to some mythical origin—the liberation of our supposedly innate but repressed libido, or the restoration of our so-called "natural" democratic rights.

The point here is not simply to dwell on the purportedly shocking revelation concerning the symptomatic link—what one might call the equiprimordiality—of totalitarianism and democracy, but rather to show that the ideal of the liberal individual (whose right to freedom is accompanied by an inborn capacity for tolerance, and whose healthy conscience is the sign of an innate moral disposition, and so on), is a construction whose supposedly natural status is a fiction. This amounts to dismantling the idea that totalitarian governments are a *secondary* formation, the corruption of an origin, or the *perversion* of what would otherwise be a natural system of equally distributed justice. *That* story of the origin and its subsequent perversion is a myth, in the sense in which Lacan uses the word when he writes that the Oedipus myth is the attempt to give epic form to what is in fact the operation of a structure. This is where Rousseau is more radical than other "state of nature" theorists. His explanation of the social contract relies on the idea that originally, before any conventions or institutional constraints were established, human nature took a certain form, but as his argument unfolds, it becomes clear that this original state is purely mythical, a fiction that his own political discourse confronts as such. This is in sharp contrast to other state-of-nature theorists, who rely unequivocally on an idea of "human nature" that is always *pre-supposed rather than demonstrated* (as is suggested by the Hobbesian model, in the fact for example that when I agree to leave your acorns alone if you agree to leave mine alone, I am *already* operating as the rational agent whose existence is supposed to be *generated* by the social contract, and not presupposed as original—since originally nature is said to have been merely violent and aggressive, and thus dependent upon the arrival of law for its rational coherence). We thereby see that the symbolic order forces upon us a confrontation with the equiprimordiality of two opposed positions which an historical account would regard according to a genetic narrative, as sequential, and also as hierarchically ordered in such a way that one position can be regarded as natural, while the other is treated as a cultural product—the choice being left open as to whether one prefers a "return to nature," or a celebration of the "higher law" of culture, though in either case the common origin has been repressed.

THE "HISTORICAL SENSE"

In his essay on Nietzsche, Foucault distinguishes the work of the historian from the first genealogical insights that go under the name of "the historical sense": "The historical sense," he writes,

> gives rise to three . . . modalities of history [all of them deployed against the pious restoration of historical monuments]. The first is parodic, directed against reality, and opposes the theme of history as reminiscence or recognition.

The *historian*'s gaze is thereby distinguished from that of the satirical genealogist:

> The *historian* offers this confused and anonymous European, who no longer knows himself or what name he should adopt, the possibility of alternate identities, more individualized and substantial than his own. But the man with historical sense will see that this substitution is simply a disguise. Historians supplied the Revolution with Roman prototypes, romanticism with knight's armor, and the Wagnerian era was given the sword of the German hero. The genealogist will know what to make of this masquer-

ade. He will not be too serious to enjoy it; on the contrary, he will push the masquerade to its limit and prepare the great carnival of time where masks are constantly reappearing. . . . In this, we recognize the parodic double of what the second *Untimely Meditation* called "monumental history." . . . Nietzsche accused this history, one totally devoted to veneration, of *barring access* to the actual intensities and creations of life. The parody of his last texts serves to emphasize that *"monumental history" is itself a parody.* Genealogy is history in the form of a concerted carnival. (*LCMP,* 160–61, emphasis added)

FICTION

Parody is of course only one of the lessons Foucault takes from Nietzsche. If we ask more generally about the relation of genealogy to fiction, we may recognize the peculiar "distance" that genealogy inhabits—not the transcendental distance that allows a perfect view of the past, and not the distance of escape, the distance of an imaginary world that takes us away from reality, but the distance of words. In an essay on Robbes-Grillet, Foucault writes:

What if the fictive were neither the beyond, nor the intimate secret of the everyday, but the arrowshot which strikes us in the eye and offers up to us everything which appears? In this case, the fictive would be that which names things, that which makes them speak, and that which gives them in language their being already apportioned by the sovereign power of words. . . . This is not to say that fiction is language: this trick would be too easy, though a very familiar one nowadays. It does mean, though, that . . . the simple experience of picking up a pen and writing creates . . . a distance. . . . If anyone were to ask me to define the fictive, I should say . . . that it was the verbal nerve structure of what does not exist.[11]

Later in the same essay, Foucault returns to the word "distance":

I should like to do some paring away, in order to allow this experience to be what it is. . . . I should like to pare away all the contradictory words, which might cause it to be seen too easily in terms of a dialectic: subjective and objective, interior and exterior, reality and imagination. . . . This whole lexicon . . . would have

> to be replaced with the vocabulary of distance. . . . Fiction is not
> there because language is distant from things; but language is
> their distance, the light in which they are to be found and their
> inaccessibility. (149)

Thus, when we ask (in regard to Jonathan Swift and his satirical text)
how the inverted image is not just an entertaining fiction, a journey to
the underground world of the Marquis de Sade, or the exotic dun-
geons of Bicêtre, but rather an image that reflects back upon the normal world, the "arrowshot" that returns to "strike us in the eye," we
cannot understand this in terms of the opposition between "fiction and
truth." This answer, even if it proceeds beyond opposition to a sort of
dialectical interplay, in which the imaginary and "reality" interact, is
insufficient, because it does not adequately confront the role of *language*.[12] If we wish to understand language, then, we cannot rest content with a dialectical solution, according to Foucault: "reality and
imagination," Foucault writes, "this whole lexicon . . . would have to
be replaced." When we speak of fiction, then, we are no longer in the
realm of truth and falsity; we have passed from the image to the word,
from the opposition between reality and imagination to the symbolic.

IMAGE AND WORD

This discrepancy between the image and the word is the source of
Foucault's constant preoccupation with the difference between seeing
and saying, perception and verbalization, the level of visibility and
the function of the name. If, as we have seen, the relation between
the image and reality is not a matter of productive negation, in which
the encounter with an alien image cancels out our self-knowledge
and requires us to be transformed; if the dialectical account of the
image and reality somehow obscures the role of language, perhaps
this is because there is a difference between the image and the word,
a gap or void that, according to Foucault, is not sufficiently confronted by phenomenology. Perhaps "distance" names the lack that
separates the symbolic domain from that of perception, evidence,
and light. "Fiction is not there because language is distant from
things; but language is their distance, *the light* in which they are to
be found *and their inaccessibility*"(149, emphasis added). Perhaps
"distance," in naming the lack of any dialectical relation between

speech and vision, also amounts to a refusal of all attempts to generate a stable historical unfolding, the gradual emergence of an origin, or the teleological production of something that had to be gradually constructed through the handing-down of a common tradition. Perhaps "distance" is the name for why Foucault refuses to participate in the Husserlian response to the crisis of the human sciences (see *Archaeology of Knowledge*, 204).

In that case, language would not only destabilize the usual dialectic between fiction and truth; it would also call for a reconfiguration of the concept of history, one in which things would retain their inaccessibility, beyond all phenomenological retrieval, even the retrieval that might seem to operate in archaeology itself. This would bring archaeology very close to what Foucault speaks of as fiction. Such a revision of historical knowledge is evident in the remark already cited, where Foucault remarks that his work does not aim "to dissipate oblivion, to rediscover in the depths of things . . . the moment of their birth (whether this is seen as their empirical creation, or the transcendental act that gives them origin); it does not set out to be a recollection of the original or a memory of the truth. On the contrary, its task is to *make* differences" (205, original emphasis).

Such a making of differences, such a disruption of phenomenological retrieval, can only be grasped through maintaining the *space* that separates the image and the word, the instability that keeps the relation of perception and language perpetually subject to dislocation. In *The Birth of the Clinic*, for instance, his analysis shows that modern medicine was organized precisely through a mapping of discourse (the physician's case history), a discourse that was intended to coincide with the space of corporeal visibility, and Foucault shows that this perfect formalization of seeing and speech can be maintained only through a metaphysics of the subject, a modern philosophical anthropology. The first sentence of *The Birth of the Clinic* reads: "This book is about space, about language, and about death; it is about the act of seeing, the gaze."[13] In *The Order of Things*, we find a similar gesture, when Foucault discusses the image painted by Vélazquez: in one sense, it would be possible to regard this painting as a complete display, a Gestalt, the manifestation of all the techniques of representation at work in Classical thought, the very image of representation, in which the distance between the visible world and its verbal representation would be definitively closed within the confines of the encyclopedia.[14] In order for this to be possible, Foucault says, all that is necessary is that we give a name to the one spot at which the surface of the painting seems incomplete (the mirror at the back which does not reflect, but which should show the subjects being painted, who will eventually appear on the canvas whose back we see in the painting called *Las Meniñas*): This hole could be filled with the proper name, "King Philip IV and his wife, Mariana" (9). Foucault continues:

> But if one wishes to keep the relation of language to vision open, if one wishes to treat their incompatibility as a starting-point for speech instead of as an obstacle to be avoided . . . then one must erase those proper names. (9)

The play of substitutions then becomes possible in which, as Foucault shows, the royal subjects change place with the spectator of the painting, who also becomes the object of the painter's regard. In this opening, this void that marks the relation between the image and the word, we can begin to approach what Lacan calls the question of the real.

REPRESSION AND POWER

Let us now see if we can carry these remarks over into Foucault's analysis of power. In an interview with Bernard Henri-Lévi, Foucault remarks that movements of humanitarian reform are often attended by new types of normalization.[15] Contemporary discourses of liberation, according to Foucault, "present to us a formidable trap." In the case of sexual liberation, for example,

> What they are saying, roughly, is this: "You have a sexuality; this sexuality is both frustrated and mute . . . so come to us, tell us, show us all that. . . ." As always, it uses what people say, feel, and hope for. It exploits their temptation to believe that to be happy, it is enough to cross the threshold of discourse and to remove a few prohibitions. But in fact it ends up repressing. (114)

Power, according to Foucault, is therefore not properly understood in the form of juridical law, as a repressive, prohibitive agency that transgression might overcome, but is rather a structure, a relation of forces, such that the law, far from being simply prohibitive, is a force that generates its own transgression. Despite the claims of reason, the law is always linked to violence in this way, just as the prison, in the very failure of its aim at reform, reveals that at another level it is an apparatus destined to produce criminality (Lacan's remarks on the "aim" and "goal" of the drive would be relevant here). This is why Foucault rejects the model of law, and the idea that power is a repressive force to be overthrown. Transgression, liberation, revolution, and so on are not adequately grasped as movements *against* power, movements that would contest the law or displace a prohibition; for these forms of resistance in fact belong to the apparatus of power itself. Transgression and the law thus have to be thought otherwise than in the juridical, oppositional form of modernity, which is invested with all the drama and pathos of revolutionary narratives; we are rather concerned with a structural relation that has to be undone.

We can see here why Foucault says that genealogy is not simply a form of historical investigation. It does not aim at recovering lost voices, or restoring the rights of a marginalized discourse (speaking on behalf of the prisoners, or recovering the discourse of madness). Genealogy does not participate in this virtuous battle between good and evil, but is rather an operation that goes back to the origins, the first moments when an opposition between madness and reason took shape, and came to be ordered as a truth.[16] This distinction between genealogy and historical efforts at recovering lost voices bears directly on Foucault's sense of the ethical dimension of genealogy: "What often embarrasses me today," he says,

> is that all the work done in the past fifteen years or so . . . functions for some only as a sign of belonging: to be on the "good side," on the side of madness, children, delinquency, sex. . . . One must pass to the other side—the good side—but by trying to turn off these mechanisms which cause the appearance of two separate sides . . . that is where *the real work* begins, that of the present-day historian.[17] (120–21, emphasis added)

BEYOND GOOD AND EVIL

This is not to say that no difference exists between the fascist and the liberal, madness and reason. This game of dissolving all differences by showing that you can't tell one thing from another is not what is at stake.[17] The point is rather to refuse to reanimate the forces of moral approbation and censure—denouncing the enemy and congratulating oneself on having achieved a superior stance—and rather to ask how one is to conduct an analysis. Foucault's work often reaches just such a point, where he seems to pass beyond good and evil.

In books like *Discipline and Punish*, and even as early as *Madness and Civilization*, he says that, as terrible and oppressive as the imprisonment of the insane may be, as intolerable as the torture and public humiliation of criminals may seem to us today—we who look back with our enlightened eyes—it is not our censure of this barbarism that Foucault wishes to enlist. What really matters, for us today, is not the deficiency of the past, but the narrative that reassures us about our own grasp on the truth, our possession of more humane and rational methods. As horrific as the tale of the torture of Damiens may be in the opening pages of *Discipline and Punish*—and it is a story, a little image or vignette, that frames this long mustering of documentary evidence, as Vélazquez's artful painting frames the meticulous and patient discourse on knowledge in *The Order of Things* (see also the opening of *The Birth of the Clinic*)—this scene of torture, which captures the eye and rouses the passions, is not offered up as a spectacle for our contempt. To be sure, it does tempt the appetite of our moral indignation, our satisfaction in ourselves, our certainty that we have arrived at a better way. But the genealogy of the prison is not the story of the progressive abandonment of an unjust system of monarchical power, and the emergence of a more democratic legal order; it is the story of the formation of the modern police state, a network of normalization *which is concealed by the conventional history* of law and justice. That history is a narrative written by the conquerors, in which the truth *about the present* is lost.

COUNTER-MEMORY

It is the same in *Madness and Civilization*. Foucault's work is often written *against* a prevailing narrative, as a kind of counter-memory: it is usually said, he tells us, that the liberation of the insane from their condition of imprisonment constitutes an improvement, a sort of scientific advance—a greater understanding of the insane, and a progressive reform of the barbaric practices which previously grouped the insane together with the criminal and the poor. But this story only serves the interests of the present; it is not the true history, but a history written by the conqueror. For the fact is that the organization of this supposedly liberal and scientific discipline of psychiatric knowledge only served to produce greater and more diversified forms of subjugation, a greater and more subtle surveillance of the minutiae of interior mental life. The body has been freed, Foucault says, only for the soul to become a more refined and effective prison: you watch too much TV, you eat too much, you don't get enough exercise, you waste your time, you criticize yourself too much, and you should be ashamed for feeling guilty about all this, for dwelling so much on your pathetic problems. This is "the genealogy of the modern 'soul'."[18] "Th[is] soul is the effect and instrument of a political anatomy." It was once the body that was put in prison, but now "the soul is the prison of the body" (*DP*, 30). And it is on the basis of this modern psychological soul that "have been built scientific techniques and discourses, and the moral claims of humanism" (*DP*, 30), whose handbooks can be found on the bestseller lists, and whose various institutional forms are distributed across the entire social network, from outpatient clinics to recreational packages. It is *that* contemporary regime, and not the earlier incarceration of the insane, that captures Foucault's attention. It is the story we tell ourselves, and not the barbarism of the past, that Foucault wishes to interrogate. That is why he does not simply produce a history for us, but also tells us the usual story, and asks us to think about who it is that tells that story, *who is speaking* in the received narrative.

In *The History of Sexuality*, we find a similar gesture: it looks as if the Victorians repressed sex, and perhaps it could be shown that repression is not an adequate concept, that in fact power does not operate by means of repression, but that there was rather an incitement to discourse, a complex production of sexuality. And yet, however much ink has been spilled over this thesis, the central focus of this first volume is not simply on whether there was "repression" among the Victorians, or something more complex, but also on the way in which the usual story of liberalization is a history written by the conquerors, their fiction.

We may return here to our basic question. In fact it is incorrect to say that whereas the Victorians repressed sex, we have liberated it. Our knowledge of the past should be altered in this respect. But Foucault does not simply drop the usual history, in order to replace it with a better one. He is not simply interested in the truth, a better method, a more accurate history. He does not simply reject the false narrative, but asks: If it is so often told, what satisfactions does the received story contain? This is a question about the present and not about the Victorian era. If this story of repression is told so often, who does it please and who does it celebrate? Who is the subject that enunciates this history? For the story of liberated sexuality, or the promise of its liberation, does contain its satisfactions: even if it is not the truth, Foucault writes at the beginning of the first volume, the narrative of sexual repression among the Victorians has its reasons, and "is easily analyzed," for we find that "the sexual cause—the demand for sexual freedom . . . becomes legitimately associated with the honor of a political cause."[19] The received history is thus a fiction that has its reasons. How now? These brave Europeans! That they should need to tell such tales about their ancestors! "A suspicious mind might wonder," says Foucault (*HS*, 6).

The oppressiveness of Victorian life is not what interests Foucault; what concerns him is, rather, *our story*, the narrative we have consented to believe.[20] There may be a reason, he writes,

> that makes it *so gratifying for us* to define the relationship between sex and power in terms of repression: something that one might call the speaker's benefit. If sex is repressed . . . then the mere fact that one is speaking about it has the appearance of a deliberate *transgression*. . . . [O]ur tone of voice shows that we know we are being subversive, and *we ardently conjure* away the present and appeal to the future, whose day will be hastened by the contribution we believe we are making. Something that smacks of revolt, of promised freedom, of the coming age of a different law, slips easily into this discourse on sexual oppression. Some of the ancient functions of prophecy are reactivated therein. (*HS*, 6–7, emphasis added)

HISTORY, THEORY, FICTION

In short, it is true that Foucault wishes to tell us a different history, to show us that sex in the nineteenth century was not in fact repressed, but rather incited to speak, articulated in many new discursive forms, and not simply silenced or prohibited. It is also true that this argument, this revised *history*, contributes at another level to a *theoretical* elaboration of power. But we cannot be satisfied with this operation of knowledge. For in addition to the revised history, and beyond the theoretical doctrine, what ultimately drives Foucault is a desire, not to construct a more accurate history (the truth about the past—that of the historian) or to erect a great theoretical edifice (a universal truth—that of the philosopher), but to dismantle the narratives that still organize *our present experience* (a truth that bears on the position of enunciation).[21] "I would like to explore not only these discourses," Foucault writes,

> but also the will that sustains them. . . . The question I would like to pose is not "Why are we repressed?" but rather, "Why do we say, with so much passion and so much resentment against our most recent past, against our present, and against ourselves, that we are repressed?" (*HS*, 8–9)

It is the same in *Discipline and Punish*, when Foucault responds to an imaginary reader who wonders why he spends so much time wandering among obsolete systems of justice and the obscure ruins of the torture chamber. "Why?" he replies. "Simply because I am interested in the past? No, if one means by that writing a history of the past in terms of the present. Yes, if one means writing a *history of the present*" (*DP*, 31, emphasis added). It is this counter-memory, this interplay between one story and another, that leads us to consider the relation between history, theory, and fiction.

TRANSGRESSION AND THE LAW

Although Foucault's refusal of the repressive conception of power appears in his discussion of the Victorians, one does not have to wait for the *History of Sexuality* to find this thesis on power, this rejection of the theory of power as prohibition, the so-called repressive hypothesis, which generates so many discourses of resistance and liberation.

Already in 1963, Foucault formulated a similar claim in his "Preface to Transgression."[22] Curiously enough, this formulation also has to do with sexuality.

Foucault begins his essay with the same focus on the present: "*We like to believe* that sexuality has regained, in contemporary experience, its full truth as a process of nature, a truth which has long been lingering in the shadows" (*LCMP*, 29, emphasis added). But as Bataille and others have shown us, transgression is not the elimination of the law by means of a force or desire that might be thought to pre-exist all prohibition. It is not the restoration of an origin, a return to immediacy, or the liberation of a prediscursive domain, by means of which we might overcome all merely historical and constituted limits.[23] On the contrary, "the limit and transgression depend on each other" (*LCMP*, 34). "Transgression," Foucault writes, "is not related to the limit as black to white, the prohibited to the lawful, the outside to the inside" (*LCMP*, 35). Long before his final books on the relation between sexuality and ethics, these remarks already have consequences for our conception of the ethical. Transgression is not the sign of liberation; it "must be detached from its questionable association to ethics if we want to understand it and to begin thinking from it. . . . It must be liberated from the scandalous or subversive" (*LCMP*, 35). This is what would be required if we were to think the obscure relation that binds transgression to the law.

Let us add that these reflections on the limit, on power and transgression, are not simply formulated as an abstract philosophical question, as though it were a theoretical matter of understanding power correctly. On the contrary, Foucault's claims make sense only if they are seen as part of his understanding of history. It is a question of the *contemporary* experience of transgression, in which the concept of the limit does not take a Kantian form, or entail a line that cannot (or should not) be crossed (a logical or moral limit), but is rather *a fold*, the elaboration of a strange non-Euclidean geometry of space, another mathematics, in which the stability of inside and outside gives way to a limit that exists only in the movement that crosses it (like a Moëbius strip, the "other side" of which constantly disappears as one circles around its finite surface—as if the point at which one might pass from one side to the other were constantly receding, so that the mathematization of space, the difference between one and two, were constantly being destabilized).[24]

In short, this concept of transgression has a historical location: it is clearly bound up with the epoch in which anthropological thought has been dismantled. Foucault puts the history very concisely in the "Preface to Transgression," where he uses the categories of "need," "demand," and "desire." In the eighteenth century, Foucault writes, "consumption was based entirely on need, and need based itself exclusively on the model of hunger." This formulation will be developed in *The Order of Things* when Foucault elaborates the Enlightenment's theory of exchange and its political economy, in their fundamental dependence on the concept of natural need. "When this element was introduced into an investigation of profit," when, in other words, the natural foundation of need was reconfigured by an economics that aimed to account for the *superfluity* of commodities, an economics that went beyond natural law, explaining the genesis of culture through *a demand that exceeded all natural need* (what Foucault calls "the appetite of those who have satisfied their hunger"), then the Enlightenment theory of exchange gave way to modern philosophical anthropology: European thought

> inserted man into a dialectic of production which had a simple anthropological meaning: if man was alienated from his real nature and his immediate needs through his labor and the production of objects . . . it was nevertheless through its agency that he recaptured his essence. (*LCMP*, 49)

For *contemporary* thought, however, this shift from need to demand will be followed by yet another dislocation, a shift from demand to desire, in which the conceptual framework of modernity no longer functions; and this time, instead of labor, sexuality will play a decisive role, obliging us to think transgression differently than in the form of dialectical production.

This new formation is not a return to "nature," but an encounter with language. "The discovery of sexuality," Foucault argues, forces us into a conception of desire that is irreducible to need or demand (the requirements of nature or the dialectical self-production of culture that characterizes anthropological thought). "In this sense," Foucault writes, "the appearance of sexuality as a fundamental problem marks the transformation of a philosophy of man as worker to a philosophy based on *a being who speaks*" (*LCMP*, 49–50). The same historical shift is stressed in *Madness and Civilization*: this book, which might at first glance seem to include an indictment of Freud, as one of those who participate in the modern psychiatric imprisonment of madness, in fact argues that Freud marks an essential displacement in relation to psychiatry, a displacement that coincides with what the "Preface to Transgression" regards as the end of philosophical anthropology:

> That is why we must do justice to Freud.[25] Between Freud's *Five Case Histories* and Janet's scrupulous investigations of *Psychological Healing*, there is more than the density of a *discovery*; there is the sovereign violence of a *return*. . . . Freud went back to madness at the level of its *language*, reconstituted one of the elements of an experience reduced to silence by positivism; . . . he restored, in medical thought, the possibility of a dialogue with unreason. . . . It is not psychology that is involved in psychoanalysis. (*MC*, 198)

The break with psychology that arrives with Freud marks the end of philosophical anthropology.

LACAN

If, as we have seen, resistance belongs to the apparatus of power, and is consequently not so much a threat to power, as a product, an effect of power (just as the totalitarian state is structurally linked to the founding of the democratic community, which would seem to be opposed to it in every respect), then it is the obscure, symptomatic relation between the two that Foucault's conception of power obliges us to confront.

Lacan says something similar about transgression and the law: we do not enjoy despite the law, but precisely because of it. This is what the thesis on *jouissance* entails: *jouissance* is not the name for an instinctual pleasure that runs counter to the law (despite the biological paradigm that still governs so many readings of Freud). It is not the fulfillment of a natural urge, or a momentary suspension of moral constraint, but quite the contrary: it is Lacan's name for Freud's thesis on the death drive, the name for a dimension of unnatural suffering and punishment that inhabits human pleasure, a dimension that is possible only because the body and its satisfaction are constitutively denatured, always already bound to representation. *Jouissance* is thus tied to punishment, organized not in defiance of the repressive conventions of civilization, or through the transgression of the moral law, but precisely in relation to the law (which does not mean "in conformity with it"). This is precisely Foucault's thesis on the productive character of power, even if it does not entail a complete theoretical overlap with Lacan in other respects.

Slavoj Žižek reminds us of Lacan's paradoxical reversal of Dostoevski here: "against [the] famous position, 'If god is dead, everything is permitted,'" Lacan claims instead that "if there is no god . . . everything is forbidden." Žižek remarks:

> How do we account for this paradox that the absence of Law universalizes prohibition? There is only one possible explanation: *enjoyment itself, which we experience as "transgression," is in its innermost status something imposed, ordered*—when we enjoy, we never do it "spontaneously," we always follow a certain injunction. The psychoanalytic name for this injunction, for this obscene call, "Enjoy!" is superego.[26]

We find here, in the relation between the law and transgression, not a simple opposition of outside and inside, prohibition and rebellion, cultural conventions opposed to natural desires, but rather a paradoxical relation of forces. Such a force cannot be grasped in terms of the Newtonian system of natural forces, the smooth machinery in which every action produces an equal and opposite reaction, a physics of libido based on natural law, or a theory of charge and discharge, tension and homeostasis. We are faced here with a more peculiar form of power, one that takes us away from natural law toward the law of language, in which force is tied to representation.[27]

Here the space of the body is given over to the unnatural network of discourse and its causality. In this framework, the relation between law and transgression is such that the rule of law appears not to "repress" or "prohibit," but to produce its own exception, not to function but to malfunction, thereby making manifest the incompleteness of the law, the impossibility of closure, the lack that destabilizes the structural, symbolic totality. As a result, moreover, the symbolic order itself appears to function only on the basis of this exception, this peculiar instability, this excess—as though the very rule of law somehow depended upon a level of malfunction and perverse enjoyment (what Freud called the "death drive," and what Lacan formulates in terms of *jouissance*). Now this is precisely how the prison seems to function in relation to the "criminal element" that it supposedly aims at eliminating. For the prison acts not simply as a limit or prohibition "preventing" crime, but carries within it a perverse productivity, a level of sadistic enjoyment that Kafka represented so well, by generating the illusion that behind the mechanical operation of a neutral, anonymous, bureaucratic law there lay an obscure level of sadistic enjoyment, a peculiar agency that *wants* the criminal to exist, in order to have the pleasure of inflicting punishment. This Other who is imagined to enjoy is one aspect of the father, a perverse manifestation Lacan gestures toward with the word "père-version." This is the point of *jouissance* that marks the excess that always accompanies the law, a dimension of subjectivity that Freud called "primary masochism." This excess is not a natural phenomenon, a primordial force that disrupts the polished machinery of culture; it is rather a peculiar feature of culture itself, an effect of language, which includes its own malfunction—the "remainder" or "trace" of what did not exist before the institution of the law, but remains outside, excluded, in an "a priori" fashion that is logical rather than chronological. This is what Lacan understands as the relation between the symbolic and the real.

THE MYTH OF ORIGINS AND THE ORIGIN OF MYTH

Freud explains this relation between the law and transgression in *Totem and Taboo*, by giving us two equiprimordial aspects of the father. This conception of the paternal function does not simply reduce to the figure of prohibition or law, as is so often said, but reveals a primordial split by which the law is originally tied to a perversion of the law. We should note here that in this text, which seeks to account for *the origin of the law*, Freud does not conceive of desire as a natural fact that would eventually, with the advent of culture, come to be organized by various prohibitions. He does not seek, in other words, to provide a genesis, a genetic narrative, in which the law would be subsequent to desire, like the imposition of a convention or social contract upon what would otherwise be a natural impulse; nor, conversely, does he follow the usual historicist argument according to which desire is simply the product of the law, the effect of various cultural prohibitions. Freud's account in effect abandons the genetic narrative and gives us instead an account of the origin that is strictly and rigorously mythical. That is the radicality of *Totem and Taboo*.

Freud's mythic account thus gives us two simultaneous functions for the father: one is the father of the law, the giver of language and symbolic exchange, the father who represents the limiting function of castration; the other is the father of the Primal Horde, the mythical figure who, before he is murdered, possesses all the women, and is therefore outside the law, the one whose enjoyment has no limit, who does not rule with the even hand of disinterested justice, but rather takes an obscene pleasure in arbitrary punishment, using us for his sport, devouring his children like Chronos, feeding his limitless appetite on our sacrifices and enjoying the pure expression of his will. This is "the dark god," as Lacan puts it: not the Christian god of love and forgiveness, who keeps together the sheepish flock of the human community, but the god of terror and indifferent violence, the god of Abraham and Job, so much more clearly grasped in the Judaic tradition.[28]

THE SYMBOLIC AND THE REAL

We can therefore see in Freud the same relation between prohibition and this peculiar excess, between the law and violence, that Foucault develops in his remarks on power. This explains why Foucault argues that the contemporary experience of sexuality is a central place in which the relation between law and transgression demands to be rethought, beyond the legislative, prohibitive conception that characterizes modernity. This obscure, symptomatic twist by which the law is bound to its own transgression, to a dimension of excess, violence, and suffering, can perhaps be seen in its most conspicuous form in

America. With all its defiant freedom and carefree self-indulgence, America does not show itself as the land of freedom and pleasure, but may be said to display the most obscene form of superego punishment: You must enjoy, you must be young and healthy and happy and tan and beautiful. The question, "What must I do?" has been replaced with the higher law of the question: "Are we having fun yet?" That is American Kantianism: "Think whatever you like, choose your religion freely, speak out in any way you wish, but you must have fun!"[29] The reverse side of this position, the guilt that inhabits this ideal of pleasure, is clear enough: Don't eat too much, don't go out in the sun, don't drink or smoke, or you won't be able to enjoy yourself!

Žižek argues that racism is another symptom in which the moral law reveals its dependence on this excess: the reason given for hating the Jews is that they have too much money; blacks have too much fun; the gay community has too much sex; and so on. The belief that the law sets a limit to pleasure will always produce a locus in which the "stolen" pleasure resides, a place where we can locate the "original" satisfaction that has supposedly been given up, or "lost": namely, in the other—or in the paranoia that confuses the other with the Other of *jouissance*. The myth of an original state of nature, a natural plenitude that was lost when we agreed to sign the social contract, would thus be linked by psychoanalysis to the mythology that is always constructed in order for racism to operate.)

Thus, as Foucault argues in his thesis on power, it is not a matter of overcoming repression, of liberating pleasure from moral constraint, or defending the insane against the oppressive regime of psychiatry, but of undoing the structure that produced these two related sides. Such is the distance between the Kantian position and that of Foucault and Lacan: the law no longer serves as a juridical or prohibitive limit, but as a force, an imperious agency that does not simply limit, but *produces an excess* that Kant did not theorize, a dimension of punishment and tyranny that it was meant to eliminate.[30] This is the kind of logic addressed by Foucault when he asks, for example, whether the very failure of the prison as an institution, the malfunction of the law, the fact that the prison seems to be a machine for organizing and proliferating criminality, is not in fact part of the very functioning of the prison, so that the law includes this excess which seems on the surface to contradict it. Lacan puts Kant together with Sade in order to show the logical relation between them, in the same way that we might speak of the obscure relation between the Rights of Man and the Reign of Terror—two formations which, from an imaginary point of view, are completely opposed and antithetical, but which turn out to have an obscure connection.

In Lacan's terminology, the establishment of the symbolic law, the (systemic) totalization of a signifying structure, cannot take place without producing a remainder, an excess that marks the limit of formalization. Something similar occurs in Foucault: where the Kantian formulation gives us an anthropology, a form of consciousness that is able, freely, to give itself its own law, and thereby to realize its essence, Foucault speaks instead of an apparatus that produces the criminal, the insane, and the destitute, all *in the name of the law*—so that the excess of Sade is the strict counterpart of Kant, and not his contradiction or antithesis. It should come as no surprise that Foucault mentions, in his account of Kant's text "What Is Enlightenment?" that it raises, among other things, the question of "making a place for Jewish culture within German thought." This text, which Kant wrote in response to a question that had been answered two months earlier by Moses Mendelssohn, is part of Kant's effort to elaborate a "cosmopolitan view" of history, in which the promise of a community of Man would be maintained; it is thus, according to Foucault, "perhaps a way of announcing the acceptance of a common destiny." And yet, as Foucault points out, history produced for us a paradoxical perversion of this common destiny. Contrary to everything Kant might have hoped for, Foucault remarks, "we now know to what drama that was to lead."[31] It is this product, this excess, this remainder which accompanies the very morality meant to exclude it, that Foucault addresses by his formulation of power as a relationship that does not take the form of justice and law (nor, we might add, of *mere* tyranny, mere "force" or exploitation, the simple "opposite" of law), but is rather a productive force, an agency of perpetual malfunction, by which the law of language never arrives without those corporeal effects that Lacan calls *jouissance*.[32]

CONCLUSION

The canonical reception of Foucault has stressed two aspects of his work: on the one hand, its contribution to theory or method (the theory of power or discourse or sexuality, the method of archaeology or genealogy), and on the other hand, its status as historical knowledge, and thus its contribution to the current return to history that is sometimes regarded as an antidote to structuralism. There are good reasons for insisting on these two aspects of his work, and both play an important role in his thinking. But it would be hasty to pretend that "theory" and "history" can be given the status that is so quickly attributed to them today. For as we have argued, Foucault refuses to lay claim to a meta-language (a "theory of power," for example, or an "archaeological method" that would function as a transcendental framework, surveying history from above, as if it had no place of birth and paid no heed to its own historical conditions, it own position of enunciation). He also refuses to present his documentary material as "knowledge about the past," in the mode in which the discipline of history traditionally presents itself.

As a result, the canonical story about Foucault, which is organized around the twin axes of "theory" and "history," can only proceed if it represses several crucial features of his thought: above all (1) its status as a "history of the present" (as opposed to knowledge about the past); (2) its interest in the "limits of formalization" (as opposed to the systematic aims of structuralist thought); and (3) its explicitly "fictional" character. Each of these features in Foucault's work can be clarified through a parallel with Lacanian psychoanalysis. The first issue can be formulated in terms of the "position of enunciation." Here, Foucault is seen to aim more at disrupting the place of the speaking subject—namely, our current arrangement of knowledge—than at producing an account of the past. The second issue can be formulated in terms of what Lacan calls "the real," namely, a traumatic element that has no imaginary or symbolic form, which is lacking any representation, but that haunts the systemic organization of conscious thought, marking its incompleteness, the impossibility of its closure, as madness marks the stories that are told about madness. Here, Foucault is regarded as aiming neither at a "structural linguistics" (the so-called archaeological period, in which an object such as madness would be nothing more than what discourse produces), nor at a "return to history" (the so-called genealogy, in which a narrative would unfold the various constructions that have developed around madness), but rather as aiming to encounter the "real" in a Lacanian sense—to provoke the destabilization of our contemporary arrangement of knowledge by touching on the elements of trauma within it (such as "transgression," in his early work, or "sexuality" in his later work). Finally, the third issue, "fiction," obliges us to stress the degree to which Foucault's work presented itself as a kind of action, a kind of praxis or intervention, rather than as a "documentary" form of knowledge. Here, the status of Foucault's "historical" research comes very close to the "fictions" produced in the course of analysis. This point also makes it possible to give more weight to the references Foucault constantly made to works of art, references that have always been slighted (and not by accident) by those who have wished to present his work either as "positive historical research" or as a new methodology or meta-language.

This does not mean that Foucault and Lacan coincide in every respect—far from it. But it does suggest that these two thinkers cannot simply be opposed to one another (as if Foucault simply hated psychoanalysis and regarded it as one more confessional discourse, or as if Lacan was simply an ahistorical thinker whose work had no bearing on the structures of human time and the peculiar contemporary formations of the law). If, in the canonical reception, Lacan and Foucault have been conveniently opposed to one another, our brief remarks might serve to intervene in that narrative, and allow us to address their relation in a way that does greater justice to its complexity.

And finally, if it is indeed the case that Foucault's work is animated at its deepest philosophical level by an effort to think differently, to pursue a mode of thought that—for all its impressive theoretical rigor, and for all its meticulous documentary detail—remains at its heart irreducible to either theory or history, and somehow closer to fiction, open in its core to a conceptual movement, and directed always to those points in our own conceptual framework that are no longer secure, no longer convincing or animated by life; if indeed Foucault's work in this sense is a writing aimed at the real, then his work can no longer be adequately grasped either as a form of historical knowledge (as the new historicism sometimes pretends, hoping to make Foucault an ally in their effort to document the contingent formation of the world), or as one more form of transcendental reflection (as is commonly said whenever Foucault is characterized as a "structuralist" or "archaeologist"), then it might be said that in this respect, too, Foucault's work, like psychoanalysis, amounts to a displacement of the common alternative between the "universalism" of theory and the "particularism" of history—the very terms that have been most frequently mobilized in the reception of Foucault. This curious mechanism, in which "reception" is at the same time a "forgetting," should come as no surprise. For in fact, the alternative between structure and history, natural essence and cultural construction, is now sufficiently old, sufficiently comfortable and familiar, that we settle into it quite placidly today, taking refuge from thought, and mobilizing instead (as if it were a sign of life) all those welcome and customary passions with which "essentialism" and "historicism" are currently invested—allowing these dying forces to wage their tired war yet one more time, to raise their voices within us, where they continue to denounce one another from the height of their increasingly tedious moral conviction, as if no other story could be told. And having thus settled into their comfortable roles, historicism and essentialism hurl their well-worn accusations back and forth at one another, enjoying their exchange, and even winking occasionally at one another, as if, beneath all the tumult and noise, they were quite calm and content, as though admitting after all that in their very opposition to one another, they share a common ground, enjoying their old game, and perhaps even celebrating a certain friendship in rehearsing this debate—like their grandparents, the *Geisteswissenschaften* and *Naturewissenschaften*, who taught them how to play.

In the midst of this conversation, Foucault's laughter would hardly be welcome. A certain air of seriousness is necessary if this opposition is to be maintained, so that these old passions can keep some semblance of their force. We can therefore understand why the "theoretical" and "historical" aspects of Foucault's work are so easily digested today, and made so central to our reception of his work, allowing us, as they do, to channel our truths along the familiar pathways, where structure and history, like nature and culture, sex and gender, all play their accustomed parts. These debates have also provided an easy framework for the reception of psychoanalysis, even (or perhaps especially) if they produce conflicting accounts, in which psychoanalysis is at one and the same time a radical version of social construction, and a regressive form of naturalism—two accounts that share a common horizon, insofar as they have both agreed in advance that the language of psychoanalysis ("desire," the "body," "sexual difference," and so on) must first be translated into more familiar terms, before we can enjoy our disagreements about it. It is no surprise that Foucault's work has likewise been translated, recast in the form of a mythical narrative which neatly divides it in half, so that the archaeological aspect of his work can be assigned to a specific period of the narrative, and construed as "structuralist" and "ahistorical," while the genealogical work could be neatly separated off, and registered as a "return to history" in which the earlier work is somehow repudiated. Such a narrative labor of translation and splitting is not unfamiliar to psychoanalysis, and it has certainly made for an easier reception of Foucault's work. But this story has also allowed us to overlook in his writing what would otherwise disrupt us—above all, the laughter that animates it, and the fiction in which it takes root: "The uneasiness that makes us laugh when we read Borges," Foucault writes, "is certainly related to the profound distress of those whose language has been destroyed" (*OT*, xix). Our language, too, has suffered a dislocation, even if it continues to repeat familiar slogans, investing them with all the passions of the past, and presenting them as new discoveries. From a genealogical point of view, the debate between nature and culture as it functions in contemporary discourse could thus be seen as a way of "translating" psychoanalysis, concealing and even forgetting it, so that anxiety might be kept at bay. For it is just this uneasiness and anxiety, emphasized by Foucault, that hover at the edge of contemporary thought, and make it so easy for us to go to sleep in the face of psychoanalysis, preferring to rely on exhausted narratives, in which psychoanalysis either demonstrates for once and for all the new truth about the "social construction of subjectivity," or fails to live up to this truth, adhering instead to a regressive and unacknowledged "naturalism," an account of "sexual difference" that somehow appears to be ahistorical. We can hardly mind the repetition of these new "discoveries" and "proofs," particularly when they carry such an aura of old friendship. And the fact that these debates only obscure what is most unfamiliar—and most historically momentous—about Freud's work, is hardly cause for alarm. For it means, of course, that psychoanalysis has a future.

Afterword

Rediscovering Drive in Freud

An Interview with Charles Shepherdson, by Jessica Miller
for The Psychoanalytic Institute of New England (PINE)

JESSICA MILLER: Can you say a bit about your interest in psychoanalysis in the context of your background as an academician, particularly your training in philosophy.

CHARLES SHEPHERDSON: Initially, my exposure to Freud was slight. I had read certain canonical texts and enjoyed them, but it was really only after reading Lacan, whom I encountered through a phenomenology institute in Italy, that I began to study Freud very seriously. This is one of the great advantages of Lacan—one of his gifts to psychoanalysis, really—that he forces his readers to go back to the actual text of Freud. One can't simply refer to concepts, like the superego or the unconscious, as if their meaning were obvious simply because they are basic terms in Freud. Later figures in the history of psychoanalysis often seem to use Freud's terms fairly easily, as if they had an established or canonical sense, but they become mysterious and obscure in Lacan, and one has to go back and puzzle over the details that he points to in Freud's writing. This impetus for close reading fit very easily with my academic training. So my path to psychoanalysis was a little indirect. I did my doctoral work in literature, and specifically on poetry, but at the time when French theory was hitting the academic scene in the United States. Everybody was reading Heidegger and Derrida and Foucault—what eventually became "postmodernism." My literature program had a very conservative heritage, and didn't deal with these developments, which was fortunate, because it meant that I had to go to the philosophy department to learn about this new material. And it turned out to be one of the best programs for continental philosophy in the country, so I was lucky. Instead of reading second- and third-hand accounts, as literary critics often do, I was forced to read Kant and Husserl and Heidegger, and this made an enormous difference when I eventually encountered Lacan. The analytic community doesn't normally have this philosophical background, though there are some important exceptions. This is one of the difficulties facing psychoanalysis, I think: as far as the French analytic tradition is concerned, philosophers are the best prepared to tackle it, yet there has been very little by way of interface between the two fields. Literary theory and film theory have done much more than philosophy to absorb Lacan, but it has happened in a haphazard fashion. I think the American reception of Lacan has been crippled partly by this. It was received in a nonclinical domain, without a clear sense of what was conceptually at stake. Then there is the foreignness of the French philosophical tradition, in this country.

JM: Well, Lacan is so involved in a dialogue with Freud. Plus he is speaking very specifically about the clinical encounter. Can you explain then what is it about Lacan's interpretation of Freud which has captured the focus of the academicians?

CS: For me, reading Freud invariably meant reading him as a philosopher, a theorist of consciousness and subjectivity, a theorist of representation and meaning. Descartes and Kant talked about these things. Of course the Freudian unconscious was a new development, and for the academic community Lacan gave people the opportunity to talk about desire, the body, and sexuality, which was a very important development. But for me, the unconscious was simply another philosophical category to deal with. And for academics generally, I think Freudian concepts have basically been incorporated in terms of the disciplines that were willing to read him, whether it was film or anthropology or literature. But then, when I went to the École Freudienne in Paris, and later to the Australian Centre for Psychoanalysis in Melbourne, I heard Lacan discussed from a more clinical perspective. This gave me a very different view of Lacan, and took me back to Freud in a different way. I now find it difficult to address the material without thinking in clinical terms. This doesn't mean my earlier philosophical concerns were inappropriate, but only that I had a new sense of the extreme tension and discontinuity between philosophy and psychoanalysis as disciplines or modes of knowledge.

JM: For clinicians, then, what might be the link between Freud and philosophy?

CS: I think it's a question of understanding clearly what psychoanalysis is as a specific form of knowledge. I taught last year at Emory University in the Psychoanalytic Studies Program. It's an academic program, with people from various departments, but there is also a Psychoanalytic Institute there, connected with the university hospital, which trains analytic candidates. This is fairly rare. The institutes have mainly kept themselves isolated from university life, so analysts have not had to deal directly with the theoretical developments that have produced such an enormous upheaval in the academy. At the same time, academics have very little exposure to the clinical side of psychoanalysis. Both sides have suffered from this isolation, I think, but for clinicians it has perhaps been especially damaging. They haven't been obliged to theorize in a rigorous or developed way, and practice can easily become its own safe haven, where one works by intuition, as if the conceptual detail were merely academic or not really relevant; but this protection from the university also means that the clinical community hasn't had the opportunity to develop a strong account of what they are doing, and present that account to the public. I think this is why the atmosphere of analytic work is so besieged today— between psychopharmacology and all kinds of psychotherapeutic practices, it isn't very clear what precisely defines the psychoanalytic enterprise. And on the academic side, because we mainly have so little exposure to the clinical aspects of analysis, it is very easy for the analytic terminology to be quickly displaced onto other fields, where it can be extremely fertile, but also tends to lose its conceptual specificity. The situation at Emory began to break this down, and it's a very healthy thing, but there's still a lot of confusion and misunderstanding, and a lot that needs to be explored.

JM: I think this is a dilemma with many unfortunate ramifications.

Psychoanalysts have reasons to keep private the clinical domain but what has happened is that culturally they are completely isolated, and they have formed a closed world unto themselves. Many people outside of this circle don't realize that psychoanalysis still exists. I get asked fairly frequently, when I have an occasion to identify myself as a psychoanalyst, even sometimes in clinical circles, "Is that still done?"

CS: Yes. So what we have is people working in the academy, in the biomedical model, and in various models from cultural studies, and then the clinical practice of analysis, which is isolated from academic life, and which has thereby avoided the obligation—and also the opportunity—to identify its own domain more rigorously. In Europe, there are departments of psychoanalysis in universities—you can get a Ph.D. in psychoanalysis—but there is no such thing in the United States. As a result, psychoanalysis is measured by reference to paradigms from medicine or literary study that distort its specificity. We hear that Freudian theory is a "pseudo-science,' as if it aimed to be a science like medicine, or that it's a form or philosophy or social theory.

JM: Furthermore, how is a Freudian theory to be distinguished from other kinds of therapy that we don't call psychoanalysis? The psychoanalysts themselves may believe that they have adequately addressed this question, but in terms of public perception, I don't think that's the case. Perhaps we could use your discussion of anorexia to illustrate the tensions which exist between the separate intellectual approaches and the need to identify the uniquely psychoanalytic endeavor.

CS: When I began to try to think clinically, anorexia seemed like precisely the kind of example that would help define the psychoanalytic approach to embodiment. The "body" in anorexia is not simply a biological phenomenon—there are physical symptoms, but it isn't a matter of organic causality, as in most medical diseases. So, anorexia enables us to distinguish between the "body" and the "organism." Lacan insisted that our relation to the symbolic order—language and representation—gives the human being a body that cannot be adequately grasped through natural laws. That's in Freud too, and it's basic to the phenomenological tradition of European philosophy. But it's hard to see clearly what it means. In the academic world, many people who object to scientific naturalism argue that our psychic and physical existence is socially formed, shaped by conventions and beliefs that change over time, and vary from culture to culture. There's a somewhat tedious debate between scientific arguments that appeal to biology, and arguments that stress the social construction of subjectivity—including anorexia. People have argued that anorexia is a twentieth-century construction, generated by images of women, fashion magazines, and certain cultural ideals of femininity. This nature-nurture alternative is a dominant framework for debate today. It's used to discuss everything—race, homosexuality, depression, intelligence, and so on. But it seems to me that anorexia doesn't belong on either side of this debate. It's a symptom that escapes biomedical causality, and is also irreducible to the accounts of subjectivity that cultural studies rely on. So psychoanalysis ought to be able to provide a distinctive theoretical account—of both subjectivity and embodiment—that would break with this alternative.

JM: So, what might be the distinctive theoretical position of psychoanalysis within the nature-nurture debate? Or rather, not within it perhaps, but beyond it?

CS: The *DSM* manual notes that anorexia is far more common among women whose sisters and mothers are anorexic than it is in the general population. This doesn't mean it's genetic. But it suggests that it isn't merely a general "social" phenomenon. Lacan highlights the family structure, and speaks of a symbolic inheritance—a nonbiological transmission of anorexia. It isn't just a question of the particular woman, in relation to cultural ideals of femininity. It's an inheritance that passes symbolically from mother to daughter, around the question of femininity. So "femininity" is neither a biological concept, nor a broadly social construction, but something more particular to the mother-daughter relation, like a dialect specific to the family, where the signifiers for femininity are handed down. This requires its own theoretical articulation, and this is where psychoanalysis has something really radical and distinctive to offer.

JM: I'm still not following the distinguishing aspect of psychoanalysis. Why can't language and symbolic transmission be subsumed by theories of social construction?

CS: Partly because accounts of the general social milieu can't explain why one subject rather than another becomes anorexic. Many women are exposed to the cultural representations, but they aren't all anorexic. It's a question of the particularity of the subject. And psychoanalysis also has the concept of the drive, which we don't find in social theory. If we want to be more precise about anorexia, we have to say that it's a question of the oral drive. When Freud distinguishes between the instinct and the drive—which Lacan always insisted on—it was in order to isolate a bodily phenomenon that doesn't follow biology. The drive is not an instinct.

JM: Because the instinct is a biological mechanism . . . ?

CS: Exactly. In anorexia, the oral drive appears as a refusal to eat. It's exactly opposed to hunger, the biological instinct of self-preservation. It's the same with reproduction: the sexual drive is not governed by the instinct to reproduce. Freud's discovery was to show that sexuality in the human is denatured, it doesn't follow a developmental path directed toward procreation. It shows up through the transformed reality that representations make possible, which is why "sexuality" in Freud's sense is a uniquely human problem, distinct from biological sex. The animal knows what to do, and we don't. That's also why there is a history of sexuality—it's not so tightly bound to the mechanisms of evolution. So the symptom in anorexia is a "sexual" symptom in that sense. It's an oral drive that cuts against the grain of nature, disrupting the instinct and causing an unnatural or nonbiological suffering. And we might also add that there is a paradoxical "pleasure" in this suffering—there is "oral *jouissance*" in anorexia, Lacan says, a kind of deadly "satisfaction" that is uniquely human.

JM: So far your discussion of the oral drive seems straight out of Freud. Does Lacan re-work the concept of drive in any way which could counter the accusation that "drive" is reductionistic, so frequently used as an excuse for its dismissal?

CS: I think Lacan's terminological innovations are a way of clarifying what is already in Freud. Lacan distinguishes between need, demand, and desire. These are not really Freudian terms, but they try to articulate what Freud was saying.

JM: I think the distinction between need, demand, and desire is so useful to consider clinically. Can you expand on this?

CS: Well, let's take these terms in relation to anorexia and the oral drive. "Need" is a biological category; it designates the organic necessity for food. "Demand" involves the relation to the other. When the child asks for food, the need of the organism may be fulfilled, but the child is also asking for love. So the term "demand" isolates this aspect and distinguishes it from "need." To put it very simply, demand is a demand for love, for recognition from the other, which is sought when the child asks for food. So what is the child really eating, when it eats—or when it refuses to eat?

JM: It's a very useful terminology in regard to the object relation, because the object of need is "milk," while the object of demand is "the breast."

CS: Yes, and usually the two objects go together. But anorexia is an oral demand in which the need of the organism is compromised. But demand has more than one side to it, because in one sense the demand for food is a form of speech, a verbal demand addressed to the other, but in another sense it has a corporeal dimension, since demand is not only addressed to the other, but is also an oral demand for an object. And the object, food, is no longer a natural object, but a symbolic one—it carries within it the other's love. So when we talk about the relation to the breast, we are talking about this strange, ambiguous relation between the body and speech, the oral satisfaction of the body and the symbolic relation to the other. In anorexia, something in the symbolic relation to the other has gone wrong, and has consequences at the level of the body. The "oral demand" has been somatized, rather than verbalized, and it compromises the needs of the organism.

JM: This is a psychoanalytically derived conception of "conflict" beyond the notions of thematic conflict or a conflict of affects. It's not even a conflict of drives. It's a conflict between drive and something else; between drive and desire.

CS: Yes, you can say that anorexia is a somatized demand, in which the subject's desire is compromised. Instead of having access to her desire, the anorexic is stuck in this oral demand, and we see a kind of repetition compulsion, where nothing else is possible for her. And the symptom is condensed around the question of femininity. Eugénie Lemoine-Luccioni has a beautiful formulation in which she says it is "a 'No' addressed to the mother" (no period, no breasts, no maternity, etc.). This "No" is an oral demand which appears, not as speech, but as a bodily symptom in which her desire is sacrificed. That's the oral drive—a somatized demand. And desire is what appears "beyond demand," Lacan says. It's really a reformulation of what we find in Freud. What matters for psychoanalysis is that even the most elementary, preverbal relation to food is not a matter of naturalistic "nurturing," but is already a relation to the other, a demand that is either answered or not—a demand that allows the child to encounter the mother's desire.

JM: In this case, are you referring to the mother's desire to feed her child or not, as construed by the child? Is the mother's desire then the child's formulation in answer to the enigma of what the mother wants?

CS: Well, I was trying to get at what you said about the object-relation. When the child is fed, it isn't just a question of "nurturing" in a naturalistic sense. And it isn't just a question of demand either. When the child is fed, it always encounters the mother's desire—through her attention, her neglect, her obsessive overconcern, her perfect comfortableness—in all sorts of ways. But Lacan says that the mother's desire appears, not as her love for the child, or her desire to feed the child, but at the point where the child isn't the only object of attention for her. That's the point when the child faces the enigma of what the mother wants. The famous "lack" that Lacan talks about emerges in this experience where demand is not always answered, and the child shows aggression, or passivity, or other sorts of responses to this lack. It's not a lack at the level of the child's "needs," as if it involved a "deficit." It's not the lack of a "real" object, and it's not a bad lack, a deficiency. In fact, it's only this encounter with the mother's desire that allows the child to separate from her, and move beyond its demand for love. That emergence of subjectivity is what development—if you want to use the word—means, and not anything naturalistic. In that sense, the child's desire depends on the desire of the mother.

JM: But you were also saying something about the object.

CS: Lacan says that the anorexic is "eating the nothing." The "object" of the oral drive is not food, but "the nothing." The anorexic is trying to introduce a lack where it hasn't been sufficiently established—and it happens at the level of the body. The desire of the mother, which is where lack appears, hasn't registered for the child, who is therefore stuck in demand. And this has corporeal consequences. The anorexic wants a lack to be introduced, and as long as it isn't there, she is stuck trying to make a lack appear, and her desire is lost. That's why Lacan says desire depends on the "object of lack." It's an "object" because it all happens at the level of the body, not just "psychologically." As long as she is stuck with this oral demand for "the nothing," desire remains impossible for her, and, there are all sorts of bodily consequences, in perceptual distortion, body image, and so on. I heard a Lacanian, Paola Mieli, speaking in New York last week about something similar in body-piercing, tattooing, self-cutting, cosmetic surgery, and other corporeal incisions. That's the difference between the human and the animal—the human body depends on this "object of lack," and if it doesn't get registered, the body can't emerge, and desire is compromised. For me, one of the real enigmas is how all this relates to sexual difference.

Notes

INTRODUCTION

1. Already the first sentence of this book must therefore be reconsidered—as the epigraph suggests.

2. I have developed this argument in more detail in "The Epoch of the Body: Need and Demand in Kojève and Lacan," *Perspectives on Embodiment: The Intersections of Nature and Culture*, ed. Gail Weiss and Honi Fern Haber (New York: Routledge, 1999), 183–211.

3. These remarks are developed in chapters three and four, and also in an earlier article that was preparatory to this book, "Vital Signs: The Place of Memory in Psychoanalysis," *Research in Phenomenology* [special issue, "Spaces of Memory"] 23 (1993): 22–72.

4. On the emergence of biology as a discipline, see William Coleman, *Biology in the Nineteenth Century: Problems of Form, Function and Transformation* (New York: Wiley and Sons, 1971), and Georges Canguilhem, *A Vital Rationalist: Selected Writings from Georges Canguilhem*, ed. François Delaporte (New York: Zone Books, 1994), especially "Epistemology of Biology," 67–90. On the emergence of history as a discipline, see Maurice Mandelbaum's magisterial book *History, Man, and Reason: A Study in Nineteenth-Century Thought* (Baltimore: Johns Hopkins University Press, 1971); Georg G. Iggers, *The German Conception of History: The National Tradition of Historical Thought from Herder to the Present* (Middletown, CT: Wesleyan University Press, 1968); and Friedrich Meinecke, *Historism: The Rise of a New Historical Outlook*, trans. J. E. Anderson with a foreword by Sir Isaiah Berlin (London: Routledge and Kegan Paul, 1972).

5. In making this claim, as he does in *The Order of Things: An Archae-*

ology of the Human Sciences, trans. Alan Sheridan (New York: Random House, 1970), Foucault is clearly following Merleau-Ponty. See Maurice Merleau-Ponty, "Phenomenology and the Sciences of Man," in *The Primacy of Perception: and other essays on phenomenological psychology, the philosophy of art, history, and politics*, ed. with an introd. by James M. Edie (Evanston, IL: Northwestern University Press, 1964).

6. Michel Foucault, *The Birth of the Clinic: An Archaeology of Medical Perception*, trans. Alan Sheridan (New York: Random House, 1973).

7. Monique David-Ménard, *Hysteria from Freud to Lacan: Body and Language in Psychoanalysis*, trans. Catherine Porter (Ithaca, NY: Cornell University Press, 1989).

8. I have discussed Freud's early text on organic and hysterical paralysis further in "*Adaequatio Sexualis*: Is There a Measure of Sexual Difference?" *From Phenomenology to Thought, Errancy, and Desire: Essays in Honor of William J. Richardson, S.J.*, ed. Babette Babich (Dordrecht: Kluwer, 1995), 447–73.

CHAPTER 1

1. Paris: Seuil, 1976. *The Dividing of Women or Woman's Lot*, trans. Marie-Laure Davenport and Marie-Christine Réguis (London: Free Association Books, 1987). See the article by Lemoine-Luccioni excerpted as "The Fable of the Blood" in *Returning to Freud: Clinical Psychoanalysis in the School of Lacan*, ed. and trans. by Stuart Schneiderman (New Haven, CT: Yale, 1980). References will be to this translation and will appear in the text.

2. *Diagnostic and Statistical Manual of Mental Disorders*, Third Edition (Washington, D.C.: American Psychiatric Association, 1980), 67 (emphasis mine). They also note that the disorder is found 95 percent of the time in females, and that it carries a mortality rate of 15–21 percent, adding that "many of the adolescents have delayed psychosexual development, and adults have a markedly decreased interest in sex."

3. In the interview "Questions," Irigaray writes: "When I speak of the *relation to the mother*, I mean that in our patriarchal culture the daughter is absolutely unable to control her relation to her mother. Nor can the woman control her relation to maternity, unless she reduces herself to that role alone." Luce Irigaray, *Ce sex qui n'en est*

pas un (Paris: Minuit, 1977). *This Sex Which Is Not One*, trans. Catherine Porter (Ithaca, NY: Cornell, 1985). References will henceforth appear in the text, French pagination first, English second, here, 140/143. Translations are occasionally modified.

4. This is a point that has been made both by Joan Copjec, in "Cutting Up," in *Between Feminism and Psychoanalysis*, ed. Theresa Brennan (London: Routledge, 1989), 227–46, and by Jacqueline Rose, in *Sexuality in the Field of Vision* (London: Verso, 1986); see "Feminism and the Psychic," esp. 7–9, and "Femininity and Its Discontents," esp. 83–93.

5. I have tried to show elsewhere why the analogy between the term "symbolic order" and the idea of "sociohistorical conditions" is seriously flawed *from the psychoanalytic point of view* (which is not to say its use in other ways is illegitimate, but only that the distinction between the psychoanalytic understanding of the symbolic and that of cultural studies must be acknowledged), in "On Fate: Psychoanalysis and the Desire to Know," in *Dialectic and Narrative*, ed. Tom Flynn and Dalia Judowitz (New York: State University of New York Press, 1991), 271–302.

6. See *This Sex*, 45–49, 135–38/45–49, 136–40, and *Le Corps-a-corps avec la mere* (Montreal: La Pleine Lune, 1981).

7. Eleanor Kuykendall, for example, writes: "The ethical imperative that Irigaray would draw . . . is to cease to pursue the psychic separation between mother and daughter required by partiarchy," and to "consider the possibility of a matriarchal ethic to replace that patriarchal imperative to separate mother and daughter." "Toward an ethic of nurturance: Luce Irigaray on Mothering and Power," in *Mothering: Essays in Feminist Theory*, ed. Joyce Trebilcot (Totowa, NJ: Rowman and Allanheld, 1984), 269. I would argue virtually the opposite: in our culture, the more pressing need is to make possible a place for the "woman" that does not reduce to that of the "mother."

8. As Margaret Whitford—whom I would like to thank here for a number of helpful remarks on a draft of this paper, and for her generous encouragement—has written, "there is no suggestion that communities of women . . . will automatically be idyllic." In fact, she says, "women suffer from an inability to individuate themselves, from [what Irigaray, in *L'Ethique de la difference sexual* (Paris: Minuit, 1984), calls] 'confusion of identity between them.' . . . The problem

is well known from Nancy Chodorow's work, but Chodorow and Irigaray are quite different. . . . Irigaray accepts the clinical view that women have difficulty in separating from their mothers. However, she presents this psychoanalytic data as a symptom in the symbolic order. She argues that the clinical picture also applies to metaphysics; *in metaphysics too*, women are not individuated: *there is only the place of the mother*" (110–12, italics mine). See "Rereading Irigaray," in *Between Feminism and Psychoanalysis*, 106–26. For some brief remarks on Chodorow and Lacan, see Toril Moi, "Patriarchal Thought and the Drive for Knowledge," in the same volume, 189–205.

9. We recall Freud's remark, in "Some Observations Towards a Comparative Study of Organic and Hysterical Paralysis" (1888), that the hysterical symptom itself does not follow the lines of anatomy, but rather those of *ordinary language*: what is paralyzed, he notes, is "the arm as far up as the shoulder," or the common *idea* (one might say image) of the parts of the body. Does the symptom in its nonorganic determination, then, correspond to the *image* of the body, or to the *language*?

10. This is not to say, "Anne-Marie is a lesbian," just like that (it is not what she says, either). Rather, there is a question *there*, which is also *refused*: child (not yet "woman") or mother (but not "woman") or even man (that is: not "woman," see note 23)—this is the series of responses among which Anne-Marie vacillates. In other words, one must not reduce her *question* to a *choice*, for this is precisely what she has attempted to do by marrying—a solution that does not close the case. The point is, then, that hysteria and homosexuality are not one and the same (see "Man or Woman?" below). This is why it is correct to insist that a woman can love another woman as a woman, but also why it is incorrect to say that psychoanalysis treats homosexuality as if one partner were always in effect "masculine," and the other "feminine."

11. One might place here the remarks by women, either pregnant or with infants, to the effect that "Everyone has a right (or claims the right) to talk to you when you're pregnant." The child makes her "the mother"—as though with this "symbiosis," the woman is for a time not a particular person, *a* woman, any longer. This period disappears of course as soon as the child is old enough to appear as a "person."

12. The singular is used advisedly: It is a matter of the meaning given to *La femme*.

13. See Elizabeth Gross, "Philosophy, Subjectivity, and the Body: Kristeva and Irigaray," in *Feminist Challenges: Social and Political Theory*, ed. Carole Pateman and Elizabeth Gross (Boston: Northeastern University Press, 1987), 125–43. Irigaray "wishes," Gross writes, "to create discourses and representations of women and femininity that may positively inscribe the female body as an autonomous concrete materiality . . . Irigaray's aim is to destabilize the presumed norm . . . to speak about a positive model or series of representations of femininity," and her work therefore has "a political goal absent in Kristeva, the creation of autonomous images, models and representations of women and femininity" (138 and 143).

14. See section III, on the notion of the "future." Of course one might try to find an apparent "privilege" of the verbal *over* the image, here, which could then be shifted so as to imply a "privilege" of the symbolic *over* the imaginary (it is in fact never a question of such a hierarchy, since both elements are constitutive of the subject's very being), and one might then take such a view to imply, through another shift, a privilege of the father over the mother (it being assumed that the symbol and the image can be gendered in this way). This is Jane Gallop's concern in "Keys to Dora," *In Dora's Case: Freud, Hysteria, Feminism*, ed. Charles Bernheimer and Claire Kahane (New York: Columbia University Press, 1985), 200–20. But it should be clear that the relation between the image and the symbol is not (A) a relation in which it is a matter of choosing one over the other, since they are equiprimordial—both necessary, yet not identical to each other, nor (B) a relation that can be *narrated* according to a linear history in which the image would be *superceded* by the symbol. This view has also been used not only to misconstrue Irigaray as positing an autonomous and "prehistoric" femininity that might be recaptured; it has also been used, I think mistakenly, to interpret Kristeva's account of the relation between the semiotic and the symbolic.

15. I have written elsewhere (see note 5) on the word "limit," which marks the difference between the *totality* of the body given with the image, and the *unity* of the body given with the register of lack. This word plays a decisive but unacknowledged role in Lacan's text "The Rome Discourse," particularly in the second section, "Symbol and Language as Structure and Limit of the Field," and in the third section, where the link between "limit" and "death" is clearly marked. Jacqueline Rose has given some brief but precise remarks on this dis-

tinction in "The Imaginary," in *Sexuality in the Field of Vision*, where she discusses *unity* in connection with *repetition* and the topology of the torus. This topic is also addressed by Michèle Montrelay (see note 22).

16. Monique David-Ménard, *Hysteria from Freud to Lacan: Body and Language in Psychoanalysis*, trans. Catherine Porter (Ithaca, NY: Cornell University Press, 1989), 130–31.

17. Marie-Hélène Brousse has suggested, on this basis, the possibility of a relation between motherhood and the structure of perversion—an argument which would be worth pursuing here, and which she presented at the Kent State conference on psychoanalysis and literature in 1989 and 1990, and at the École Freudienne in Paris, in 1990.

18. Other instances of this "no exit" are possible: In her presentation of a case of transexualism at the Saint-Anne hospital in Paris, in 1990, Dr. Gorog stressed that her (anatomically male) client was not to be regarded as a man who wished to become a woman, but was rather a woman who was born into a man's body that she wished to be rid of. This is, at least as a starting point, a question of identification rather than of (biological) "truth." One central concern, for the analyst, was to *keep the question open*—neither to convince the subject that s/he should not want an operation (the attempt at "normalization"), nor simply to agree to the operation, since the details of the case (the subject as a child had been sexually abused by an uncle and male schoolteachers, and had a complex relationship with his grandmother, who held black masses and is connected with his belief that he is the reincarnation of Veronica Putnam, a Dutch witch) suggested that such an operation would not in fact resolve the client's problem, which appeared to be less a "hysteric's" problem of identification than a problem of psychosis. For such a subject, the possibility of the question is a crucial point of orientation, more important than a secure but entirely meaningless choice.

19. As Rosi Braidotti points out, the importance of the term "difference," in current discussions, has to do not simply with the critique of neuter subjectivity and the assertion of a difference between men and women; it also has to do with insisting upon differences between women. "The Politics of Ontological Difference," in *Between Feminism and Psychoanalysis*, 89–105.

20. Willy Apollon, Daniele Bergeron, and Lucy Cantin, on the basis of their work with psychotics in Quebec, have suggested that Marilyn Monroe's history was essentially that of a psychotic who protected

herself against a psychotic break by a precarious identification with "The Woman," an identification which was lost when her career began to unravel. Their work was presented at the Kent State conference on psychoanalysis and literature in 1989 and 1990.

21. See Catherine Millot, *Horsexe* (Paris: Point Hors Ligne, 1983), ch. 4. This is what Lacan, from a different starting point, proposes in *Encore* (Paris: Seuil, 1975), with the account of the feminine relation to the law, in which "universality" has a different function than for masculinity. See "A Love Letter," in *Feminine Sexuality*, ed. J. Mitchell and J. Rose (New York: Norton, 1982).

22. Michèle Montrelay, *L'Ombre et le nom* (Paris: Editions de Minuit, 1997), 119–46. See "The Story of Louise," in *Returning to Freud*, 75–93.

23. As Lacan puts it: "In this labor [of analysis] which [she] undertakes to reconstruct *for another*, [she] rediscovers the fundamental alienation that made [her] construct it *like another*, and which has always destined it to be taken from [her] *by another*" *E*, 249/42.

24. This point—her relation to the other—should be developed in connection with the idea of love, in particular transference-love (a topic crucial to Kristeva's recent work). At this juncture, the analysand prefers a relation of love and identification, both in regard to the new husband she has found during the course of analysis and in regard to the person of her analyst, to a relation of desire, since the latter would threaten the imaginary structure of her ego, which is beginning to decompose: That is the reason for the sudden anxiety she shows at the prospect of a continuation of the analysis. As there is not time to develop this here, let me only cite Freud's 1914 paper, "On Narcissism: An Introduction." Freud speaks here of "choosing a sexual ideal after the narcissistic type which possesses the excellences to which [she] cannot attain. This is the cure by love, which [she] generally prefers to cure-by-analysis . . . [she] usually brings expectations of this sort with [her] to the treatment and directs them toward the person of the physician. . . . [P]artially freed from [her] repressions . . . [she] withdraws from further treatment in order to choose a love-object, leaving [her] cure to be continued by a life with someone [she] loves. We might be satisfied with this result, if it did not bring with it all the dangers of a crippling dependence upon [her] helper in need" (*SE* 14: 91). See also Octave Mannoni, *Freud: The Theory of the Unconscious* (London: Verso, 1985), 134–38, et passim.

25. There are a number of complications that I have had to omit here, one of which is that, in her relation to men, Anne-Marie has also been able to adopt what she herself speaks of as the role of the man—another position that keeps to one side the question of her desire. "[S]he becomes virile" (66), Lemoine-Luccioni writes. "When she is not maternal, Anne-Marie becomes a man" (70).

26. See especially Freud's *Three Essays on the Theory of Sexuality* (*SE*, 7:123–245) and "The Instincts and Their Vicissitudes" (*SE*, 14:109–40). See also Jean Laplanche, *Life and Death in Psychoanalysis*, trans. Jeffrey Mehlman (Baltimore: Johns Hopkins, 1976), esp. chs. 1 and 2.

27. Janet Sayers has written that for Irigaray, "Femininity is essentially constituted by female biology"; Kate McKluskie has written that Irigaray puts forth an "anatomical determinism" and "is able to deny the need for language," thereby returning us to "the ghetto of inarticulate female intuition." It should no longer be possible to speak, as Lisa Jardine has recently done, of Irigaray's "reintroduction of feminine biology" or to call it, as she does, "a kind of essentialist strategy," which she then reproaches as a "catastrophe" that "reinforces all that has been oppressively said about women *as* body." This reading, which does not even understand in the most basic way what the word "body" means, is simply irresponsible, a non-reading, in which Irigaray is nowhere to be found. Janet Sayers, *Biological Politics: Feminist and Anti-Feminist Perspectives* (London: Tavistock, 1982). Kate McKluskie, "Women's Language and Literature: A Problem in Women's Studies," *Feminist Review* 14 (summer 1983). Lisa Jardine, "The Politics of Impenetrability," in *Between Feminism and Psychoanalysis*.

28. Although there is a relation between the self-regulation of the organism and the satisfaction of pleasure, one must be careful here not to collapse the idea of pleasure entirely into the idea of biological life functions: Freud makes a distinction between the interests of self-preservation and sexual libido very early, in order to indicate that pleasure is linked to a whole series of psychoanalytic problems that set it *against* the animal maintainance of life—problems including autoaffective pleasure, narcissism, and a number of economic problems in the relation between the ego (as "love-object") and the external world. Pleasure is therefore understood as continuous with biological needs only by those who refuse the Freudian position which sees a conflict between these two ideas. It should not be difficult to see, how-

ever, that the human "organism" has some capacity to seek pleasure at a cost to its organic self-maintainance—as the advertisement suggests which depicts a man pointing a handgun toward his brain by way of the opening in his nostril, a depiction labeled "cocaine." To see pleasure as continuous with the biological understanding is not a psychoanalytic position, then; but it is the position taken by ego-psychology, for which the ego is seen as the balancing point by which the subject maintains a "state of equilibrium" between external reality and internal impulses—and in this view the ego is taken as an "adaptational" function of the subject. This is not at all, however, the position of Irigaray and Kristeva, for whom there is a distinction between sexuality and the satisfaction of organic needs. For these feminists, the domain of sexuality and the problem of pleasure must not be modeled on the needs of the organism, but must be seen as in conflict with it, and indeed as revealing a number of complex problems in the "unnatural" formation of identity.

29. See Jean Laplanche, *Life and Death in Psychoanalysis*, 23 (original italics). See also Foucault's remarks on the function of the "norm" in *The Order of Things*, ch. 10.

30. On speaking, see Jacques Lacan, (*E*, 296–99/83–85); on the distinction between seeing and looking, cf., for example, Lacan's remarks in his discussion of the gaze, in *Seminar XI*. See also Stuart Schneiderman, "Art According to Lacan," in *Newsletter of the Freudian Field* 2, no. 1 (spring 1988); and on eating, *SXI*, 165–66.

31. Susan Bordo has collected some interesting material on anorexia from the journals of students, but the use that she makes of the traditional opposition between the spirit and the flesh, as a conflictual pair that makes sense of the anorexic's relation to her body—a relation of attempted mastery or transcendence, on her account—differs from the psychoanalytic argument, which does not see the "flesh" as equivalent to "matter" precisely because the body is constituted in a much closer relation to the signifier, and because the "spirit" or psyche is nothing but embodied, as the clinical material suggests. This is not to say that the traditional dichotomy is *psychologically* irrelevant to the anorexic. "*Anorexia Nervosa*: Psychopathology as the Crystalization of Culture" in *Feminism and Foucault: Reflections on Resistance*, ed. Irene Diamond and Lee Quinby (Boston: Northeastern University Press, 1988), 87–117.

32. See Parveen Adams, "Versions of the Body" in *m/f*, nos. 11–12 (1986), 27–34.

33. See the discussion of the concept of energy in Jacques Lacan's Seminar, Book II, 1954–55, *The Ego in Freud's Theory and in the Technique of Psychoanalysis*.
34. See Freud, "Papers on Metapsychology" (*SE*, 14:148). The concept of erotogenic zones concerns the organization, not originally given, of the body, both in its surface (the skin and mucous membranes) and internally (organs, fantasized or organic); it is generally also a concept that addresses the exchange between the internal and external, and is therefore constitutive of the subject's distinguishing between itself and the outer world—this is one register of the stress placed on the oral and anal drives as dealing with "exchange" and object-relations. Laplanche and Pontalis write: "Although the existence and predominance of definite bodily zones in human sexuality remains a fundamental datum in psychoanalytic experience, any account of this fact in merely anatomical and physiological terms is inadequate. What has to be given consideration too is that these zones, at the beginning of psychosexual development, constitute the favored paths of exchange with the surroundings, while at the same time soliciting the most attention, care—and consequently stimulation—from the mother." Jean Laplanche and J.-B. Pontalis, *The Language of Psychoanalysis*, trans. D. Nicholson-Smith (New York: Norton, 1973), 155.
35. *Hysteria From Freud to Lacan: Body and Language in Psychoanalysis*, 3, 22.
36. See Elizabeth Grosz, *Sexual Subversions: Three French Feminists* (Sydney: Allen and Unwin, 1989), ch. 3; *Jacques Lacan: A Feminist Introduction* (New York: Routledge, 1990), chs. 3 and 6; and note 13.
37. The philosophical stakes should be clear: any discussion that sets Platonism *against* historicism thereby takes over uncritically the very categories of metaphysics (in particular the "temporal" and "eternal") that orient our current discussion as to whether gender is "cultural" or "biological," the shortcomings of which Irigaray is working to overcome. For a discussion of this problem in another context, see Rodolphe Gasché's remarks on historicism in "Of Aesthetic and Historical Determination" in *Post-Structuralism and the Question of History* ed. Derek Attridge, Geoff Bennington, and Robert Young (Cambridge, UK: Cambridge University Press, 1987), 139–61.
38. See J.-A. Miller, "How Psychoanalysis Cures According to Lacan," *Newsletter of the Freudian Field*, vol. 1, no 2 (Fall 1987), 4–30, esp.

19–22. I would also note that my use of the word "feminine," here and throughout the essay, is not meant to be restricted to the cultural aspects of "femininity" to which the word normally refers in English. The English language has the word *feminine* for the so-called constructions of gender, and the word *female* for the natural and biological aspects of sex. The French has only one word, *féminité*, which makes it unclear whether nature or culture is the reference. I want to preserve this ambiguity, and accordingly I use the word "feminine" as an equivalent for the French word.

39. Joan Copjec, in "Cutting Up," objects to what she calls "the argument for construction" for similar reasons:

> Consider, for example, certain analyses of the hystericization of women's bodies, of the "invention of hysteria." According to these, an investigation of turn-of-the-century medical practices . . . will tell us not how hysteria was studied, but, more accurately, how it was constructed as a historical entity. . . . In these examples, the social system of representation is conceived as lawful, regulatory, and on this account the cause of the subject [who wants] what social laws want it to want. The construction of the subject, then, depends on the subject's taking social representations as images of its own ideal being, on the subject's deriving a "narcissistic pleasure" from these representations.

Copjec claims that this argument cannot give an adequate account of desire, that is to say, of the discrepancy between (A) the subject who is constructed in accordance with the ideals of the symbolic order, and (B) discontent, symptoms, pain, and lack. *Between Feminism and Psychoanalysis*, 228–29. This objection points out that, in order to explain how the subject can at the same time *suffer* the consequences of accepting these ideals, the "constructionist" has recourse only to a vague notion of a violated "human nature" that is entirely unsatisfactory. The suggestion is that in current discussions of gender there is generally an impasse in the binary system that simply *opposes* the social to the natural, and Copjec argues that this impasse is more adequately overcome by the triad of Imaginary, Symbolic, and Real that is found in Lacan.

40. See John Forrester, ". . . a perfect likeness of the past," in *The Seductions of Psychoanalysis: Freud, Derrida, Lacan* (Cambridge, UK: Cambridge University Press, 1990), 90–96.

41. The same difficulty regarding the "prehistoric" presents itself in Kristeva's conception of the semiotic and the symbolic: It is tempting to pretend that these two domains can be put into a temporal sequence that we can then *narrate* as a history of repression, as though the semiotic were a "prehistoric femininity" that is subsequently replaced by a symbolic dimension that would be temporally later; but in so doing, we would obliterate altogether one of the central tasks that Kristeva is exploring with this distinction, namely, the task of conceptualizing the nonlinear temporality that belongs *both* to poststructuralist accounts of the "end" of metaphysics and historical change, *and* to the psychoanalytic conception of personal history, psychic time, and human "development"—a conception that offers us a whole series of temporal problems ranging from its view of memory, group identifications, the relation to ancestry, and *nachtraglichkeit*, to the thesis that the unconscious does not know the time of history. The semiotic and symbolic cannot be ordered sequentially, then, but must be seen as mutually constitutive and equiprimordial. The problem here, then, is to understand not how the (original) semiotic is replaced by the (later) symbolic, according to a narrative time (a reading that will always be nostalgic), but rather how the *conjunction* of these two *gives rise* to the possibility of time. One of the misfortunes suffered by some feminist writers is that their philosophical concerns are sometimes neglected in favor of what is taken to be their more "immediately relevant" claims—while it should be clear from their texts that these writers claim, as immediately relevant and pressing, the need for a rethinking of the basic concepts of the Western tradition, which has been formative for women. One would have to explore this temporal question in connection with Kristeva's essay "Women's Time," to begin to address this adequately, but for our purposes here it is enough to insist that the body, in Irigaray's work, cannot serve as a prehistoric origin any more than the semiotic can in Kristeva, because the body is always already involved in a historically determinate order of representation. See Tina Chanter, "Female Temporality and the Future of Feminism," in *Abjection, Melancholia and Love: The Work of Julia Kristeva*, ed. John Fletcher and Andrew Benjamin (New York: Routledge, 1990), 63–79.
42. "Rereading Irigaray," 117, 120 (emphasis mine).
43. I in no way mean to suggest that Irigaray is *only* psychoanalytic in

her point of view, or that she has no questions about her relationship to some aspects of psychoanalytic theory—for it is perfectly clear that one of her central concerns is to reread the traditional psycho-analytic literature with the wariest of eyes, as she does other texts. I mean only to highlight here some features of her work, since she is a trained and practicing analyst, and since the reception of her work has hitherto tended to focus on other aspects of her work.

44. One can perhaps appreciate at this point why Foucault, in *The Order of Things*, for all his severe reservations about psychoanalysis, nev-ertheless situates it not with Marxism and phenomenology, which he regards as the most tortured and comprehensive forms of the mod-ern philosophy of "Man," but rather as a "counterscience" that repudiates the figure of "Man" as a metaphysics. See *The Order of Things*, 327, 340–43, 351–55, 373–86.

45. See Iris Marion Young, "The Ideal of Community and the Politics of Difference" in *Feminism/Postmodernism*, ed. Linda J. Nicholson (New York: Routledge, 1990), 300–23.

46. "Rereading Irigaray," 108.

47. "The Pirate's Fiancee: Feminists and Philosophers, or Maybe Tonight It'll Happen," in *Feminism and Foucault: Reflections on Resistance.*

48. Jacqueline Rose, "Julia Kristeva: Take Two," in *Sexuality in the Field of Vision*, 159.

49. The "remainder," taken first and one might think "negatively" as waste, has also been important to Irigaray's work on what of woman is "excess," that is to say, what is not inscribed, what does not enter entirely into symbolization, what escapes the system that has been given for its articulation. Derrida has discussed this notion of "remainder" in relation to Hegel's thought, and Irigaray has devel-oped the idea in regard to the Hegelian notion of "speculation," which is clearly meant to include Lacan's work; an adequate account would have to address the fact that *le reste*, the remainder, which is not inscribed, is precisely linked by Lacan to the real.

50. Meaghan Morris has noted this, against Monique Plaza: "Irigaray's text itself infuriatingly resists definition as feminine; for her the fem-inine is conditional and future tense, an interrogative mood . . . the feminine is suspended and explored." See "The Pirate's Fiancee."

51. One might elaborate here Kristeva's interest in the pre-Oedipal rela-tion to the mother (and the "father of individual prehistory"), show-ing that this "period" is for similar reasons not simply a period in

time which subsequently is repressed, as many genetic accounts of child development suggest, but is rather a moment which perpetually *returns*, as do the anal drives, for example. This is why, for both those who argue for the "end of metaphysics" and those who work in psychoanalytic theory, the question of how history happens cannot be detached from the problem of repetition, which is precisely what characterizes the drives and metaphysics.

52. Arleen Dallery indicates the stress French feminism tends to place upon the task that would remain *after* (or of course while) equal rights and recognition are—more or less, tentatively—secured: "Not only has woman's voice or experience been excluded from the subject matter of western knowledge, but even when the discourse *is* 'about' women, or women are the speaking subjects, it still speaks according to phallocratic codes." See "The Politics of Writing (The) Body: *Ecriture Feminine*," in *Gender/Body/Knowledge*, ed. Alison Jaggar and Susan Bordo (New Brunswick, NJ: Rutgers University Press, 1989), 53.

CHAPTER 2

1. Julia Kristeva, "Stabat Mater," *Histoires d'amour* (Paris: Denoël, 1983), 225–47. The text will be cited from the English translation, "Stabat Mater," trans. León S. Roudiez, *The Kristeva Reader*, ed. Toril Moi (New York: Columbia University Press, 1986), 160–85. Also available in Julia Kristeva, *Tales of Love*, trans. Leon Roudiez (New York: Columbia University Press, 1987), 234–63.

2. The literature on Kristeva is extensive. For examples of different and often quite conflicting views, see Judith Butler, "The Body Politics of Julia Kristeva," *Gender Trouble: Feminism and the Subversion of Identity* (New York: Routledge, 1990), 79–91; Janice Doane and Devon Hodges, *From Klein to Kristeva: Psychoanalytic Feminism and the Search for the "Good Enough" Mother* (Ann Arbor, Mich.: University of Michigan Press, 1992); Nancy Fraser, "The Uses and Abuses of French Discourse Theories for Feminist Politics," *Revaluing French Feminism: Critical Essays on Difference, Agency, and Culture*, ed. Nancy Fraser and Sandra Lee Bartky (Bloomington: Indiana University Press, 1992), 177–93; Elizabeth Grosz, *Sexual Subversions: Three French Feminists*; Alice Jardine, "Introduction to Julia Kristeva's 'Women's Time,'" *Signs* 7, no. 1 (1981): 5–12; Ann Rosalind Jones, "Writing the Body: Towards an Understanding of

L'Écriture Féminine," *Feminist Studies* 7, no. 2 (summer 1981); Dorothy Leland, "Lacanian Psychoanalysis and French Feminism: Towards an Adequate Political Psychology," *Hypatia* 3, no. 3 (winter 1989): 81–103; Kelly Oliver, *Reading Kristeva: Unraveling the Double-Bind* (Bloomington: Indiana University Press, 1993); Jacqueline Rose, "Julia Kristeva: Take Two," *Sexuality in the Field of Vision*, 141–64; Madelon Sprengnether, *The Spectral Mother: Freud, Feminism, and Psychoanalysis* (Ithaca, NY: Cornell University Press, 1990), esp. 212–36; see also collected essays in *Body/Text in Julia Kristeva: Religion, Women, and Psychoanalysis*, ed. David Crownfield (Albany: State University of New York Press, 1992). In *Ethics, Politics, and Difference in Julia Kristeva's Writing*, ed. Kelly Oliver (New York: Routledge, 1993), see esp. Tina Chanter, "Kristeva's Politics of Change: Tracking Essentialism with the Help of a Sex/Gender Map," 179–95; Alice Jardine, "Opaque Texts and Transparent Contexts: The Political Difference of Julia Kristeva," 23–31; Alison Weir, "Identification with the Divided Mother: Kristeva's Ambivalence," 79–91; and Ewa Ziarek, "Kristeva and Levinas: Mourning, Ethics, and the Feminine," 62–78.

3. Despite of its difficulties, this narrative is now virtually canonical in the reception of Lacan, and governs both the "staging" of Lacan's thought and that of the Oedipal and pre-Oedipal "periods." This narrative staging provides the path of reading (or avoidance) taken for example by Peter Dews in *The Logics of Disintegration: Poststructuralist Thought and the Claims of Critical Theory* (London: Verso, 1987). Consider a single, "introductory" sentence, apparently devoted to the most elementary and neutral description, an orienting device, supposedly prior to the analysis itself, yet marked by a series of formidable narrative elements: "Shortly after the *Discours de Rome*, a rapid and remarkable shift of emphasis begins to take place in Lacan's teaching, clearly visible in the disjunction between the first (1953–54) and second (1954–55) *Seminars*, in which the theory of the ego and the imaginary, which had been the central concern of the first phase of Lacan's teaching, is displaced from its primary position by the theory of a new register which Lacan refers to as the 'Symbolic.'" Here, the two periods of the canonical history are laid down, organizing in advance virtually everything that will be said, and with this division we find a clear narrative structure—a "rapid and remarkable shift," representing what we are to recognize as a "dis-

junction" (rather than an elaboration), and further characterized as a change in which a "first phase" is "displaced" by a "new register" that would appear not only to have been absent in the beginning, but also to entail a radical decentering of the "central concern" of Lacan's early work from its "primary position." Such a history is by no means neutral, and its stages are then elaborated with decisive consequences that disorient the entire reading, dividing Lacan between an "early" Hegelianism and a "later" turn to Saussure and "linguistics" in which the first stage is not reworked, but simply shed like a skin, never to return. In the process, moreover, Lacan is translated back into "the ancestors," returned to the fathers (Hegel and Saussure), in such a way that psychoanalysis itself disappears, as if history never presented us with anything but the same familiar story—which of course then allows Dews to protest that Lacan "hasn't said anything new" and "denies history."

4. Martin Heidegger, "Letter to Father Richardson," in William J. Richardson, S. J., *Heidegger: Through Phenomenology to Thought* (The Hague: Martinus Nijhoff, 1974), viii–xxiii; cited from xviii and xxii.

5. "Television," trans. Denis Hollier, Rosalind Krauss, and Annette Michelson in *Television: A Challenge to the Psychoanalytic Establishment*, ed. Joan Copjec (New York: Norton, 1990), 30, translation modified.

6. I have discussed this reductive periodizing in the reception of Foucault in "A Loss for Words: Literature and Method in Foucault's *The Order of Things*," *Literature and Psychology* 40, no. 4: 1–27.

7. *The Spectral Mother*, 214.

8. *The Spectral Mother*, 215.

9. The question mark is omitted from the English translation.

10. Lacan writes of "la métaphore paternelle" that it concerns the "name" rather than the "real father" (*père réel*): "le Nom-du-Père, soit la métaphore qui substitue ce Nom à la place premièrement symbolisée par l'opération de l'absence de la mère." (*E*, 557/200)

11. The phrase "real father" is an early usage of the term "real" which does not coincide with the more developed use of the term as designating the "impossible" or foreclosed element, the function of lack that is closely related to the "object a," objects of the drive which are characterized by their containment of the void. "Real" here thus means "actual," and is not the "real" in the "Lacanian" sense.

12. The question of the father in psychoanalysis is extremely complex, and the changes in Freud's views, as well as Lacan's reformulations, merit extended discussion (see ch. 4). We will not develop it here since we are principally concerned with the mother. But it should be said that, as Russell Grigg puts it, "in Freud's work the normative function of the father tends gradually to give way to the pathological," thereby leading Lacan to distinguish the Oedipal father, who appears to regulate the relation to the mother, mediating the otherwise overwhelming, "devouring" power of the maternal figure, and the father of *Totem and Taboo*, who does not so much serve to mediate, but rather "himself has assumed the power, obscurity, and cruelty of the omnipotence his function was supposed to dissipate." One of the consequences of this shift in Freud is that it now becomes difficult to understand why the child is said to identify with the father, given this latter characterization. The problem is partly resolved by Freud's distinction between the ego ideal and the superego, but in Lacan, the matter is formulated somewhat differently, by reference to the imaginary and symbolic father, who correspond to different forms of lack, namely, "privation" and "castration." See Russell Grigg, "Freud's Problem of Identification," *Newsletter of the Freudian Field* 1, no. 1 (spring 1987), 14–18. See also the remarks of Slavov Žižek on the the father in *For They Know Not What They Do: Enjoyment as a Political Factor* (New York: Verso, 1991) and *Enjoy Your Symptom: Jacques Lacan in Hollywood and Out* (New York: Routledge, 1992).

13. The three most familiar discussions of schema R in English are perhaps the following: André Green, "Logic of Lacan's *objet (a)* and Freudian Theory: Convergences and Questions," *Interpreting Lacan*, ed. Joseph H. Smith and William Kerrigan (New Haven, CT: Yale University Press, 1983), 161–91; Richard Boothby, *Death and Desire: Psychoanalytic Theory in Lacan's Return to Freud* (New York: Routledge, 1991); Robert Samuels, *Between Philosophy and Psychoanalysis: Lacan's Reconstruction of Freud* (New York: Routledge, 1993).

14. To be somewhat more precise, we should note that the field of "reality" does not *come between* the imaginary and symbolic triangles. As Lacan's notes to this essay indicate—notes added some ten years after its writing—the intrusion of the symbolic makes the fields of the imaginary and reality *overlap*. The imaginary and reality thus share half the diagram, a single triangle. This corresponds to Freud's dis-

cussions of the "perception-consciousness system," where the construction of the ego is shown to produce a relation to the world that is governed by "consciousness" rather than immediate "perception." As Freud sometimes says, for the human animal, under the influence of the pleasure principle, reality is a "hallucinated" reality. See the notes to Jacques Lacan, "D'une question préliminaire à tout traitement possible de la psychose," (*E*, 553–54, note 1/223, note 18).

15. Freud uses the phrases "flight from reality," "loss of reality," "turn from reality," and "withdrawal from reality." He also distinguishes the various relations to reality that characterize diagnostic categories such as paraphrenia, psychosis, neurosis, melancholy, and mourning (as well as among "intellectuals"). See especially "Mourning and Melancholy," 14:243–58; and "The Loss of Reality in Neurosis and Psychosis," 19:183–87.

16. Two of Heidegger's lectures on language, "The Essence of Language" and "Poetry and Thinking: On Stephan Georg's 'The Word'" (the latter translated simply as "Words"), begin with a reference to this line from Stephan Georg's poem "Das Wort." See Martin Heidegger, *Unterwegs zur Sprache* (Pfullingen: Neske, 1959), published in English as *On the Way to Language*, trans. P. Hertz and J. Stambaugh (New York: Harper and Row, 1971). See also the discussion by Robert Bernasconi, *The Question of Language in Heidegger's History of Being* (Atlantic Highlands: Humanities Press, 1985), 49–64.

17. Lacan's "Rome Discourse," "The Function and Field of Speech and Language in Psychoanalysis," has a particularly clear account of his early position in regard to object-relations theory. The essay is divided into three main parts (and an introduction), the second of which treats this topic, arguing that in the theoretical discussion of "the concept of libidinal object relations . . . a clear-cut reaction is taking place in favour of a return to the technical pivot of symbolization" (*E*, 243/35), a matter which he elsewhere (in "Aggressivity in Psychoanalysis") credits Melanie Klein with having recognized better than others: "Only Melanie Klein, working on the child at the very limit of the appearance of language, dared to project subjective experience back to that earlier period when observation nevertheless enables us to affirm its dimension" (*E*, 115/20).

18. A series of important articles has addressed the question of the relation between (and relative priority of) sexual difference and Heidegger's conception of ontological difference, beginning with the work

of Jacques Derrida and Luce Irigaray. See Jacques Derrida, "*Geschlecht*: différence sexuelle, différence ontologique," *Psyché: Inventions de l'autre* (Paris: galilée, 1987), 395–414, first published in *Cahiers de l'Herne (no. 45): Martin Heidegger,* ed. Michel Haar (Éditions de l'Herne: Paris, 1983), 419–30, and simultaneously in English as "Geschlecht: Sexual Difference, Ontological Difference," *Research in Phenomenology* 13 (1983), 65–83; Luce Irigaray, *Éthique de la différence sexuelle* (Paris: Minuit, 1984), trans. Carolyn Burke and Gillian C. Gill, *An Ethics of Sexual Difference* (Ithaca: Cornell University Press, 1993); David Farrell Krell, *Daimon Life: Heidegger and Life-Philosophy* (Bloomington: Indiana University Press, 1992), esp. ch. 8, "Something Like Sexes, Something Like Spirit," 252–91; see also the extended discussion of this issue in Tina Chanter, *Ethics of Eros: Irigaray's Rewriting of the Philosophers* (New York: Routledge, 1995).

19. Michèle Montrelay, "The Story of Louise," in *Returning to Freud.* This text also uses the term "symbolic mother."

20. In Lacan's words: "There is no longer any way, therefore, of reducing this Elsewhere to the imaginary form of a nostalgia, a lost or future Paradise; what one finds is the paradise of the child's loves, where, *Baudelaire de Dieu!*, something's going on, I can tell you" (*E,* 548/193).

21. For an excellent analysis of Lacanian objections to the "good enough mother," see Parveen Adams, "Mothering," *The Woman in Question,* ed. Parveen Adams and Elizabeth Cowie (Cambridge: MIT Press, 1990), 315–27.

22. *FS,* 80. This translation differs considerably from—and generally improves upon—the one available in *Écrits: A Selection*, especially in this instance.

23. For a brief, lucid account of the terms "gift" and "debt," see Moustafa Safouan, *Le Structuralism en psychanalyse* (Paris: Seuil [Points], 1968), esp. 55–69.

24. This allows the child to pass from primary to secondary narcissism (in Freud's language), or (in accordance with schema R) from (e) to (I), thereby giving rise to the ego ideal. We may recognize the extent to which Lacan's apparently strange language has some precedent in Freud if we note that Freud also speaks of "demand" when it comes to this distinction between the ego and the ego ideal. In *Group Psychology* he writes:

> We have been driven to the hypothesis that some such agency [he calls it "conscience"] develops in our ego which may cut itself off from the rest of the ego and come into conflict with it. We have called it the "ego ideal," and by way of functions we have ascribed to it self-observation, the moral conscience, the censorship of dreams, and the chief influence in repression. We have said that *it is the heir to the original narcissism* in which the childish ego enjoyed self-sufficiency; *it gradually gathers up* from the influences of the environment *the demands* which that environment makes upon the ego and which the ego cannot always rise to; so that a man, when he cannot be satisfied with his ego itself, may nevertheless be able to find satisfaction in the ego ideal which has been differentiated out of the ego. (18:109–10, emphasis added)

Freud adds in a footnote,

> A far more fundamental and comprehensive psychological analysis would have to intervene at this point. A path leads from identification by way of imitation to empathy, that is, to the comprehension of *the mechanism by means of which we are enabled to take up any attitude at all towards another* mental life. (emphasis added)

25. Jacques-Alain Miller has given an especially clear account of the paternal metaphor in these terms in "To Interpret the Cause: From Freud to Lacan," *Newsletter of the Freudian Field* 3, nos. 1 and 2 (spring/fall 1989): 30–50.

26. This is the "overlapping of two lacks" discussed in *Seminar XI* under the heading of "alienation" and "separation," 203–15. See also Parveen Adams, "Representation and Sexuality," *The Woman in Question*, 233–52.

27. Treatments of *jouissance* by Lacan are numerous and the term is used in several ways. English readers might begin with the section titled "The paradox of *jouissance*" in *Seminar VII: The Ethics of Psycho-analysis 1959–60*, ed. Jacques-Alain Miller, trans. Dennis Porter (New York: Norton, 1992), 167–240. First published as *Le Seminaire, Livre VII: L'ethique de la psychanalyse, 1959–60*, ed. Jacques-Alain Miller (Paris: Seuil, 1986). References will henceforth appear in the text preceded by *SVII* (for *Seminar VII*), French pagination first, English second.

28. These remarks of Freud have been very usefully discussed by Cather-

ine Millot, "The Feminine Superego," trans. Ben Brewster, 294–306.

29. A more developed treatment would have to discuss the fact that "denial" is the mechanism of perversion, which means that this figure of the virgin, this "maternity," is a form of feminine perversion. That Kristeva means this seriously is clear from the fact that she speaks of "the paranoid lust for power" that, in the figure of the Virgin Mary, changes "a woman into a Queen of Heaven" (180). Such statements have been read as a misogynistic attack on the idea of "women's empowerment" (as a social goal), but I think it would be more correct to recognize that what is at stake is not the demeaning of "women" in sociological terms, or of women's "empowerment," but rather a psychoanalytic "analysis" of the figures that have regulated femininity and its possible identifications, not only restricting them to a few familiar forms, but also to forms that have too often been attended by pathological results. This perhaps takes us back to her concern with paranoia, melancholy, and the like.

30. Jacques Derrida, "The Art of Memoires," *Memoires: for Paul de Man* (New York: Columbia University Press, 1988), 47–88, esp. 48–49.

31. See Slavoj Žižek, *For They Know Not What They Do: Enjoyment as a Political Factor* (New York: Verso, 1991), 220–21; see also the discussion of the sexuation graph on pp. 121–23.

32. It is clear from this that femininity as masquerade is in large part a way in which the woman who takes this position "participates in man's fantasy." But from the point of view of psychoanalysis, one also has to ask what it is *in the woman* that contributes to this participation. As Lacan puts the question in his "Guiding Remarks for a Congress on Feminine Sexuality" (*FS*, 86–98), "Even given what masochistic perversion owes to masculine invention, is it safe to conclude that the masochism of the woman is a fantasy of the desire of the man?" (FS 92).

33. Eugénie Lemoine-Luccioni, *Partage des femmes*, 74; *The Dividing of Women or Woman's Lot*, 60.

34. Thus Lacan writes in "Guiding Remarks": "Man here acts as the relay whereby the woman becomes this Other for herself as she is this Other for him" (*FS*, 93).

35. For more detailed discussion of the question of perversion, see *Traits de perversion dans les structures cliniques*, ed. Navarin Press, Fondation du Champs Freudien (Paris: Navarin, 1990).

36. Sarah Kofman, *The Enigma of Woman: Woman in Freud's Writings*

(Ithaca, NY: Cornell University Press, 1985). For some interesting remarks on ancient figures such as the sphinx, see Jean-Joseph Goux, *Oedipus, Philosopher*, trans. Catherine Porter (Stanford, CA: Stanford University Press, 1993).

37. See Élie Doumit's untitled discussion in *Lacan avec les philosophes* (Paris: Albin Michel, 1991), 265–76; the volume collects the papers of a conference held under this title at the Collège International de Philosophie.

38. This is Lacan's notorious but not very clearly understood statement in "God and the *Jouissance of The Woman*" (*FS*, 146).

39. Marie-Hélène Brousse, "Feminism With Lacan," *Newsletter of the Freudian Field* 5, nos. 1 and 2 (spring/fall, 1991): 113–28; cited from 126.

40. See "The Freudian Thing" (*E*, 401–36/114–45), esp. section 3, "The Thing Speaks of Itself."

CHAPTER 3

1. Catherine Millot, *Horsexe: Essay on Transsexuality*, trans. Kenneth Hylton (New York: Autonomedia, 1990). References will appear henceforth in the text.

2. Georges Canguilhem, *The Normal and the Pathological*, intro. Michel Foucault, trans. Carolyn R. Fawcett and Robert S. Cohen (New York: Zone, 1991), and Michel Foucault, *The Order of Things*, esp. 356–61. These books were both published in French in 1966.

3. In *Life and Death in Psychoanalysis*, Jean Laplanche writes: "Are we suggesting, since deviance is necessarily defined in relation to a norm, that Freud himself would rally to the notion of a sexual instinct? . . . Such is not the case, [for] the *exception*—i.e. the perversion—*ends up taking the rule along with it*" (p. 23). See Freud, 7:160. In his *History of Sexuality* Foucault contrasts psychoanalysis with the theories of "degeneration" that were used at the turn of the century not only to account for the "regressive" character of homosexuality, but to establish pseudo-evolutionary models of racial "advancement" and "primitivism." According to Foucault, the distance Freud took from such models, which aimed at a developmental ranking, made it possible for psychoanalysis to avoid more than other theories of the time the fascist movements and eugenics programs that were contemporaneous with it. See *The History of Sexuality: An Introduction*, trans. Robert Hurley (New York: Vintage, 1990), 150.

4. Slavoj Žižek, *For They Know Not What They Do: Enjoyment as a Political Factor* (New York: Verso, 1991). Further references will appear in the text.

5. Joan Copjec, "m/f, or Not Reconciled," *The Woman in Question*, 10–18. References will henceforth appear in the text.

6. A similar claim is made by Parveen Adams in the same volume, in her discussion of Nancy Chodorow's proposal that the psychic constitution of men and women would be different if men and women shared equally in the task of parenting, so that women would not be confined to the position of maternity, and men would not be excluded from this position. Such an argument, Adams points out, is a "sociologized" version of psychoanalysis, one that situates contingent historical formations at the same level as psychic structure; but more important for our present discussion is Adams's concern with the danger of such a recommendation, which, however desirable for other reasons, proposes to "manage" or institutionalize a "correct" form of parenting, to resolve what Lacan calls the "impossibility" of the sexual relation by recourse to a social arrangement. Chodorow thus would seem to risk advocating the same kind of normalizing function that has classically characterized the great humanitarian and philanthropic reforms of educational psychology in the past. Psychoanalysis remains wary of the cost that such normalization will entail—however laudable such a solution may be in its spirit and intentions, and however useful it might be as an improvement over other arrangements. See "Mothering," 315–27.

7. Elizabeth Grosz suggests that in stressing the "symbolic" aspect of the trauma, Freud may have been covering up actual facts of empirical abuse, treating them as "mere fabrications." One is surely right to be wary on this point, but it would be a mistake to argue that psychoanalysis regards the trauma as merely "fictional," in the trivial sense of reducing it to a matter of indifference; it would be a mistake, that is, to refuse the specific difficulty psychoanalysis seeks to address, in the name of restoring a presymbolic "reality," as though any discussion of the effect of language amounted to a simple dismissal of such things as child abuse. See *Jacques Lacan: A Feminist Introduction*, 51–59.

8. The case of "Emma" is probably the most famous example. Here, two scenes overlap: an early experience of molestation by a shop owner, which at the time "meant nothing" to the child, in the sense that it did not produce any traumatic response, and another scene

that occurred several years later in the same place. In that incident, the young woman, now at the age of puberty, is laughed at by adolescent boys, the later scene being in itself not traumatic, just a "normal" unpleasant experience, but yet functioning in such a way as suddenly to confer meaning retroactively on the earlier scene, and producing in the young woman a phobia whose unconscious character is evident from the fact that she says she does not understand why she has a phobia and cannot enter into shops. This overlapping is a structure given only with the action of the signifier: the status of the trauma thus has to be understood as belonging, not to either event in itself, but to their relation. For three of the most useful texts on this subject, see Freud, "Studies on Hysteria" (2:48–105); Laplanche, *Life and Death*, 38–44; and Michèle Montrelay, "The Story of Louise," in Stuart Schneiderman, *Returning to Freud*, 75–93, a case excerpted from *L'Ombre et le nom* (Paris: Minuit, 1977).

9. Constance Penley, "Missing *m/f*," *The Woman in Question*, 7.
10. "A Note on the Distinction Between Sexual Division and Sexual Differences," *The Woman in Question*, 102.
11. Marjorie Garber, *Vested Interests: Cross-Dressing and Cultural Anxiety* (New York: Routledge, 1992), 75–77, 93.
12. An excellent account of the history underlying the terms "sex" and "gender" in the reception of French feminism is Tina Chanter, "Kristeva's Politics of Change: Tracking Essentialism with the Help of a Sex/Gender Map," in Kelly Oliver, ed. *Ethics, Politics, and Difference in Julia Kristeva's Writing*, 179–95.
13. Luce Irigaray, "The Female Gender," in *Sexes and Genealogies*, trans. Catherine Porter (New York: Columbia University Press, 1993), 107.
14. To be precise, we would have to distinguish between *various forms of historicism*. See Maurice Mandelbaum, *History, Man, and Reason: A Study in Nineteenth-century Thought* (Baltimore: Johns Hopkins University Press, 1971). For an excellent example of the difference between a "humanist" historicism (in which "sexual difference" is not made problematic, but simply presupposed, in favor of a historical analysis of "gender"), and a more radical historicism, see the essays by Isaac Balbus and Jana Sawicki in *After Foucault: Humanistic Knowledge, Postmodern Challenges*, ed. Jonathan Arac (New Brunswick, NJ: Rutgers University Press, 1988). Jana Sawicki

argues convincingly that one can see such a "return of essentialism" in Issac Balbus's article. Judith Butler's recent book is clearly another effort, on the part of what might be called a radical historicism, to encounter precisely this problem, that is, not simply to demonstrate the constructed character of gender, but to think through the impasses of the historicist tradition, to follow through the implications of sexual difference for the theory of history, rather than taking for granted a conception of history that can then simply be put to use in the analysis of various constructions of "gender." See *Bodies That Matter: On the Discursive Limits of "Sex"* (New York: Routledge, 1993).

15. See the essays collected in *Poststructuralism and the Question of History*, especially Rodolphe Gasché, "Of Aesthetic and Historical Determination," 139–61.

16. In *The Birth of the Clinic*, Foucault gives an extremely useful account of the emergence of the term *lesion* and its role in the rise of modern medicine, the formation of "organic medicine" as distinct from the "science of diseases" that had governed the Enlightenment. Foucault points out that the concept of the lesion, in what was apparently a merely technical discussion of "the seat of disease," in fact reveals the decisive elements that organize the concept of the "body" in organic medicine. Freud then would seem to break with this organic model described by Foucault. See *The Birth of the Clinic*, 186–91.

17. For a useful discussion of the way Freud's theory disrupts the available models of scientific reasoning (on hypnosis, hysteria, animal magnetism, cathartic medicine, and so on), see Léon Chertok and Isabelle Stengers, *A Critique of Psychoanalytic Reason*, trans. Martha Noel Evans (Stanford, CA: Stanford University Press, 1992).

18. For two different discussions of this and similar passages, see Chertok and Stengers, *A Critique of Psychoanalytic Reason*, 26–45; and Monique David-Ménard, *Hysteria From Freud to Lacan*, 1–16.

19. For further development of the difference between the *presentation* of the image and the *logic* of the symbolic in Lacan and Aristotle, see Charles Shepherdson, "Vital Signs: The Place of Memory in Psychoanalysis," *Research in Phenomenology* 23 (1993): 22–72.

20. For an excellent account of this "inscription of the void" and its role in the constitution of the body, see Michèle Montrelay, "The Story of Louise," in *Returning to Freud*; see also Julia Kristeva's discussion of metaphor in "Freud and Love: Treatment and its Discontents," *The*

Kristeva Reader. I have discussed this inscription of lack in "On Fate: Psychoanalysis and the Desire to Know," *Dialectic and Narrative*, 271–302, esp. 294–302.

21. Julia Kristeva, "Freud and Love," 244.
22. See, for the two most often discussed examples, "The Origin of the Work of Art" and "The Thing," in *Poetry, Language, Thought*, ed. and trans. Albert Hofstadter (New York: Harper and Row, 1971).
23. A similar difficulty obtains with the term "negation," as Joan Copjec has clearly shown. See her discussion of Brentano and Foucault in "Missing m/f."
24. Leslie Martin Lothstein, *Female-to-Male Transsexualism: Historical, Clinical, and Theoretical Issues* (Boston: Routledge and Kegan Paul, 1983).
25. A similar difficulty appears in the legal context when, as discussions of Jack Kevorkian have made clear, it is said that subjects should have the right to die, *if they are mentally competent*—which means that in certain cases, someone else will decide upon the subject's competence, that someone else will (and "ought to") protect the subject against the choices that subject might make, and that a person's free choice may not be in the person's own interest.
26. The recent, popular *Brain Sex* provides a good example of such a test, without the slightest ironic distance, a test designed to reveal through some "twenty questions" the degree of intrauterine hormonal testosterone to which one was exposed before birth, and to rank the respondent accordingly, on a sliding scale of masculinity and femininity. Anne Moir and David Jessel, *Brain Sex: The Real Difference Between Men and Women* (New York: Dell, 1989).
27. See also Moustapha Safouan, "Contribution to the Psychoanalysis of Transsexualism," in *Returning to Freud*, pp. 195–212.
28. Lothstein relates a series of cases that are illuminating in this regard.
29. It should also be clear from this that Millot's position clarifies what often remains unclear in the secondary literature—namely, whether transsexuals are homosexual or not. Excessive focus on "behavior" without sufficient attention to structural positions (that is, to the structural difference between phallic and symbolic identification) has led clinicians to orient themselves by reference to what a subject "does," which in fact shows very little. Millot's account would suggest that whereas the homosexual position is "normal," in that one finds desire, a relation to the other, and so on, the position *horsexe* is structured by a demand in which desire is eclipsed.

30. As Jacqueline Rose points out, Lacan became more and more concerned with the terms "certainty," "knowledge," and "belief" as he developed his account of sexual difference. See *Feminine Sexuality*, 50. Irigaray has taken up precisely these terms in "La Croyance Même," an essay on "belief" and sexual difference addressed to Derrida (in *Sexes et Parentés*, Paris: Minuit, 1987), 37–65. Derrida has responded (to her and others) in *Memoires of the Blind: The Self-Portrait and Other Ruins*, trans. Pascale-Anne Brault and Michael Nass (Chicago: University of Chicago Press, 1993), a text that opens with the question, "Do you believe?" (1).

CHAPTER 4

1. These statements recur throughout Lacan's texts. The first can be found, for example, in *Écrits*, 265/55 and 549/193, and in *Seminar XI*, 131; the second can be found in *Seminar XI*, 21; the third in *Seminar XI*, 157.
2. Jacques-Alain Miller, "Extimité," *Lacanian Theory of Discourse: Subject, Structure, and Society*, ed. Mark Bracher, Marshall Alcorn, Jr., Ronald J. Cortell, and Françoise Massardier-Kenney (New York: New York University Press, 1994), 74–87; cited from 85.
3. Miller, "Extimité," 80.
4. Nestor Braunstein dates this moment from about 1958, in *La Jouissance: un concept lacanien* (Paris: Point Hors Ligne, 1990). Philippe Julien dates the moment somewhat later: "[F]rom 1964 on, Lacan distanced himself from the period of the fifties. More and more, he came to doubt the creative power of speech, asserting finally in 1980 that it has none" (63). And again: "Such was Lacan's teaching on the transference and termination of analysis in 1960–61. Let us note that everything depends on the precise relationship *between* the symbolic and the imaginary dimensions. But what about the *real*? Lacan had used the term since 1953, but had not yet introduced the *real* as such. He did so in 1964" (102). See Philippe Julien, *Jacques Lacan's Return To Freud: The Real, the Symbolic, and the Imaginary*, trans. Devra Beck Simiu (New York: New York University Press, 1994).
5. The sixth international meeting of the Freudian Field (Rencontre international du Champ freudien) in Paris focused on this theme. The papers are collected in *Traits de perversion dans les structures cliniques*. Many of the presentations stress the difference between the *clinical designation* of "perversion," understood as a category distinct from neurosis and psychosis, and the *trait of perversion* within

the "normal" subject. It is the latter that concerns us here, a perverse "remainder" or "surplus effect" within the law *as such*, and not merely in "exceptional" cases.

6. Slavoj Žižek has often discussed this issue. For an account that also focuses on the "two fathers," see *Enjoy Your Symptom: Jacques Lacan in Hollywood and Out* (New York: Routledge, 1992), ch. 5.

7. Russell Grigg, "Freud's Problem of Identification," *Newsletter of the Freudian Field* 1:1 (spring 1987), 15.

8. Jacques-Alain Miller, "To Interpret the Cause: From Freud to Lacan," *Newsletter of the Freudian Field* 3 (spring/fall 1989), 49.

9. Catherine Millot, *Nobodaddy: L'Hystérie dans le siècle*, (Paris: Point Hors Ligne, 1988), 74. All translations are mine.

10. Jacques-Alain Miller, "A Reading of Some Details in *Television* in Dialogue with the Audience," *Newsletter of the Freudian Field* 4:1, 2 (spring/fall 1990), 17.

11. One can see here that at least two distinct conceptions of *jouissance* are possible (leaving aside here the question of "feminine *jouissance*"), two modes of transgression in relation to symbolic law: one in which it designates an original state of presymbolic "plenitude" that is lost, and yet continually sought by the subject, and a second in which it designates a relation to an "object" that comes into being only *after* the symbolic order has been established. I have discussed this in more detail in "The Intimate Alterity of the Real" in *Postmodern Culture* 6:1 (May 1996).

12. I discuss this relation between law and *jouissance* (in which the two terms are no longer simply oppositional) and its relation to Foucault's thesis on the "repressive hypothesis" and his treatment of law and transgression, in ch. 5.

13. Intersubjectivity is thus not given at the outset, or guaranteed as an inevitable part of biological development, but has to be constructed, in a process that depends on some kind of representation. Most commentators agree on this point, but differences arise on how the subject—and intersubjectivity—are constituted, what precisely the relation to the mother consists of, what role is played by the father, and how sexual difference is established in the process. For a useful summary of the issues from a non-Lacanian perspective, see Jessica Benjamin, *Like Subjects, Love Objects: Essays on Recognition and Sexual Difference* (New Haven, CT: Yale University Press, 1995), esp. chs. 1, 2, and 3.

14. This law before the law could be approached in several different ways, among them: (1) by discussing the status of the "unary trait" in Lacan, and its relation to the proper name; (2) by distinguishing in more detail the "object of the drive" (the breast, feces, gaze, voice, etc.—which we have only touched on above); and (3) by elaborating the difference between demand and desire. On the first point, see Philippe Julien, *Jacques Lacan's Return to Freud: The Real, the Symbolic, and the Imaginary*. On the second point, as Jacqueline Rose points out, it would be a matter of showing that the first two objects (oral and anal) correspond roughly to the imaginary, while the latter two (the gaze and the voice) correspond roughly to the symbolic. See Jacqueline Rose, "The Imaginary," *Sexuality in the Field of Vision*, 167–97. On the third point, see my "The Epoch of the Body: Need and Demand in Kojève and Lacan," *Perspectives on Embodiment*.

15. See the entry on "Primary Identification" in Jean Laplanche and J.-B. Pontalis, *The Language of Psychoanalysis*, 336.

16. I follow Russell Grigg, Stuart Schneiderman, and Jacqueline Rose in preferring the title "The Meaning of the Phallus" to "The Signification of the Phallus," on the ground that the French "*sens*" and "*signification*" correspond more normally to the English "sense" and "meaning" (Alan Sheridan, and the translators of Seminars I and II, render them as "meaning" and "signification" respectively). It should also be recalled that Lacan delivered "The Meaning of the Phallus" in German, where "Meaning" (French "*signification*") was *Bedeutung* (a point he stresses in the essay). The German distinction between *Sinn* and *Bedeutung* would thus correspond to *sens* and *signification* (the English "sense" and "meaning").

17. See Janice Doane and Devon Hodges, *From Klein to Kristeva*, esp. ch. 3; Alison Weir, *Sacrificial Logics: Feminist Theory and the Critique of Identity* (New York: Routledge, 1996), 173–83; Kelly Oliver, *Reading Kristeva: Unraveling the Double-Bind*, ch. 3; Jessica Benjamin, *Like Subject, Love Objects*, ch. 3; Jacqueline Rose, "Julia Kristeva—Take Two," *Sexuality in the Field of Vision*, 141–64.

18. Jessica Benjamin for example suggests in ch. 3 of *Like Subjects, Love Objects* that by stressing the "father of individual prehistory" Kristeva is maintaining a classical Freudian position in which the only possible alternative to an "engulfing" or "undifferentiated" relation to the mother lies in "paternal authority." She argues that a second alternative would lie in a more adequately developed account of the

complexity—and indeed the symbolic dimension—of the maternal relation itself, thereby demystifying the archaic image of the mother as omnipotent, utopian, and undifferentiated. Benjamin writes:

> The issue is not the idea that only the father can represent the third term, a concrete, literal notion that all feminists might question (Rose 1982). Rather, the issue is whether we believe that an external force must "break" the dyad, whether we even think that the dyad is "asocial" or a "unity." We might instead view this representation of a third term as an effect generated by the symbolic space within a social, differentiated maternal dyad. (96)

As long as this is not recognized, she argues, psychoanalytic theory will inevitably remain patriarchal, and "a rendition of the oedipal solution would emerge, in which paternal power appears to be a necessity of culture." We would suggest that although there are significant differences between Benjamin's position and Lacan's, she has come closer here to Lacan's position than she seems to recognize: that is to say, the necessity of mediation within the maternal relation to the child, as a mediation that need not be actually grounded in the father as a male person, but that must nevertheless be introduced as a principle of "representation" (what Benjamin calls the "representation of a third term"), *is precisely what Lacan means by the "paternal function."* The "paternal metaphor" is intended not to assert the power of the "father" as a male person, and thereby to assert patriarchy as a "necessity of culture," but to break the identification between the "paternal function" and the male person—which is close to what Benjamin advocates here. In my view, therefore, Kristeva's discussion of the "father of individual prehistory" cannot amount to a turn toward paternal authority, unless one already, and I think mistakenly, *presupposes* that this "father" is the psychological individual, sexually marked as "male" in a more or less biological way—unless, that is, one takes this "father" to be in effect identical with its meaning in ordinary language. For Kristeva, it is not a question of the "mother" and "father" in any ordinary sense, but a question of understanding how language emerges, how the field of representation, mediation, and difference comes into being— a question of what transcendental philosophy would have called their "conditions of possibility," and of how this comes to be attached, with more or less stability, to "sexual difference"—which, again, is not identical with the difference between the "mother" and "father" in the ordinary sense.

19. As Jacqueline Rose puts it, with the symbolic law,

the mother is refused to the child in so far as a prohibition falls on the child's desire to be what the mother desires (not the same, note, as a desire to possess or enjoy the mother in the sense normally understood).

Thus, if incestuous desire (which is not, strictly speaking, desire, but rather its capitulation) means anything, it means that the child's initial demand for the mother, a demand for full and immediate presence, is "phallic," and that desire is only possible beyond demand. Rose adds:

Castration means first of all this—that the child's desire for the mother does not refer *to* her but *beyond* her, to an object, the phallus, whose status is first imaginary (the object presumed to satisfy her desire) and then symbolic (recognition that desire cannot be satisfied). Jacqueline Rose, "Introductuon II," *FS*.

20. Freud himself speaks of the substitution that occurs in the "fort-da game" in terms of this symbolic operation. He argues that the disappearance of the mother—which gives rise to the question, "Where is she going? What does she want? (and perhaps especially) Why am I not enough for her?"—is given an explanation by reference to the father, who is not present as such, but who is present as a symbolic reference, a signifier, a name, the one who is away in the war and who has "gone to the front" as Freud says. In the game played with the spool, which is thrown away and pulled back again in the movement of the "fort-da game," we see, according to Freud, "the child's great cultural achievement—the instinctual renunciation" which the child makes, "in allowing his mother to go away without protesting" (*SE*, 18:15). As Lacan points out, *it is not mastery over the mother that the child attains*, by replacing her with a symbolic substitute that he can control, *but precisely the reverse*: if the child is jubilant in playing this game, it is a sign of his renunciation of instinct, the loss of the maternal object, *the abandonment of incestuous desire*, and *the acceptance of symbolic mediation* in which presence and absence alternate, and the symbolic movement of desire becomes possible. For Lacan, the symbolic aspect of the paternal function allows us to

see the crucial link between the "fort-da game" and the origin of language. See *SXI*, 239: "To say that it is simply a question for the subject of instituting himself in a function of mastery is idiotic. . . . The exercise with this object [the spool of thread] refers to an alienation, and not to some supposed mastery."

21. One can see here that the child's desire depends on the desire of the Other, and that a correlation exists, according to Lacan, between two lacks—in the subject and in the Other—which are not identical, but which depend on one another. Lacan discusses this clearly in *Seminar XI*, where he speaks explicitly of the "overlapping of two lacks." For an excellent commentary of this issue, see Parveen Adams, "Representation and Sexuality," in *The Woman in Question*, ed. Parveen Adams and Elizabeth Cowie (Cambridge: MIT Press, 1990), 233–52.

22. We can hear this sacrificial note sounded in the cry of the child, in the moment when the cry passes from "need" to "demand." As Michèle Montrelay points out, even when all its needs have been fulfilled, the child is still able to cry, and *this* cry, which no longer asks for food or warmth or some organic necessity, has passed "beyond" need, becoming the first appeal to the Other, the first demand in the symbolic order, at once an acknowledgment of maternal desire—a recognition that *the Other is lacking*—and also an effort to put an end to that lack. The cry can thus be understood as a "sacrificial demand" in the sense that with it, the child proposes itself as the object to fill the lack in the Other—the cry thus being a "demand" that seeks the closure of desire. For psychoanalysis, therefore, what is crucial is not only the difference between "need" and "demand," but the further operation ("castration") by which desire can find its place "beyond demand." Michèle Montrelay, "The Story of Louise," *Returning to Freud*, 75–93.

23. As Sylvia Rodríguez, an Australian analyst, once said to me in conversation, "there is all the difference in the world between saying to the child, 'Do this for me, dear,' and saying 'Do this because you must,' or because 'everyone has to.'" The first maintains the imaginary "bondage" of love (what Lacan calls the demand for love), while the second opens the symbolic field of "the They," the anonymous domain of "it is necessary"—the third party *which is the precondition of intersubjectivity*. This should suggest that paternal authority, as an imaginary power (I stress this word power partly with Foucault in mind), is precisely an abdication of the law.

24. For an extended discussion of the castration complex as a specific moment within the Oedipus complex, see the anonymous paper published in *Feminine Sexuality* as "The Phallic Phase and the Subjective Import of the Castration Complex" (*FS*, 99–122).

25. Jacqueline Rose gives an excellent, extended treatment of three forms of identification in Freud's *Group Psychology* and their relation to the imaginary and symbolic in Lacan. We disagree, however, with her remark that "the problem of sexual difference clearly informs the first two categories," since it does not arise in the first form of identification, mentioned above. See Jacqueline Rose, "The Imaginary," in *Sexuality in the Field of Vision*. See also the useful distinctions between "internalization," "incorporation," and "introjection" (terms that are often used interchangeably), in *Psychoanalytic Terms and Concepts*, ed. Burness E. Moore, M.D., and Bernard D. Fine, M.D. (New Haven, CT: Yale University Press, 1990), under "internalization," 102–103.

26. Laplanche and Pontalis, *The Language of Psychoanalysis*, 336.

27. It should be clear that on this account, there would be a distinction between identification and object-choice even where they might appear to coincide or converge on the same point—for example, in the case of a subject who identifies with one sex and also takes that sex as an object. This is particularly important for the question of homosexuality, and of whether it is possible to desire another woman "as a woman," or to desire a man "as a man." It is often said that psychoanalysis imposes a compulsory heterosexuality, and is it surely the case that this tendency exists, not only among certain psychoanalysts (who consider homosexuality a disorder that might be cured), but also by virtue of the very structure of the Oedipus complex, which *seems* to split object-choice and identification in two different directions, in precisely this "compulsory" fashion (so that a man who chooses another man as his object would automatically be regarded as having a "feminine" identification, and thus viewed in terms of a "heterosexual" object-choice). I would therefore stress this *seeming*, which relies on a symmetry that the diagrams do not finally sustain, since the problem they articulate is a conceptual distinction (which is also a distinction in the psyche), between identification and object-choice, and not an "empirical" distinction between two "actual objects," one representing identification and the other object-choice.

28. The question of sexual difference is famously addressed by Freud in "Female Sexuality," where the question of "paternal identification"—understood here as symbolic identification (and not as the "father of individual prehistory")—is said to be a particularly problematic issue for the girl. If the boy is usually led to give up the initial identification with the mother by identifying with the father, it is not so with the girl. "With the small girl," Freud says, "her first object, too, was the mother. How does she find her way to her father? How, when, and why does she detach herself from her mother?" (*SE*, 21:225). In fact, Freud adds, even when she does make this "turn towards the father," it may be that "her father *merely takes over the heritage* of an equally strong attachment to her mother" (227), in which case (1) it remains highly obscure what differentiates the "mother" and "father," and what relation there can possibly be between "sexual difference," and the terms "father" and "mother"; and (2) it would seem that the father inherits or perpetuates (or maintains a genealogical link with) precisely some of the features of the "first object" which he was meant to overcome. This is precisely our question, this "turning towards the father," which has a different structure in each of the two sexes, and which Lacan comes to regard as a question of "*père-version.*"

29. Some writers have developed a feminine ethics on this basis, arguing that women tend to have more fluid ego boundaries and a greater capacity for empathy. What Freud regards as the "insufficient development of a superego" and a "less commanding conscience" are thus read as positive phenomena, capable of generating a different sense of "justice." Others have argued that the very model of "proper subjectivity" is modeled on the specific individuation of the boy, and is therefore specifically masculine without having been recognized as such.

30. Many critics have taken issue with Freud's account, from numerous perspectives. Let us refer the reader at this point only to Luce Irigaray, "Body Against Body: In Relation to the Mother," *Sexes and Genealogies*, 9–21.

31. For a discussion of the antinomies in Kant, and their relation to the question of sexual difference, see Joan Copjec, *Read My Desire: Lacan Against the Historicists* (Cambridge: MIT Press, 1994), pp. 201–36; and Slavoj Žižek, *Tarrying with the Negative: Kant, Hegel, and the Critique of Ideology* (Durham, NC: Duke University Press, 1993), 45–80 (which includes remarks on Copjec's formulations).

32. We should be wary of speaking too easily of Lacan's "use" of Saus-

sure, and of his "linguistic interpretation" of Freud, for these observations mean not only that the "father" is regarded as a linguistic function in some sense, but also that language is now regarded as carrying within it a relation to mortality that linguistic theory would not normally be led to encounter. As Heidegger would say, only *mortals* speak, and all speech carries a mark of mortality. Those who wonder whether computers can "communicate" would therefore do well to read Freud a little.

33. In the essay on psychosis, where psychosis is understood as a failure of the paternal function, Lacan asks us to imagine this as a deficiency in the *signifier*. Where the place of the signifier ought to have been established, it (and not the actual father) remains inadequate: "to the appeal of the Name-of-the-Father responds, not the absence of the real father, for this absence is more than compatible with the presence of the signifier, but the inadequacy of the signifier itself" (E 557/200).

34. This version of schema R, which is somewhat more complex than the version given in Lacan's *Écrits*, is taken from André Green, "Logic of Lacan's *objet (a)* and Freudian Theory: Convergences and Questions," *Interpreting Lacan*, Psychiatry and the Humanities, vol. 6, ed. Joseph Smith and William Kerrigan (New Haven, CT: Yale University Press, 1983), 161–91. Green's diagram, however, puts a capital phi (Φ) in place of Lacan's lower case phi (ϕ) thereby confusing the phallic signifier with the phallus as an imaginary object. See page 64.

35. On the "possible" and "impossible," and more generally Lacan's use of the categories of modal logic, see Robert Samuels, *Between Philosophy and Psychoanalysis: Lacan's Reconstruction of Freud* (New York: Routledge, 1993), a book that also contains a helpful discussion of *Totem and Taboo*.

36. See *Totem and Taboo* (*SE*, 13:146–56). I put quotations around the word "saves" in order to recall that the Greek text plays out the entire tragedy around this remarkable word (*soter*, "savior"). In the beginning, the Chorus comes to Oedipus saying, "You, father Oedipus, who have been our recourse in the past, who saved us from the Sphinx, we come to you now again, seeking help." And Oedipus, being called by that name (*soter*), is willing to assume it, saying in reply "Do not be afraid my children, for I will save the city." And at the end of the play, when he recognizes what he has done, Oedipus says that his entire destiny has been governed by an obscure law of which he was unaware, and that the gods have "saved" him, "set him aside" for their own reasons: "I have been saved for a terrible purpose by Apollo," he says.

37. Freud speaks of the "fixation" of infantile libido, as Samuels points out in *Between Philosophy and Psychoanalysis*.

38. We should offer a correction to Laplanche and Pontalis here, for in their definition of the "ego ideal," they assert that in 1923, in *The Ego and the Id*, "ego ideal and superego appear as synonymous," and that in 1933, with the *New Introductory Lectures*, there is "a distinction between the two terms," one of which designates the function of the ideal (symbolic identification), while the other designates the dimension of unconscious guilt and the sense of inferiority. See Laplanche and Pontalis, *The Language of Psychoanalysis*, 144–45. The issue is somewhat more complicated by the fact that Laplanche and Pontalis see a distinction between the ego ideal and the superego in "On Narcissism" (written just as the final essay in *Totem and Taboo* was completed), even though the term "superego" itself is not used there. Thus, they see this distinction being made in 1914, and then disappearing again until 1933.

39. Martin Heidegger, *Being and Time* (New York: Harper and Row, 1962), 281. Pagination follows that of the seventh (and subsequent) German editions, *Sein und Zeit* (Tubingen: Neomarius Verlag, 1953), which is given marginally in the English edition.

40. One could say that this feature is already present in the Oedipal drama, in the sense that Antigone and the other children of Oedipus inherit a "fate" from the father that corresponds closely to the concept of a "return" of the pathological father beyond the law. One could say that already for Oedipus himself, there is an inheritance from Laius, who responded to the oracle by leaving his son to die on the hillside. From Laius to Labdacus and back to the "prehistory" of Cadmus, we would thus *always already be in the version of the father* given in *Totem and Taboo*. This is correct, as far as the Greek drama goes (which always exceeds the reading we may wish to find in it). But insofar as we are concerned with a shift in Freud's work (and indeed Lacan's) from the early accounts of the Oedipus complex to the account given in *Totem and Taboo*, the distinction may have some validity. Certainly is has a *conceptual* validity, even if it is unclear in the texts themselves whether the distinction is clearly operative.

41. Catherine Millot, *Nobodaddy: L'Hystérie dans le siècle*, 74.

42. I have discussed this in more detail in "Vital Signs: The Place of Memory in Psychoanalysis," *Research in Phenomenology* [special issue, "Spaces of Memory"] 23 (1993): 22–72.

43. See Martin Heidegger, *Being and Time*, 280–301.

CHAPTER 5

1. Friedrich Nietzsche, *On The Genealogy of Morals*, trans. Walter Kaufmann (New York: Vintage, 1967).
2. This chapter was first given as a lecture at the Collegium Phaenomenologicum in Perugia, Italy, in 1993. I thank the directors, Charles C. Scott and Philippe van Haute, for the invitation, and for their hospitality.
3. "The Concern for Truth," *Michel Foucault, Politics, Philosophy, Culture: Interviews and Other Writings*, ed. Lawrence D. Kritzman (New York: Routledge, 1988), 262.
4. Michel Foucault, *The Archaeology of Knowledge*, trans. A. M. Sheridan-Smith (New York: Pantheon Books, 1972), 206.
5. In *The Archaeology of Knowledge*, Foucault conjures up an imaginary interlocutor, who challenges him to distinguish his work from structuralism, and then upon hearing Foucault's reply, says,

   > I can even accept that one should dispense, as far as one can, with a discussion of the speaking subject; but I dispute that these successes [of archaeology, as distinct from structuralism] give one the right *to turn the analysis back on to the very forms of discourse that made them possible*, and *to question the very locus in which we are speaking today*. (202, emphasis added)

   Instead, the interlocutor argues, we must acknowledge that "the history of those analyses . . . retains its own transcendence." Foucault replies, "It seems to me that the difference between us lies there (much more than in the over-discussed question of structuralism)" (202).
6. Slavov Žižek, *For They Know Not What They Do*, 13.
7. In his essay on psychosis, Lacan makes it explicit that the categories of "reality" and the "imaginary" not only *overlap*, but are themselves structured *through* the symbolic. Thus, "reality" no longer has the status of a "true reality" that one might oppose to an "imaginary" or "fictional" construction, and in addition, the fact that these two categories are in some sense mutually constitutive is itself the result of language. Thus, whereas the animal might be said to "adapt to reality" (in the usual sense of that word), the human being "adapts" (if one can still use this word) by means of representations that are constitutive of both "reality" and the "imaginary." See Jacques Lacan, "On a Question Preliminary to Any Possible Treatment of Psychosis" (*E, 531–83/179–225*).

8. Foucault makes the following remark in an interview with François Ewald: "The history of thought means not just the history of ideas or representations, but also an attempt to answer this question. . . . How can thought . . . have a history?" See "The Concern for Truth," 256.

9. Jacques Derrida, "Cogito and the History of Madness," *Writing and Difference*, trans. Alan Bass (Chicago: University of Chicago Press, 1978), 34. Henceforth cited in the text as *WD*.

10. To develop this properly, one would have to explore Foucault's remarks on the specifically modern form of "the origin," as he explains it in *The Order of Things*. As he says in "The Retreat and Return of the Origin," for modern thought, the origin "is very different from that ideal genesis that the Classical Age had attempted to reconstitute . . . the original in man is that which articulates him from the very outset upon something other than himself. . . . Paradoxically, the original, in man, does not herald the time of his birth, or the most ancient kernel of his experience. . . . [I]t signifies that man . . . is the being without origin . . . that man is cut off from the origin that would make him contemporaneous with his own existence" (331–32).

11. Michel Foucault, "Distance, Aspect, Origine," *Critique*, November 1963, 20–22. Cited from Raymond Bellour, "Towards Fiction," in *Michel Foucault: Philosopher*, trans. Timothy J. Armstrong (New York: Routledge, 1992), 148–56.

12. See Jean Hyppolite's remarkable but succinct discussion of Hegel on just this point, in *The Structuralist Controversy: The Languages of Criticism and the Sciences of Man*, ed. Richard Macksey and Eugenio Donato (Baltimore: Johns Hopkins, 1970). Hyppolite's account suggests that what we are here calling "dialectic" in fact refers not so much to Hegel as to a received version of "dialectic."

13. Michel Foucault, *The Birth of the Clinic: An Archaeology of Medical Perception*, ix.

14. A relevant discussion of this painting from a Lacanian perspective is Pierre-Gilles Guéguen, "Foucault and Lacan on the Status of the Subject of Representation," *Newsletter of the Freudian Field* 3, nos. 1–2 (spring/fall 1989): 51–57.

15. "Power and Sex," *Michel Foucault, Politics, Philosophy, Culture*, 110–24.

16. See "Power and Sex," 112.

> A few years ago, historians were very proud to discover that
> they could write not only the history of battles, of kings and
> institutions, but also of the economy . . . feelings, behavior,
> and the body. Soon, they will understand that the history of
> the West cannot be dissociated from the way its 'truth' is pro-
> duced. . . . The achievement of 'true' discourses . . . is one of
> the fundamental problems of the West.

17. Bernard Henri-Lévi points out that because Foucault suggests that
    there is *a relation* between the (mistaken) thesis asserting sexual
    repression and those practices which aim at liberation, he has some-
    times been misunderstood to argue that they are the same: "Hence
    the misunderstanding of certain commentators: 'According to Fou-
    cault, the repression or liberation of sex amounts to the same thing'"
    ("Power and Sex," 114). Foucault replies that the point was not to
    erase the difference between these two (or between madness and rea-
    son), but simply to consider the way in which the two things were
    bound to one another, in order to recognize that the promise of lib-
    eration takes part in the same conceptual arrangement that produced
    the idea of repression, to such a degree that the very aim of libera-
    tion often "ends up repressing" (as in the case of psychoanalysis, per-
    haps). This is why Foucault regards psychoanalysis with such
    suspicion, despite the connections we are pursuing between Foucault
    and Lacan. The question is whether psychoanalysis indeed remains
    trapped within the modern discourses of liberation that were born
    alongside what Foucault regards as the "monarchical" theories of
    power (what he also speaks of as the "repressive hypothesis"), or
    whether, as Foucault sometimes suggests, psychoanalysis in fact
    amounts to a disruption of that paradigm, just as genealogy does.
18. Michel Foucault, *Discipline and Punish: The Birth of the Prison*
    (New York: Vintage, 1977), 29. Henceforth cited in the text as DP.
19. Michel Foucault, *The History of Sexuality: An Introduction*, trans.
    Robert Hurley (New York: Vintage, 1978), p. 6. Henceforth cited in
    the text as HS.
20. Jana Sawicki's response to a paper by Issac Balbus shows very clearly
    the difference between a genealogical perspective and the "modern"
    discourses of liberation. These two papers offer an admirable exam-
    ple of the contrast between a "Marxist" analysis and a feminism that
    is influenced in part by genealogy. In her remarks, Sawicki shows
    how the promise of a liberated future is haunted by the "most viru-

lent" forms of humanism, in the sense that Balbus' call for liberation carries with it a normative component that escapes his analysis. See Isaac Balbus, "Disciplining Women: Michel Foucault and the Power of Feminist Discourse" and Jana Sawicki, "Feminism and the Power of Foucaultian Discourse," in *After Foucault: Humanistic Knowledge, Postmodern Challenges*, ed. Jonathan Arac (New Brunswick, NJ: Rutgers University Press, 1988).

21. Just as with psychoanalysis, there is here a focus on the past, and an elaboration of general principles, but the final word bears on the subject who is speaking, for that is where the reality of history lies.

22. Michel Foucault, "Preface to Transgression," *Language, Counter-Memory, Practice*, 29–52. The essay was first published as "Hommage à George Bataille" in *Critique*, nos. 195–96 (1963), 751–70.

23. At the end of *HS*, Foucault makes a similar point: sex is the most refined *product*, and not the *origin*; it is what one might call a discursive effect and not a "natural" basis that is shaped by various restrictions or prohibitions. The question we are asking, with Lacan, however, is whether sex is *simply* or *entirely* discursive. To speak of the real is not to speak of a prediscursive reality such as sex, but it is to ask about what remains outside representation (as madness, for Foucault, is left in silence or in shadow by the discourses of reason).

24. I am thinking here of Lacan's reflections upon the body itself as structured by such limits—the eyes, ears, and other orifices seeming to participate in just this dislocation of Euclidean space. See Jeanne Granon-Lafont, *La topologie ordinaire de Jacques Lacan* (Paris: Point Hors Ligne, 1985). I have discussed this briefly in "The Intimate Alterity of the Real," *Postmodern Culture* 6 (May 1996).

25. See Derrida's recent remarks on this sentence in "Etre juste avec Freud," in *Penser la folie: Essais sur Michel Foucault* (Paris: Galilée, 1992), 141–95.

26. Slavoj Žižek, *For They Know Not What They Do*, 9–10.

27. It is true that the "mechanics" of libido at one point occupied Freud, when he still believed it possible to measure libido according to a model of charge and discharge, homeostasis and tension. But something always disturbs this model, and Freud's use of such paradigms always follows them *to the limit*, to the point where they collapse, rather than elaborating them as a satisfactory answer. This does not keep his commentators from taking the bait, and putting their faith in an engine Freud has dismantled.

28. See the end of "Vital Signs: The Place of Memory in Psychoanalysis," *Research in Phenomenology* 1993, 22–72.
29. See Foucault's "What Is Enlightenment?" trans. Catherine Porter, in *The Foucault Reader*, ed. Paul Rabinow (New York: Pantheon, 1984), esp. 35–36. See also Žižek's remarks on Kant in *For They Know Not What They Do*, 203–209 and 229–37. In "What Is Enlightenment?" Foucault's question is very close to Lacan's: What linkage, what common origin, do we find between these two fathers, terror and enlightenment?
30. This thesis has been elaborated in considerable detail by Slavoj Žižek, in *The Sublime Object of Idealogy* (New York: Verso, 1989).
31. "What Is Enlightenment?" 33.
32. The discussion of Foucault and Derrida by Ann Wordsworth mentions the fact that the question of violence is one of several points at which these two thinkers, despite of their apparent conflict, come closest together. Foucault points out that madness and reason are not distinguished by natural necessity or by right, but only by the contingency of a certain formation of knowledge, and that history itself can be understood as occurring precisely because of the *inevitability* (the "law") of such contingent formations, and not as the unfolding of a fundamental "truth" of culture or human nature (teleological or merely sequentially continuous). Derrida himself says this

    > amounts to saying that madness is never excluded, except *in fact*, violently in history; or rather that this exclusion, this *difference* between the fact and the principle is historicity, the possibility of history itself. Does Foucault say otherwise? "*The necessity* of madness is linked . . . to the *possibility of history*." (WD, 310)

    Like Foucault and Lacan, so also Foucault and Derrida are much closer than their current academic reception would suggest.

Bibliography

Adams, Parveen. "Versions of the Body." *m/f*, nos. 11–12 (1986). 27–34.

———. "Representation and Sexuality." *The Woman in Question.* Ed. Elizabeth Cowie and Parveen Adams. Cambridge: MIT Press, 1990. 233–52.

———. "Mothering." *The Woman in Question.* Ed. Parveen Adams and Elizabeth Cowie. Cambridge: MIT Press, 1990. 315–27.

———. "A Note on the Distinction Between Sexual Division and Sexual Differences." *The Woman in Question.* Ed. Parveen Adams and Elizabeth Cowie. Cambridge: MIT Press, 1990.

Anonymous. "The Phallic Phase and the Subjective Import of the Castration Complex." *Feminine Sexuality.* 99–122.

Arac, Jonathan, ed. *After Foucault: Humanistic Knowledge, Postmodern Challenges.* New Brunswick: Rutgers University Press, 1988.

Balbus, Isaac. "Disciplining Women: Michel Foucault and the Power of Feminist Discourse." *After Foucault: Humanistic Knowledge, Postmodern Challenges.* Ed. Jonathan Arac. New Brunswick: Rutgers University Press, 1988.

Bellour, Raymond. "Towards Fiction." *Michel Foucault: Philosopher.* Ed and trans. Timothy J. Armstrong. New York: Routledge, 1992. 148–56.

Benjamin, Jessica. *Like Subjects, Love Objects: Essays on Recognition and Sexual Difference.* New Haven: Yale University Press, 1995.

Bernasconi, Robert. *The Question of Language in Heidegger's History of Being.* Atlantic Highlands: Humanities Press, 1985.

Boothby, Richard. *Death and Desire: Psychoanalytic Theory in Lacan's Return to Freud.* New York: Routledge, 1991.

Bordo, Susan. "*Anorexia Nervosa*: Psychopathology as the Crystalization of Culture." *Feminism and Foucault: Reflections on Resistance.* Ed. Irene Diamond and Lee Quinby. Boston: Northeastern University Press, 1988. 87–117.

Bouchard, Donald, ed. *Language, Counter-Memory, Practice: Selected Essays and Interviews.* Ithaca: Cornell University Press, 1977.

Bracher, Mark, and Marshall Alcorn, Jr., Ronald J. Cortell, and Françoise Massardier-Kenney, ed. *Lacanian Theory of Discourse: Subject, Structure, and Society.* New York: New York University Press, 1994.

Braidotti, Rosi. "The Politics of Ontological Difference." *Between Feminism and Psychoanalysis.* Ed. Theresa Brennan. London: Routledge, 1989. 89–105.

Braunstein, Nestor. *La Jouissance: un concept lacanien.* Paris: Point Hors Ligne, 1990.

Brennan, Theresa, ed. *Between Feminism and Psychoanalysis.* London: Routledge, 1989.

Brousse, Marie-Hélène. "Feminism With Lacan." *Newsletter of the Freudian Field.* vol. 5 (spring/fall, 1991), 113–28.

Butler, Judith. *Gender Trouble: Feminism and the Subversion of Identity.* New York: Routledge, 1990.

———. *Bodies That Matter: On the Discursive Limits of "Sex."* New York: Routledge: 1993.

Canguilhem, Georges. *The Normal and the Pathological.* Intro. Michel Foucault. Trans. Carolyn R. Fawcett and Robert S. Cohen. New York: Zone Books, 1991.

Chanter, Tina. "Female Temporality and the Future of Feminism." *Abjection, Melancholia and Love: The Work of Julia Kristeva.* Ed. John Fletcher and Andrew Benjamin. New York: Routledge, 1990. 63–79.

———. "Kristeva's Politics of Change: Tracking Essentialism with the Help of a Sex/Gender Map." *Ethics, Politics, and Difference in Julia Kristeva's Writing.* Ed. Kelly Oliver. Bloomington: Indiana University Press, 1993. 179–95.

———. *Ethics of Eros: Irigaray's Rewriting of the Philosophers.* New York: Routledge, 1995.

Chertok, Léon, and Isabelle Stengers. *A Critique of Psychoanalytic Reason: Hypnosis as a Scientific Problem from Lavoisier to Lacan.* Trans. Martha Noel Evans. Stanford: Stanford University Press, 1992.

Copjec, Joan. "Cutting Up." *Between Feminism and Psychoanalysis.* Ed. Theresa Brennan. London: Routledge, 1989. 227–46.

———. "m/f, or Not Reconciled." *The Woman in Question.* Ed. Parveen Adams and Elizabeth Cowie. Cambridge: MIT Press, 1990. 10–18.

———, ed. *Television: A Challenge to the Psychoanalytic Establishment.* New York: Norton, 1990.

———. *Read My Desire: Lacan Against the Historicists.* Cambridge: MIT Press, 1994.

Crownfield, David. *Body/Text in Julia Kristeva: Religion, Women, and Psychoanalysis.* Albany: State University of New York Press, 1992.

Dallery, Arlene. "The Politics of Writing (The) Body: *Ecriture Feminine.*" *Gender/Body/Knowledge.* Ed. Alison Jaggar and Susan Bordo. New Brunswick: Rutgers University Press, 1989.

David-Ménard, Monique. *Hysteria from Freud to Lacan: Body and Language in Psychoanalysis.* Trans. Catherine Porter. Ithaca: Cornell University Press, 1989.

Derrida, Jacques. "Cogito and the History of Madness." *Writing and Difference.* Trans. Alan Bass. Chicago: University of Chicago, 1978.

———. "*Geschlecht*: diveérence sexuelle, différence ontologique." *Psyché: Inventions de l'autre.* Paris: galilée, 1987. 395–414. First published in *Cahiers de l'Herne (no. 45): Martin Heidegger.* Ed. Michel Haar. Paris: Éditions de l'Herne, 1983. 419–30. "Geschlecht: Sexual Difference, Ontological Difference." *Research in Phenomenology* 13 (1983), 65–83.

———. "The Art of Memoires." *Memoires: for Paul de Man*. New York: Columbia University Press, 1988. 47–88.

———. "Etre juste avec Freud." *Penser la folie: Essais sur Michel Foucault*. Paris: Galilée, 1992. 141–95.

———. *Memoires of the Blind: The Self-Portrait and Other Ruins*. Trans. Pascale-Anne Brault and Michael Nass. Chicago: University of Chicago Press, 1993.

Dews, Peter. *The Logics of Disintegration: post-structuralist thought and the claims of critical theory*. London: Verso, 1987.

Diagnostic and Statistical Manual of Mental Disorders, Third Edition. Washington D.C.: American Psychiatric Association, 1980.

Doane, Janice, and Devon Hodges. *From Klein to Kristeva: Psychoanalytic Feminism and the Search for the "Good Enough" Mother*. Ann Arbor: University of Michigan Press, 1992.

Doumit, Élie. untitled discussion. *Lacan avec les philosophes*. Paris: Albin Michel, 1991. 265–76.

Forrester, John. *The Seductions of Psychoanalysis: Freud, Derrida, Lacan*. Cambridge: Cambridge University Press, 1990.

Foucault, Michel. "Distance, aspect, origine," *Critique*, November 1963. 20–22.

———. "Hommage à George Bataille." *Critique*, nos. 195–96 (1963). 751–70. Trans. "Preface to Transgression." *Language, Counter-Memory, Practice: Selected Essays and Interviews*. Ed. Donald F. Bouchard. Ithaca: Cornell University Press, 1977. 29–52.

———. *Madness and Civilization: A History of Insanity in the Age of Reason*. Trans. Richard Howard. New York: Vintage, 1965.

———. *The Order of Things: An Archaeology of the Human Sciences*. Trans. Alan Sheridan. New York: Random House, 1970.

———. *The Birth of the Clinic: An Archaeology of Medical Perception*. Trans. A. M. Sheridan Smith. New York: Vintage, 1975.

———. *Discipline and Punish: The Birth of the Prison*. Trans. Alan Sheridan. New York: Vintage, 1977.

———. "What Is Enlightenment?" Trans. Catherine Porter. *The Foucault Reader*. Ed. Paul Rabinow. New York: Pantheon, 1984.

———. "The Concern for Truth." *Michel Foucault: Politics, Philosophy, Culture*. Ed. Lawrence Kritzman. New York: Routledge, 1988.

———. *The History of Sexuality: An Introduction*. Trans. Robert Hurley. New York: Vintage, 1990.

Fraser, Nancy. "The Uses and Abuses of French Discourse Theories for Feminist Politics." *Revaluing French Feminism: Critical Essays on Difference, Agency, and Culture*. Ed. Nancy Fraser and Sandra Lee Bartky. Bloomington: Indiana University Press, 1992. 177–93.

Freud, Sigmund. *The Standard Edition of the Complete Psychological Works of Sigmund Freud*. 24 vols. Ed. James Strachey, et al. Trans. James Strachey. London: The Hogarth Press, 1957.

Gallop, Jane. "Keys to Dora." *In Dora's Case: Freud, Hysteria, Feminism*. Ed. Charles Bernheimer and Claire Kahane. New York: Columbia University Press, 1985. 200–20.

Garber, Marjorie. *Vested Interests: Cross-Dressing and Cultural Anxiety.* New York: Routledge, 1992.

Gasché, Rodolphe. "Of Aesthetic and Historical Determination." *Post–Structuralism and the Question of History.* Ed. Derek Attridge and Geoff Bennington. Cambridge: Cambridge University Press, 1987. 139–61.

Goux, Jean-Joseph. *Oedipus, Philosopher.* Trans. Catherine Porter. Stanford: Stanford University Press, 1993.

Granon-Lafont, Jeanne. *La topologie ordinaire de Jacques Lacan.* Paris: Point Hors Ligne, 1985.

Green, André. "Logic of Lacan's *objet (a)* and Freudian Theory: Convergences and Questions." *Interpreting Lacan* [Psychiatry and the Humanities, vol. 6]. Ed. Joseph Smith and William Kerrigan. New Haven: Yale University Press, 1983. 161–91.

Grigg, Russell. "Freud's Problem of Identification." *Newsletter of the Freudian Field,* 1:1 (spring 1987), 14–8.

Gross, Elizabeth. "Philosophy, Subjectivity, and the Body: Kristeva and Irigaray." *Feminist Challenges: Social and Political Theory.* Ed. Carole Pateman and Elizabeth Gross. Boston: Northeastern University Press, 1987. 125–43.

Grosz, Elizabeth. *Sexual Subversions: Three French Feminists.* Sydney: Allen and Unwin, 1989.

———. *Jacques Lacan: A Feminist Introduction.* New York: Routledge, 1990.

Guéguen, Pierre-Gilles. "Foucault and Lacan on the Status of the Subject of Representation." *Newsletter of the Freudian Field,* vol. 3, nos. 1–2 (spring/fall 1989), 51–57.

The Harvard Guide to Modern Psychiatry. Ed. Armand M. Nicoli, Jr., M. D. Cambridge: Harvard University Press, 1978.

Heidegger, Martin. *Sein und Zeit.* Tubingen: Neomarius Verlag, 1953. *Being and Time.* Trans. John MacQuarrie and Edward Robinson. New York: Harper and Row, 1962.

———. *Unterwegs zur Sprache.* Pfullingen: Neske, 1959. Trans. P. Hertz and J. Stambaugh *On the Way to Language.* New York: Harper and Row, 1971.

———. "The Origin of the Work of Art." *Poetry, Language, Thought.* Ed. and trans. Albert Hofstadter. New York: Harper and Row, 1971.

——— "The Thing," *Poetry, Language, Thought.* Ed. and trans. Albert Hofstadter. New York: Harper and Row, 1971.

———. "Letter to Father Richardson." William J. Richardson, S. J., *Heidegger: Through Phenomenology to Thought.* The Hague: Martinus Nijhoff, 1974. viii–xxiii.

———. *The Metaphysical Foundations of Logic.* Trans. Michael Heim. Bloomington: Indiana University Press, 1984.

Hyppolite, Jean. "The Structure of Philosophic Language According to the 'Preface' to Hegel's *Phenomenology of the Mind.*" *The Structuralist Controversy: The Languages of Criticism and the Sciences of Man.* Ed. Richard Macksey and Eugenio Donato. Baltimore: Johns Hopkins, 1970. 157–85.

Irigaray, Luce. *Ce sex qui n'en est pas un.* Paris: Minuit, 1977. *This Sex Which Is Not One.* Trans. Catherine Porter. Ithaca: Cornell, 1985.

———. *Le Corps-a-corps avec la mère*. Montréal: La Pleine Lune, 1981.

———. "La Croyance Même." *Sexes et Parentés*. Paris: Minuit, 1987. 37–65.

———. *L'Ethique de la difference sexual*. Paris: Minuit, 1984. Trans. Carolyn Burke and Gillian C. Gill. *An Ethics of Sexual Difference*. Ithaca: Cornell University Press, 1993.

———. "The Female Gender." *Sexes and Genealogies*. Trans. Catherine Porter. New York: Columbia University Press, 1993.

———. "Body Against Body: In Relation to the Mother," *Sexes and Genealogies*. Trans. Gillian Gill. New York: Columbia University Press, 1993. 9–21.

Jardine, Alice. "Introduction to Julia Kristeva's 'Women's Time.'" *Signs* 7, no. 1 (1981): 5–12.

———. "Opaque Texts and Transparent Contexts: The Political Difference of Julia Kristeva." *Ethics, Politics, and Difference in Julia Kristeva's Writing*. Ed. Kelly Oliver. New York: Routledge, 1993. 23–31.

Jardine, Lisa. "The Politics of Impenetrability." *Between Feminism and Psychoanalysis*. Ed. Teresa Brennan. New York: Routledge, 1989.

Jones, Ann Rosalind. "Writing the Body: Towards an Understanding of *L'Ecriture Féminine*." *Feminist Studies* 7, no. 2 (summer 1981).

Julien, Philippe. *Jacques Lacan's Return to Freud: The Real, the Symbolic, and the Imaginary*. Trans. Devra Beck Simiu. New York: New York University Press, 1994.

Kofman, Sarah. *The Enigma of Woman: Woman in Freud's Writings*. Trans. Catherine Porter. Ithaca: Cornell University Press, 1985.

Krell, David Farrell. *Daimon Life: Heidegger and Life-Philosophy*. Bloomington: Indiana University Press, 1992.

Kristeva, Julia. "Stabat Mater." *Histoires d'amour*. Paris: Denoël, 1983. 225–247. "Stabat Mater." Trans. Léon S. Roudiez. *The Kristeva Reader*. Ed. Toril Moi. New York: Columbia University Press, 1986. 160–85. Also available in Julia Kristeva, *Tales of Love*. Trans. Léon Roudiez. New York: Columbia University Press, 1987. 234–63.

———. "Freud and Love: Treatment and Its Discontents." *The Kristeva Reader*. Ed. Toril Moi. New York: Columbia University Press, 1986. 240–71.

Kritzman, Lawrence D., Ed. *Michel Foucault, Politics, Philosophy, Culture: Interviews and Other Writings, 1977–1984*. New York: Routledge, 1988.

Kuykendall, Eleanor. "Toward an ethic of nurturance: Luce Irigaray on Mothering and Power." *Mothering: Essays in Feminist Theory*. Ed. Joyce Trebilcot. Totowa: Rowman and Allanheld, 1984.

Lacan, Jacques. *Écrits*. Paris: Seuil, 1966. *Écrits: A Selection*. Trans. Alan Sheridan. New York: Norton, 1977.

———. *Le Séminaire, livre XI: Les quatres concepts fondamentaux de la psychanalyse*. Ed. Jacques-Alain Miller. Paris: Seuil, 1973. *The Four Fundamental Concepts of Psychoanalysis*. Trans. Alan Sheridan. New York: Norton, 1978.

———. *Le Séminaire, livre VII: L'ethique de la psychanalyse, 1959–60*. Ed. Jacques-Alain Miller. Paris: Seuil, 1986. *Seminar VII: The Ethics of Psychoanalysis 1959–60*. Trans. Dennis Porter. New York: Norton, 1992.

———. *The Seminar of Jacques Lacan, Book II: The Ego in Freud's Theory and in the Technique of Psychoanalysis, 1954–55*. Ed. Jacques-Alain Miller.

Trans. Sylvana Tomaselli, with notes by John Forrester. New York: Norton, 1988.

———. "Television." Trans. Denis Hollier, Rosalind Krauss, and Annette Michelson. *Television: A Challenge to the Psychoanalytic Establishment.* Ed. Joan Copjec. New York: Norton, 1990.

———. "Introduction to the Names-of-the-Father Seminar." Trans. Jeffrey Mehlman, in *Television: A Challenge to the Psychoanalytic Establishment.* Ed. Joan Copjec. New York: Norton, 1990. 81–95.

Laplanche, Jean, and J.-B. Pontalis. *The Language of Psychoanalysis.* Trans. Donald Nicholson-Smith. New York: Norton, 1973.

Laplanche, Jean. *Life and Death in Psychoanalysis.* Trans. Jeffrey Mehlman. Baltimore: Johns Hopkins, 1976.

Leland, Dorothy. "Lacanian Psychoanalysis and French Feminism: Towards an Adequate Political Psychology." *Hypatia* 3, no. 3 (winter 1989): 81–103.

Lemoine-Luccioni, Eugénie. *Partage des femmes.* Paris: Seuil, 1976. *The Dividing of Women or Woman's Lot.* Trans. Marie-Laure Davenport and Marie-Christine Réguis. London: Free Association Books, 1987.

———. "The Fable of the Blood." *Returning to Freud: Clinical Psychoanalysis in the School of Lacan.* Ed. and trans. Stuart Schneiderman. New Haven: Yale, 1980.

Lothstein, Leslie Martin. *Female-to-Male Transsexualism: Historical, Clinical, and Theoretical Issues.* Boston: Routledge and Kegan Paul, 1983.

Mannoni, Octave. *Freud: The Theory of the Unconscious.* London: Verso, 1985.

McKluskie, Barbara. "Women's Language and Literature: A Problem in Women's Studies." *Feminist Review* 14 (summer 1983).

Miller, Jacques-Alain. "How Psychoanalysis Cures According to Lacan." *Newsletter of the Freudian Field,* vol. 1, no 2 (fall 1987): 4–30.

———. "To Interpret the Cause: From Freud to Lacan," *Newsletter of the Freudian Field,* vol. 3 (spring/fall 1989): 30–50.

———. "A Reading of Some Details in *Television* in Dialogue with the Audience." *Newsletter of the Freudian Field,* vol. 4 (spring/fall 1990): 4–30.

———. "Extimité." *Lacanian Theory of Discourse: Subject, Structure, and Society.* Ed. Mark Bracher, Marshall Alcorn, Jr., Ronald J. Cortell, and Françoise Massardier-Kenney. New York: New York University Press, 1994. 74–87.

Millot, Catherine. *Nobodaddy: L'Hystérie dans le siècle.* Paris: Point Hors Ligne, 1988.

———. *Horsexe: Essay on Transsexuality.* Paris: Point Hors Ligne, 1983. *Horsexe: Essay on Transexuality.* Trans. Kenneth Hylton. New York: Autonomedia, 1990.

———. "The Feminine Superego." Trans. Ben Brewster. *The Woman in Question.* Ed. Parveen Adams and Elizabeth Cowie. Cambridge: MIT Press, 1990. 294–306.

Mitchell, Juliet, and Jacqueline Rose, ed. *Feminine Sexuality: Jacques Lacan and the école freudienne.* Trans. Jacqueline Rose. New York: Norton, 1982.

Moi, Toril. "Patriarchal Thought and the Drive for Knowledge." *Between Feminism and Psychoanalysis.* Ed. Teresa Brennan. New York: Routledge, 1989. 189–205.

Moir, Anne, and David Jessel. *Brain Sex: The Real Difference Between Men and Women*. New York: Dell, 1989.

Montrelay, Michèle. *L'Ombre et le nom*. Paris: Editions de Minuit, 1977.

———. "The Story of Louise." *Returning to Freud: Clinical Psychoanalysis in the School of Lacan*. Ed. and trans. Stuart Schneiderman. New Haven, CT: Yale University Press, 1980. 75–93.

Moore, Burness, M.D., and Bernard D. Fine, ed. *Psychoanalytic Terms and Concepts*. New Haven, CT: Yale University Press, 1990.

Morris, Meagan. "The Pirate's Fiancee: Feminists and Philosophers, or maybe tonight it'll happen." *Feminism and Foucault: Reflections on Resistance*.

Nietzsche, Friedrich. *On the Genealogy of Morals*. Trans. Walter Kauffman. New York: Vintage, 1967.

Oliver, Kelly. *Reading Kristeva: Unraveling the Double-Bind*. Bloomington: Indiana University Press, 1993.

———, ed. *Ethics, Politics, and Difference in Julia Kristeva's Writing*. New York: Routledge, 1993.

Penley, Constance. "Missing *m/f*." *The Woman in Question*. Cambridge: MIT Press, 1990.

Richardson, William J. *Heidegger: Through Phenomenology to Thought*. The Hague: Martinus Nijhoff, 1974.

Rose, Jacqueline. *Sexuality in the Field of Vision*. London: Verso, 1986.

———. "Julia Kristeva—Take Two." *Sexuality in the Field of Vision*. 141–64.

———. "The Imaginary." *Sexuality in the Field of Vision*. 167–97.

———. "Introduction II." *Feminine Sexuality: Jacques Lacan and the école freudienne*.

Safouan, Moustafa. *Le Structuralism en psychanalyse*. Paris: Seuil, 1968.

———. "Contribution to the Psychoanalysis of Transsexualism." *Returning to Freud*. 195–212.

Samuels, Robert. *Between Philosophy and Psychoanalysis: Lacan's Reconstruction of Freud*. New York: Routledge, 1993.

Sawicki, Jana. "Feminism and the Power of Foucaultian Discourse." *After Foucault: Humanistic Knowledge, Postmodern Challenges*. Ed. Jonathan Arac. New Brunswick, NJ: Rutgers University Press, 1988.

Sayers, Janet. *Biological Politics: Feminist and Anti–Feminist Perspectives*. London: Tavistock, 1982.

Schneiderman, Stuart, ed. and trans. *Returning to Freud: Clinical Psychoanalysis in the School of Lacan*. New Haven, CT: Yale, 1980.

Schneiderman, Stuart. "Art According to Lacan." *Newsletter of the Freudian Field*, 2: 1 (spring 1988).

Shepherdson, Charles. "On Fate: Psychoanalysis and the Desire to Know." *Dialectic and Narrative*. Ed. Tom Flynn and Dalia Judovitz. New York: State University of New York Press, 1993: 271–302.

———. "Vital Signs: The Place of Memory in Psychoanalysis." *Research in Phenomenology*, [special issue, "Spaces of Memory"], vol. 23 (1993): 22–72.

———. "A Loss for Words: Literature and Method in Foucault's *The Order of Things*." *Literature and Psychology*, 40:4 (spring 1994): 1–27.

———. "*Adaequatio Sexualis*: Is There a Measure of Sexual Difference?" *From*

Phenomenology to Thought, Errancy, and Desire. Ed. Babette Babich. Dordrecht: Kluwer, 1995. 447–73.

———. "Need and Demand in Kojève and Lacan." *Perspectives on Embodiment: The Intersections of Nature and Culture.* Ed. Honi Haber and Gail Weiss. New York: Routledge, 1999. 183–211.

———. "History and the Real: Foucault with Lacan." *Postmodern Culture*, 5:2 (January 1995).

———. "The Intimate Alterity of the Real." *Postmodern Culture*, vol. 6 (May 1996).

Silvestre, Michel. *Demain la psychanalyse.* Paris: Navarin, 1987.

Sprengnether, Madelon. *The Spectral Mother: Freud, Feminism, and Psychoanalysis.* Ithaca: Cornell University Press, 1990.

Traits de perversion dans les structures cliniques. Ed. Navarin Press, Fondation du Champs Freudien. Paris: Navarin, 1990.

Weir, Alison. "Identification with the Divided Mother: Kristeva's Ambivalence." *Ethics, Politics, and Difference in Julia Kristeva's Writing.* Ed. Kelly Oliver. New York: Routledge, 1993. 79–91.

———. *Sacrificial Logics: Fem inist Theory and the Critique of Identity.* New York: Routledge, 1996.

Whitford, Margaret. "Rereading Irigaray," in *Between Feminism and Psychoanalysis.* Ed. Teresa Brennan. New York: Routledge, 1989. 106–26.

Young, Iris Marion. "The Ideal of Community and the Politics of Difference" in *Feminism/Postmodernism.* Ed. Linda J. Nicholson. New York: Routledge, 1990. 300–323.

Ziarek, Ewa. "Kristeva and Levinas: Mourning, Ethics, and the Feminine." *Ethics, Politics, and Difference,* 62–78.

Žižek, Slavoj. *For They Know Not What They Do: Enjoyment as a Political Factor.* New York: Routledge, 1992.

———. *Tarrying with the Negative: Kant, Hegel, and the Critique of Ideology.* Durham: Duke University Press, 1993.

———. *The Sublime Object of Ideology.* New York: Verso, 1989.

Index

Adams, Parveen, 91, 219n 6
aggression, 83, 87, 122, 194
alterity, 107, 110, 129; feminine, 55
amenorrhea, 17–18, 25–26
analysis, 26, 43, 80, 98, 160, 182
anatomy, 30, 62, 85, 101, 107; change of, 101; female, 19, 31
anorexia, 11–12, 17–18, 21, 25–27, 33, 38, 115, 190–94, 205n 31
antinomy, 74–75, 134
anxiety, 184
Apollon, Willy, 202n 20
archaeology, 59, 166
Aristophanes, 70
Australian Centre for Psychoanalysis, 188
autonomy, 122, 128, 144

Bachelard, Gaston, 34
Balbus, Isaac, 235n 20
Bataille, Georges, 173
Benjamin, Jessica, 131, 225n 18, 226n 18
Bergeron, Daniele, 202n 20
biological: analysis, 18; determination, 19; determinism, 95; need, 33; norm, 32; origin, 140; phenomenon, 38; principles, 31
biology, 4, 7, 32, 39, 52, 192; and history, 17–19, 94; and sexuality, 30; vital order of, 37
biomedical model, 7, 10, 190
birth, 27, 29, 67
body, the, 3–5, 11, 15, 18, 21–24, 30, 33–35, 37, 39, 46, 52, 54, 85, 88, 93–94, 101, 110, 112, 170, 176, 184, 188, 190, 193, 195, 200n 9, 206n 34, 221n 16; and history, 30, 39; and the organism, 95–100; biological, 54; con-

struction of, 21 (see also constitution of the body); erotogenic, 6, 23; fantasy, 102, 104; female, 52; imaginary, 38–39, 97–98; limitation of, 23; perfected, 106; sexual, 112
Bordo, Susan, 205n 31
boys, 29, 128, 130–32, 230n 28 (see also child, the)
Braidotti, Rosi, 202n 19
Braunstein, Nestor, 223n 4
breast, the, 28–29, 98, 119, 193–94
Brousse, Marie-Hélène, 80–82, 202n 17

Canguilhem, Georges, 86
Cantin, Lucy, 202n 20
castration, 13–14, 73–81, 86, 108, 118, 123, 127, 141–42, 147, 213n 12, 227n 19, 228n 22; complex, 128; feminine, 76; masculine, 76; symbolic, 72
child, the, 27–30, 50, 60, 63, 66, 68–71, 74, 78, 80, 83, 120, 122–24, 126–27, 129, 132, 135–39, 140, 144, 146–47, 193–95, 213n 12, 214n 17, 215n 24, 227n 19; -mother relation, 79; as maternal phallus, 79; autonomy of, 128; demand of (see demand of child); development of, 36; female, 74, 123 (see also girls); male, 74, 123 (see also boys); sexual identity of, 128; subjective position of, 124
China, 56, 74
Chodorow, Nancy, 200n 8, 219n 6
chronological: model, 72; time, 148, 158
chronology, 59, 72, 147, 177
conscience, 121, 145–46, 149–51, 162, 216n 25, 230n 29

247

Index

prohibitions, 65, 148–49, 168, 172–73, 176–78, 227n 19; cultural, 87, 96, 178; external, 96

psychiatry, 157, 175, 179

psychoanalysis, 1–5, 8–11, 15, 18, 21, 31 32, 42–44, 46, 55, 59, 61–62, 83, 96–97, 99–100, 116, 126, 132–33, 158, 175, 179, 183–85, 187–92, 194, 205n 28, 209n 44, 212n 3, 213n 12, 217n 32, 218n 3, 219n 6, 235n 17; and history, 89–95; ethics of, 78, 119; French, 1–2, 8, 10, 94, 188; history of, 9; Lacanian, 115, 181; revision of, 44; theory of specificity in, 7–8

psychoanalytic theory, 1, 7–8, 13, 15, 55, 82, 125, 132, 209n 43, 210n 51, 226n 18; French, 2, 95, 99

psychology, 5, 37, 175

psychosis, 56, 64, 82, 101, 106, 118–19, 135, 148, 223n 4, 231n 33, 233n 7

punishment, 177, 179

racism, 179

Raymond, Janice, 108

real, the, 6, 63–66, 68, 81, 90, 98–99, 101–2, 110, 117, 137, 160, 167, 182, 194; and history, 153–85; experience, 38; relations, 136–37

realism, 161

reality, 154–56, 158–61, 165, 214n 15, 233n 7; field, 65; principle, 64, 160; testing, 160

reason, 159, 161, 168

reception theory, 55–59

Reé, Paul, 154

religion, 71, 86, 142

remainder. See le reste

reminiscences, 5, 98 (see also memory)

representation, 4–6, 19, 28–29, 31, 33, 37, 52–53, 56, 59, 61, 81, 87–88, 97, 156, 158, 160, 176, 181, 190, 192, 201n 13, 226n 18; image of, 166; laws of, 96; maternal (see maternal represenation); of sexuality, 99; paralysis (see paralysis, representation); verbal, 167

repression, 50, 51, 57, 171, 179, 208n 41; and power, 167–68; of sex (see sex, repression of)

repressive hypothesis, 96, 121, 146, 172

reproduction, 30, 32–33, 60

resistance, 20, 168, 172

rituals, 100

Robbes-Grillet, 164

Rodríguez, Sylvia, 228n 23

role(s), 85–88; conformity of, 103

Rose, Jacqueline, 51, 135, 223n 30, 225n 16, 227n 19, 229n 25

Rousseau, 162

sacrifice, 71, 86, 105–6, 150–51

Sade, Marquis de, 180

satire, 154–56, 160

Saussure, Ferdinand de, 117, 134, 212n 3, 230–31n 29

Sawicki, Jana, 235n 20

Sayers, Janet, 204n 27

schema R, 64–65, 65, 69, 72–73, 75–80, 107–8, 137, 138–39, 144–45, 215n 24(see also Lacan, Jacques; sexuation diagram); feminine side, 76–77; masculine side, 74–77, 79–80

Schneiderman, Stuart, 225n 16

Schreber, Daniel Paul, 71, 86, 105–6

science, 100–3, 105, 166

semiotic, 13, 50, 56–57, 60–63, 208n 41

set theory, 108

sex(es), 2, 23, 25, 66, 73, 94–95, 102, 106–7, 109, 124–26, 184, 192, 207n 38, 236n 23; and power, 171; in the nineteenth century, 172; procreative, 86; repression of, 170–71, 235n 17; the imperative of, 85–113; the other, 73, 106–7, 109–12

sexual: divide, 80; drive (see drive, sexual); embodiment (see embodiment, sexual); identity (see identity, sexual); instinct, 32; oppression, 171; relation, 78; stereotypes, 103–4

sexual difference, 1–2, 4, 8, 10–15, 18–19, 24–25, 37, 46–47, 49, 61, 66, 70–74, 80–81, 88–89, 91–95, 100–2, 104, 106–8, 122–23, 125–26, 128, 130–33, 139, 185, 214n 18, 221n 14, 224n 13, 226n 18, 230n 28; simulacrum of, 106–7; symbolization of, 12

sexuality, 2, 6–7, 9, 17–18, 30–31, 33–35, 37–38, 49, 51, 53, 86–88, 90–91, 93–96, 99, 111, 167, 170–71, 173–75, 178, 181–82, 188, 192, 205n 28; and the vital order, 30–39; development of,

254

36; discourse on, 85; feminine, 13, 37, 44, 51, 61; historical nature of, 35–36; infantile, 146; malleability of, 116; representation of, 99

sexuation, 72–83

sexuation diagram, 14, 74, 78, 107–8 *(see also* Lacan, Jacques; schema R); feminine side of, 76–77, 107; masculine side of, 74–77, 79–80, 107

Shakespeare, William, 149

Shepherdson, Charles, 187–95

significance, 17

signification, 67

signifier, the, 5, 18, 21–24, 28–29, 31, 37, 39, 63, 65, 70, 91, 97, 100, 117, 135, 137, 191, 227n 20, 231n 33; and the subject, 96; identification with, 83; law of, 36; of the primordial object, 138; phallic, 64, 120, 138

sisters, 18

social: conditions, 39–40, 45; determination, 43; formations, 91; order, 36, 42, 111–12; organization, 34; practices, 32, 89; roles, 89; theory, 1, 190, 192

social construction, 7–8, 91, 94–95, 145, 184, 191; of femininity *(see* femininity); of subjectivity, 191; of the subject, 18

society, 34–35, 91, 111–12; matriarchal, 37

specificity, 76

Speculum, 48

speech, 23, 30, 33, 36, 62, 67–68, 98, 166–67, 193–94, 223n 4; -act theory, 112

splitting, 57, 59, 184

Sprengnether, Madelon, 60

structuralism, 181, 233n 5

subject, the, 12, 18, 25, 35–37, 39–40, 45–46, 53, 57, 62–63, 65–67, 71, 81, 85–86, 89–90, 92–93, 99–100, 102, 104–7, 109–10, 112–13, 119, 128, 145–46, 148, 192, 205n 28, 222n 25, 228n 21; and relation to the phallus, 139; and the signifier, 96; constitution of *(see* constitution of subject); desire of, 50; embodiment of, 85; female, 40; formation of, 122; free, 106; identity of, 96; in psychoanalysis, 90, 95, 99; masculine, 41; normal, 144; social construction of, 18, 91, 99; temporality of, 148; transsexual, 102–3

subjectivity, 1–2, 8–9, 53, 57, 85, 91, 94, 101, 138, 177, 184, 188, 191, 194; construction of, 7, 91, 93, 95; gendered, 91, 93

substitution, 96, 98

superego, the, 73, 83, 90, 116, 119–21, 134, 144–47, 149–51, 179, 187, 213n 12, 230n 29, 232n 38

surgery: on demand, 101, 107; sex-change, 103, 109 *(see also* transsexuality; transsexuals)

surplus effect, the, 144, 146, 224n 5

Swift, Jonathan, 154, 165; *Gulliver's Travels,* 154

Sylvestre, Michel, 148

symbol, 19, 22–23, 34, 36, 64; relation between organism and the, 18

symbolic, the, 6–7, 13, 22, 31, 35–37, 39–40, 42, 45, 55, 60, 62–66, 69, 72, 88, 90, 97–99, 101, 107, 110, 128, 136–37, 162, 165, 177, 208n 41, 213n 14, 229n 25, 233n 7; -mother relationship, 115; and the imaginary, 45–46; and the real, 178–80; and the relation to the other, 193; castration *(see* castration, symbolic); determination, 44, 47; father as, 140 *(see also* father, symbolic); formulation, 102, 181; function, 63, 127, 138, 156; inheritance *(see* inheritance, symbolic); mediation *(see* mediation, symbolic); order, 3, 4, 12–13, 15, 19, 30, 37, 39, 57, 60, 66–68, 71, 73, 77, 85, 88, 90, 101, 103, 106, 116, 117–20, 123, 126, 135–38, 146–48, 151, 163, 190, 224n 11, 228n 22; phenomenon, 88, 138; relation to the mother, 73; relations, 110, 136; triangle *(see* imaginary triangle)

symbolization, 24, 67, 78, 90, 121, 209n 49, 214n 17

symptom(s), 18–19, 26, 33, 38, 95–96, 98, 100–1, 103–4, 110, 112, 116, 179, 190–91, 193, 200n 9; formation, 6, 110; hysterical, 4, 200n 9; somatic, 5, 17–18, 190, 194; symbolic structure of, 158

temporality, 146–51; problem of, 39–54

theory, 172, 182–83; film, 2, 188; literary, 188

time. *See* temporality